Kinds of Camera Shots

The film and video industries have names for all the kinds of shots you might take with your camcorder.

- ✔ **ELS:** Extra long-shot. This is an open or closing shot of a scene that is effective for establishing environment.
- ✔ **LS:** Long-shot. The character occupies one-half to three-quarters of the screen height.
- ✔ **MLS:** Medium long-shot. This shot shows the character's body plus a little above and below the body.
- ✔ **KNEE:** Knee shot. A three-quarter shot from the head to the knee of the subject.
- ✔ **MS:** Medium shot. This shot is from the top of the head to just below the waist.
- ✔ **MCU:** Medium close-up. This shot is often called a bust shot because it cuts from the top of the head to just above the diaphragm of the subject.
- ✔ **CU:** Close-up. This shot is from the upper forehead to the upper chest.
- ✔ **BCU:** Big close-up. This shot is a full head shot.
- ✔ **VCU:** Very close-up. This shot is a face shot, mid forehead to above the chin.
- ✔ **ECU:** Extreme close-up. This shot is a very tight face shot or a shot used for isolated details.

Adding Tracks to the Adobe Premiere Timeline

Adobe Premiere allows you to add up to 99 video and audio tracks in the Premiere Timeline window, which means that you can create layer upon layer of video and audio effects.

1. **Click the right-pointing arrow in the upper-right corner of the Timeline window.**

   A selection box appears.

2. **Select Track Options in the drop-down list.**

   The Track Options dialog box appears.

3. **Click the <u>A</u>dd button.**

   The Add Tracks dialog box appears.

4. **Type any number up to 96 in the Video Tracks box or type any number up to 97 in the Audio Tracks box.**

5. **Click OK in the Add Tracks dialog box.**

6. **Click <u>O</u>K in the Track Options dialog box.**

   You just added a video or audio track to your project.

Adobe Premiere Keyboard Shortcuts

Using the numbers on your keyboard (not the numeric pad at the far-right of your keyboard), perform these shortcuts in the Monitor, Timeline, or Clip window:

Press This Key	To Do This
2	Move forward one frame
1	Move back one frame
4	Move forward five frames
3	Move back five frames
A	Go to first frame
S	Go to last frame

Fixing Photo Imperfections with Adobe Photoshop

To remove scratches from a scanned or recorded still image, open Adobe Photoshop and follow these steps, using the Zoom and Rubber Stamp tools:

1. **Click the Zoom tool located in the tenth row, right column of the Photoshop toolbox, which is found at the far-left side of the Photoshop window.**

   The cursor becomes a spyglass with a + inside it.

2. **Draw a square around and slightly larger than the scratched area by clicking just above and to the left of the scratch. Pressing the mouse, drag diagonally over the scratch, creating a box. Release the mouse.**

   You now see a close-up of the scratched area.

3. **Click the Rubber Stamp tool located in the fourth row, left column of the toolbox.**

   As you pass the cursor over the image, the cursor becomes a rubber stamp.

   Before continuing your work, you need to select a small brush. The brush you select will directly affect the "size" of the cursor's action.

4. **Click the Brushes tab in the Colors\Swatches\Brushes palette located at the far-right side of the Photoshop window.**

   A selection of brush sizes appears.

5. **Click the brush in the top row, third from the left.**

   Now you need to collect some of the good part of the image to use for your scratch repair.

6. **To use the Rubber Stamp tool, position the cursor approximately one inch to the left of the imperfection.**

7. **Press and hold down the Alt key and simultaneously click and release your mouse.**

   You just set the angle and distance relationship for the Rubber Stamp tool.

8. **Using this setting, position the cursor over the imperfection, click and drag to deposit color and shading.**

   Voilà! Your scratch has disappeared.

The IDG Books Worldwide logo is a registered trademark under exclusive license to IDG Books Worldwide, Inc., from International Data Group, Inc. The ...For Dummies logo is a trademark, and For Dummies is a registered trademark of IDG Books Worldwide, Inc. All other trademarks are the property of their respective owners.

For Dummies®: Bestselling Book Series for Beginners

TM

BESTSELLING BOOK SERIES

References for the Rest of Us!®

Are you intimidated and confused by computers? Do you find that traditional manuals are overloaded with technical details you'll never use? Do your friends and family always call you to fix simple problems on their PCs? Then the ...*For Dummies*® computer book series from IDG Books Worldwide is for you.

...*For Dummies* books are written for those frustrated computer users who know they aren't really dumb but find that PC hardware, software, and indeed the unique vocabulary of computing make them feel helpless. ...*For Dummies* books use a lighthearted approach, a down-to-earth style, and even cartoons and humorous icons to dispel computer novices' fears and build their confidence. Lighthearted but not lightweight, these books are a perfect survival guide for anyone forced to use a computer.

Already, millions of satisfied readers agree. They have made ...*For Dummies* books the #1 introductory level computer book series and have written asking for more. So, if you're looking for the most fun and easy way to learn about computers, look to ...*For Dummies* books to give you a helping hand.

IDG BOOKS WORLDWIDE®

Digital Video FOR DUMMIES®

by Martin Doucette

IDG Books Worldwide, Inc.
An International Data Group Company

Foster City, CA ◆ Chicago, IL ◆ Indianapolis, IN ◆ New York, NY

Digital Video For Dummies®

Published by
IDG Books Worldwide, Inc.
An International Data Group Company
919 E. Hillsdale Blvd.
Suite 400
Foster City, CA 94404
www.idgbooks.com (IDG Books Worldwide Web site)
www.dummies.com (Dummies Press Web site)

Library of Congress Catalog Card No.: 99-66329

ISBN: 0-7645-0023-6

Printed in the United States of America

10 9 8 7 6 5 4 3

1B/SR/QZ/QQ/IN

Distributed in the United States by IDG Books Worldwide, Inc.

Distributed by CDG Books Canada Inc. for Canada;by Transworld Publishers Limited in the United Kingdom; by IDG Norge Books for Norway; by IDG Sweden Books for Sweden; by IDG Books Australia Publishing Corporation Pty. Ltd. for Australia and New Zealand; by TransQuest Publishers Pte Ltd. for Singapore, Malaysia, Thailand, Indonesia, and Hong Kong; by Gotop Information Inc. for Taiwan; by ICG Muse, Inc. for Japan; by Intersoft for South Africa; by Eyrolles for France; by International Thomson Publishing for Germany, Austria and Switzerland; by Distribuidora Cuspide for Argentina; by LR International for Brazil; by Galileo Libros for Chile; by Ediciones ZETA S.C.R. Ltda. for Peru; by WS Computer Publishing Corporation, Inc., for the Philippines; by Contemporanea de Ediciones for Venezuela; by Express Computer Distributors for the Caribbean and West Indies; by Micronesia Media Distributor, Inc. for Micronesia; by Chips Computadoras S.A. de C.V. for Mexico; by Editorial Norma de Panama S.A. for Panama; by American Bookshops for Finland.

For general information on IDG Books Worldwide's books in the U.S., please call our Consumer Customer Service department at 800-762-2974. For reseller information, including discounts and premium sales, please call our Reseller Customer Service department at 800-434-3422.

For information on where to purchase IDG Books Worldwide's books outside the U.S., please contact our International Sales department at 317-572-3993 or fax 317-572-4002.

For consumer information on foreign language translations, please contact our Customer Service department at 1-800-434-3422, fax 317-572-4002, or e-mail rights@idgbooks.com.

For information on licensing foreign or domestic rights, please phone +1-650-653-7098.

For sales inquiries and special prices for bulk quantities, please contact our Order Services department at 800-434-3422 or write to the address above.

For information on using IDG Books Worldwide's books in the classroom or for ordering examination copies, please contact our Educational Sales department at 800-434-2086 or fax 317-572-4005.

For press review copies, author interviews, or other publicity information, please contact our Public Relations department at 650-653-7000 or fax 650-653-7500.

For authorization to photocopy items for corporate, personal, or educational use, please contact Copyright Clearance Center, 222 Rosewood Drive, Danvers, MA 01923, or fax 978-750-4470.

is a registered trademark under exclusive license
to IDG Books Worldwide, Inc. from International Data Group, Inc.

IDG
BOOKS
WORLDWIDE

About the Author

Marty Doucette is a multimedia author, video producer, and nonlinear system integrator. He is an Indianapolis-based freelance educational program developer and writer. In the past few years, Marty has developed technical and managerial training programs for the Department of Justice, FEMA, the American Institute of Architects, and the State of Indiana. Marty has designed video production studios and frequently assists individuals and corporations in their selection of video production and post-production systems. In addition to his video production expertise, he is also the author of *Microsoft Project 98 For Dummies*. Marty manages a number of Web sites and assists individuals and corporations in their use of video and audio on the Internet.

Marty resides with his beautiful wife Lorita and their four children, Nicole, Ariel, Lindsay, and Eve in Indianapolis, Indiana.

ABOUT IDG BOOKS WORLDWIDE

Welcome to the world of IDG Books Worldwide.

IDG Books Worldwide, Inc., is a subsidiary of International Data Group, the world's largest publisher of computer-related information and the leading global provider of information services on information technology. IDG was founded more than 30 years ago by Patrick J. McGovern and now employs more than 9,000 people worldwide. IDG publishes more than 290 computer publications in over 75 countries. More than 90 million people read one or more IDG publications each month.

Launched in 1990, IDG Books Worldwide is today the #1 publisher of best-selling computer books in the United States. We are proud to have received eight awards from the Computer Press Association in recognition of editorial excellence and three from Computer Currents' First Annual Readers' Choice Awards. Our best-selling ...*For Dummies®* series has more than 50 million copies in print with translations in 31 languages. IDG Books Worldwide, through a joint venture with IDG's Hi-Tech Beijing, became the first U.S. publisher to publish a computer book in the People's Republic of China. In record time, IDG Books Worldwide has become the first choice for millions of readers around the world who want to learn how to better manage their businesses.

Our mission is simple: Every one of our books is designed to bring extra value and skill-building instructions to the reader. Our books are written by experts who understand and care about our readers. The knowledge base of our editorial staff comes from years of experience in publishing, education, and journalism — experience we use to produce books to carry us into the new millennium. In short, we care about books, so we attract the best people. We devote special attention to details such as audience, interior design, use of icons, and illustrations. And because we use an efficient process of authoring, editing, and desktop publishing our books electronically, we can spend more time ensuring superior content and less time on the technicalities of making books.

You can count on our commitment to deliver high-quality books at competitive prices on topics you want to read about. At IDG Books Worldwide, we continue in the IDG tradition of delivering quality for more than 30 years. You'll find no better book on a subject than one from IDG Books Worldwide.

John J. Kilcullen

John Kilcullen
Chairman and CEO
IDG Books Worldwide, Inc.

Eighth Annual Computer Press Awards ➣1992

Ninth Annual Computer Press Awards ➣1993

Tenth Annual Computer Press Awards ➣1994

Eleventh Annual Computer Press Awards ➣1995

IDG is the world's leading IT media, research and exposition company. Founded in 1964, IDG had 1997 revenues of $2.05 billion and has more than 9,000 employees worldwide. IDG offers the widest range of media options that reach IT buyers in 75 countries representing 95% of worldwide IT spending. IDG's diverse product and services portfolio spans six key areas including print publishing, online publishing, expositions and conferences, market research, education and training, and global marketing services. More than 90 million people read one or more of IDG's 290 magazines and newspapers, including IDG's leading global brands — Computerworld, PC World, Network World, Macworld and the Channel World family of publications. IDG Books Worldwide is one of the fastest-growing computer book publishers in the world, with more than 700 titles in 36 languages. The "...For Dummies®" series alone has more than 50 million copies in print. IDG offers online users the largest network of technology-specific Web sites around the world through IDG.net (http://www.idg.net), which comprises more than 225 targeted Web sites in 55 countries worldwide. International Data Corporation (IDC) is the world's largest provider of information technology data, analysis and consulting, with research centers in over 41 countries and more than 400 research analysts worldwide. IDG World Expo is a leading producer of more than 168 globally branded conferences and expositions in 35 countries including E3 (Electronic Entertainment Expo), Macworld Expo, ComNet, Windows World Expo, ICE (Internet Commerce Expo), Agenda, DEMO, and Spotlight. IDG's training subsidiary, ExecuTrain, is the world's largest computer training company, with more than 230 locations worldwide and 785 training courses. IDG Marketing Services helps industry-leading IT companies build international brand recognition by developing global integrated marketing programs via IDG's print, online and exposition products worldwide. Further information about the company can be found at www.idg.com.   1/26/00

Dedication

To Harley. The love of a father *and* friend cannot die. I miss you.

Author's Acknowledgments

One of the fun things about writing a book is that you can pretend that you wrote it all by yourself. My only problem is that somewhere between ten and twenty people might bonk me on the head if I tell you this. Actually, they probably wouldn't bonk me on the head because they happen to be kind in addition to being intelligent and dedicated to their crafts. Nevertheless, to avoid the risk of incoming serving spoons and baseball bats, I would like to express my gratitude to a number of people for their assistance in the writing of this book.

First, thanks to Steve Hayes, acquisitions editor at IDG, for his faith and guidance. Next, thanks to my project editor Melba Hopper. You're still speaking to me in a civil manner! I'm not sure whether that means you like me or that you are superhuman. I know the latter is true, but I hope the former is, too. Melba, thank you for being so demanding. To my technical editor, Brad Shipp, your suggestions were always well-focused and insightful. Thanks.

I would also like to thank the many talented members of IDG's production staff who helped see this book to its finish, particularly the project coordinator, Shawn Aylsworth; and Shelley Lea, supervisor of Design and Graphics. Thanks also to Steve Rath for putting together a fine index.

Thank you Mike Mount for going to bat for me. Thank you Karl Ditman for risking executive wrath to save my project. Thank you Jim Shaw for all your engineering know-how and friendly patience with me. Thank you Jim Bales for being so understanding. Thank you Barb Ham for pulling so many pieces together for me. Thank you Marsha Miller for the many ways you have helped me stay on track. Thank you Ron Clayton for knowing where it all can be found (and then finding it). And, of course, thank you Jon Bereman for all the room you have given me to let me be me, doing what I do.

And last, thank you Lorita. You are a constant interference to my picayune perspectives, ever demanding that I would see life for all of its true beauty and worth. I love you.

Publisher's Acknowledgments

We're proud of this book; please register your comments through our IDG Books Worldwide Online Registration Form located at `http://my2cents.dummies.com`.

Some of the people who helped bring this book to market include the following:

Acquisitions, Editorial, and Media Development

Project Editor: Melba D. Hopper

Acquisitions Editor: Steven H. Hayes

Copy Editor: Melba D. Hopper

Technical Editor: Brad Shipp

Media Development Editor: Marita Ellixson

Associate Permissions Editor: Carmen Krikorian

Media Development Coordinator: Megan Roney

Editorial Manager: Mary C. Corder

Media Development Manager: Heather Heath Dismore

Editorial Assistants: Paul Kuzmic, Beth Parlon

Production

Project Coordinator: E. Shawn Aylsworth

Layout and Graphics: Amy M. Adrian, Matt Coleman, Brian Drumm, Angela F. Hunckler, Kate Jenkins, Barry Offringa, Jill Piscitelli, Doug Rollison, Brent Savage, Janet Seib, Michael A. Sullivan, Brian Torwelle, Maggie Ubertini, Mary Jo Weis, Dan Whetstine, Erin Zeltner

Proofreaders: Laura Albert, Vickie Broyles, Chris Collins, John Greenough, Marianne Santy, Rebecca Senninger, Toni Settle

Indexer: Steve Rath

Special Help
Constance Carlisle, Suzanne Thomas

General and Administrative

IDG Books Worldwide, Inc.: John Kilcullen, CEO

IDG Books Technology Publishing Group: Richard Swadley, Senior Vice President and Publisher; Walter R. Bruce III, Vice President and Publisher; Joseph Wikert, Vice President and Publisher; Mary Bednarek, Vice President and Director, Product Development; Andy Cummings, Publishing Director, General User Group; Mary C. Corder, Editorial Director; Barry Pruett, Publishing Director

IDG Books Consumer Publishing Group: Roland Elgey, Senior Vice President and Publisher; Kathleen A. Welton, Vice President and Publisher; Kevin Thornton, Acquisitions Manager; Kristin A. Cocks, Editorial Director

IDG Books Internet Publishing Group: Brenda McLaughlin, Senior Vice President and Publisher; Sofia Marchant, Online Marketing Manager

IDG Books Production for Branded Press: Debbie Stailey, Director of Production; Cindy L. Phipps, Manager of Project Coordination, Production Proofreading, and Indexing; Tony Augsburger, Manager of Prepress, Reprints, and Systems; Shelley Lea, Supervisor of Graphics and Design; Debbie J. Gates, Production Systems Specialist; Steve Arany, Associate Automation Supervisor; Robert Springer, Supervisor of Proofreading; Trudy Coler, Page Layout Manager; Kathie Schutte, Senior Page Layout Supervisor; Janet Seib, Associate Page Layout Supervisor; Michael Sullivan, Production Supervisor

Packaging and Book Design: Patty Page, Manager, Promotions Marketing

◆

The publisher would like to give special thanks to Patrick J. McGovern, without whom this book would not have been possible.

◆

Contents at a Glance

Cartoons at a Glance

By Rich Tennant

page 241

page 7

page 129

page 293

page 107

page 219

page 31

page 275

Fax: 978-546-7747
E-mail: richtennant@the5thwave.com
World Wide Web: www.the5thwave.com

Table of Contents

Introduction

• •

Scenario one: Here's a pretty picture. Imagine, at this moment, thousands of people blissfully recording video with their digital camcorders or creatively editing digital video with their computers. Such a lovely, peaceful, pastoral image!

So excuse me, but I need to ask you a little question. What are you doing reading this book when you could be out there recording and editing with all those happy people? My guess is that you're smart. You probably wonder how much of the hoopla about digital video is for real. You've learned through experience that knowledge is always the key to success. So you want to know more — maybe a lot more — before you buy. You want to make sure you get the most out of what you purchase. Very smart.

Scenario two: You've just purchased a digital camcorder, and you've got a computer with nonlinear editing software. Congratulations! So why that bead of cold sweat on your brow? Why is your heart thumping a little more loudly than normal? I don't want to presume too much, but could it be that you're wondering what you're supposed to do next? As in, now what?

First, take a deep breath. You're going to be okay. You haven't made any bad decisions. In fact, you've made some great decisions in choosing digital video. You're just feeling the normal reactions of a savvy individual who has just realized something: You need basic training to be a digital videographer! Well, guess what? You've made another great decision. You bought this book.

About This Book

A well-made digital video movie is a compilation of successful decisions. This book shows you how to make those decisions. You don't need to have any prior experience. To begin, all you need is a little curiosity and the desire to have some fun.

Digital Video For Dummies takes you, step-by-step through the production (recording or shooting), postproduction (editing), and distribution (putting your end product on videotape, CD-ROM, or the Web) phases of digital video.

You find out about the kind of equipment and materials you need to get started in digital video, along with some important tricks of the trade. By the time you finish this book, you'll be beyond just shooting videos; you'll be producing *professional-looking* videos. You'll be creating graphics, making animation, and performing nonlinear editing. You'll know how to produce video that can be recorded to VHS video, CD-ROM, and the Internet.

This book provides a smorgasbord of how-to resources designed to help you get started in a wide variety of digital video projects.

The CD at the back of this book is a gold mine of sample software programs and example graphics, audio files, and movies — all awaiting your discovery.

How This Book Is Organized

This book is organized into eight parts. Each part is a logical grouping of chapters with each chapter focusing on a major point about digital video. In each chapter, you'll find enough — but not too much — specific direction to make you a budding star in digital video production.

You don't have to read this book in a chapter-by-chapter sort of way. As much as possible, each chapter is written to stand on its own. But, then again, you may find the logical order of the chapters quite helpful. Read the book any way you want. You're the boss. If you simply want to pick and choose, have at it. If you want to use this book as a step-by-step guide, go right ahead.

Part I: Doing It Digitally

The first couple of chapters in *Digital Video For Dummies* provide an overview of digital video and where it fits among all the other kinds of video production. If you haven't read or heard a lot about digital video, you're probably going to be amazed by the ascendance of this low-cost, high-quality video format. Part I isn't essential to knowing how digital video works, but it's very useful for understanding why digital video is causing such a stir.

Part II: Shooting Digital Video

One of the easiest and most important ways to maximize the potential of digital video is simply to know how to use a camcorder. I don't mean knowing how to turn it on and off; I mean knowing how to make the most of your camcorder's lens and electronic features. Your digital camcorder is a tribute to incredible breakthroughs in video technology. You need to know how to take advantage of that new technology. Part II introduces you to your digital camcorder's potential (Chapter 3).

Your digital camcorder is amazingly faithful in reproducing what it sees and hears. For that reason, the more you know about light and sound, the more advantage you can take of your camcorder's high-quality reproduction capability. Part II walks you through the time-honored practices of quality lighting (Chapter 4) and sound (Chapter 5).

Digital video offers you the opportunity to paint a beautiful picture — to capture a breathtaking moment. You may want to know some simple steps that make the most of your shots. Part II concludes by introducing you to the basics of video production planning and scene direction (Chapters 6 and 7).

Part III: Using Your Computer for Digital Video

One of the revolutionary aspects of digital video is what you can do with it on a computer. Part III describes the hardware and operating system stuff you need in order to bring video into your computer (capture) and to use your computer as a video editing workstation.

Chapter 8 tells you in plain English all the processor, RAM, operating system, and storage stuff you need to know to make intelligent decisions about your computer's configuration. Chapter 9 shows you a sample digital video capture card and its accompanying software. The chapter illustrates how painlessly and powerfully video capturing actually works.

Part IV: Editing Digital Video with Your Computer

Part IV introduces you to some awesome and easy-to-use computer software programs, all found on the CD at the back of this book. Within minutes, you'll be creating a timeline in Adobe Premiere 5.0 (Chapters 10 and 11), you'll be making illustrations with Adobe Illustrator 8.0 (Chapter 12), you'll be fixing and enhancing graphics with Adobe Photoshop 5.0 (Chapter 13), and you'll be layering video and graphics in Adobe After Effects 4.0 (Chapter 14).

Part V: Preparing Your Video for Sharing

What good is a video if it can't be seen by others? In the past, the only way to distribute video was with VHS videotapes. Those days are long gone. True, VHS is still a good way to send out your message. But nowadays, you can just as easily lay your video on a CD or encode it for playing on the Internet, or export it to a PowerPoint presentation. In Part V, you learn about the distribution available through digital video nonlinear editing, and you get some exciting suggestions for making videos everyone will want to see.

In Chapter 15, I show you state-of-the-art answers for putting video on the Web. If video for multimedia CD-ROM is your area of interest, you'll get much of the help you need in Chapter 16. Chapter 17 lays out the meat and potatoes of digital video — putting your video on tape.

Part VI: Making Cool Stuff with Digital Video

Do you want to know how to easily change ordinary photos and videos into extraordinary presentations? Part VI is the place for you. With a little imagination, you can turn two-dimensional photos into a three-dimensional adventure (Chapter 18). You can turn your neighborhood into the back lot of your own home movie production studio (Chapter 19). And you make wedding videos special and memorable (Chapter 20).

Part VI is all about having fun while making professional-quality video. You'll find that your own enjoyment is a powerful creative energy. People will want more of whatever you do. You may even consider turning your popular hobby into a profitable business.

Part VII: The Part of Tens

As if all the preceding information isn't enough, Part VII points you to a number of additional digital video resources. Chapter 21 leads you to valuable World Wide Web links. Want to know the history of digital video? No problem, I've got just the site for you. Want to know more about streaming video? I list that site, too. Want to know the compatibility of your computer with a specific capture card? Don't worry, I've got you covered.

Chapter 22 provides a dynamite list of products you may want to seriously consider for jumping into digital video. Everything from hardware to software and to advanced training opportunities — it's all in Part VII, just waiting for you.

Part VIII: Appendixes

This part has two appendixes. Appendix A gives you some helpful forms and checklists to use in video production. Appendix B tells you how to copy or install all the neato stuff from this book's CD onto your computer.

Conventions Used in This Book

Parts III and IV of this book are about using your computer as a digital media workstation. The information in these parts is helpful for anyone — no matter what kind of computer and operating system you use. For the sake of sanity though, I base all the steps and my computer and software suggestions on the assumption you are using or will be using Windows 98. The tryout software and sample files on the CD work on Windows 95, Windows 98, and Windows NT 4.0 or later operating systems. The tryout software and sample files do not work on a Macintosh operating system.

As you read this book, you'll see that some words have a letter that's underlined. These letters denote keyboard shortcuts for commands. For example, you can press the Alt key in combination with the underlined letter to choose a command quickly.

On the other hand, if you come upon two words that are joined by a little arrow, you've found commands that you're suppose to select in the given sequence. For example, if you see File⇨Print, you click the File menu and then click the Print command in the menu. Or, as I mention above, you may also be able to press Alt plus F and then press P.

Finally, from time to time, I show new or technical terms in italics. You can find a glossary with these terms at the Web site, www.digitalproduct.com. At that site, you can also find a link that takes you to the IDG Books Worldwide, Inc. Web site, where you can find information about other ...*For Dummies* books, as well as information about other books published by IDG Worldwide.

Icons Used in This Book

Tells you about other ...*For Dummies* books that can help you understand a particular function of digital video.

Alerts you when there are relevant sample files or tryout software on the CD that comes with this book.

Suggests that you commit to memory an important fact about video production or nonlinear editing.

Signals something technically wild and wonderful (if you're not already tuned into technospeak). The term may be interesting and useful, but it's not essential to doing business.

Flags a friendly little shortcut on your road to digital video production success. This icon usually signals a way to do your work easily and quickly.

Gently suggests that the future of the free world and humanity's well being for countless generations to come hinges on your next action. Actually, this icon just cautions that you're about to make a decision or perform an action that may have some kind of permanent outcome. (So maybe my first description is on the mark after all.)

Where to Go from Here

By the way, the publisher of this book loves to hear from readers. To contact the publisher (or authors of other *...For Dummies* books), visit the publisher's Web site at www.dummies.com, send an e-mail to info@idgbooks.com, or send paper mail to IDG Books Worldwide, Inc., 7260 Shadeland Station, Suite 100, Indianapolis, IN 46256.

Video producers and editors are straightforward, no nonsense types. They size up the job, determine the best course of action, begin, and never look back. The time has come. I'll see you somewhere in the book.

Part I
Doing It Digitally

The 5th Wave — By Rich Tennant

"AND TO COMPLETE OUR MULTIMEDIA PRESENTATION,..."

In this part . . .

*J*ust a few short years ago, you needed oodles and scads of money (or wealthy friends) to create high-quality video. And if you wanted to use a computer for editing, well, again, you had to have (et cetera). But not any more — technological advances in the computer industry and in digital video have changed all that. Part I tells you how.

Just what is digital video? And where does it fit among all the other kinds of video? How is digital video different from the old ways of video production? Those are good questions — each answered in Part I. The chapters in the first part of the book give you a sound background to the world of video production and the revolutionary changes being brought about by digital video.

Chapter 1

You Can Count on Your Digits

In This Chapter

▶ Video then — digital video now

▶ Easily creating the formerly impossible

▶ Digital video — the great equalizer

Something exciting has happened to the word "video." And I consider it my solemn duty to mankind to tell you what. Video wizards have "digitized" it, thereby creating (drum rolls, please) digital video!

Digital video is a new way of making and playing video. Through the radical changes made possible by advancements in computer chip technology, you can now create and play video that before could be done only with the most expensive equipment! And you can do it right on your home or office computer desktop.

In case you're wondering, in the world of video, *digital video* can refer to two things: video that is shot with a digital camcorder or video that is captured into a computer. *Capturing* is a procedure performed by a computer (via a capture card) to convert video into a computer file. In this book, I use the term digital video in both ways. I tell you how you can get the most out of a digital camcorder, and I tell you how to use your computer as a digital video workstation.

Turn to Chapter 2 for more information on capture cards and the feats they perform. And see the section "Digital versus analog," later in this chapter, for more about the advantages of digital signals.

What all this means is that you can now produce cutting-edge, professional-looking videos. With digital video — and your inherent creativity and initiative, of course — you can be a digital video artist.

What's more, the new digital video-producing equipment (which is based on the MiniDV format, a miniaturized digital video format) uses the same format as its expensively priced big brothers.

Format is geekspeak for how video and audio data is recorded on videotape. Many different formats exist, and each records data in a slightly different way. Check out Chapter 2 for information on specific kinds of video formats.

You can be a MiniDV artist *without* reducing the size of your pocketbook. Because of this breakthrough, consumers *and* professionals are flocking to the digital industry's fast-growing array of products.

I trust that no matter how timid your beginnings, by the time you finish this chapter, you, too, will be eager to join the bandwagon — whether you want to shoot video of backyard barbecues or broadcast documentaries on the migrating habits of Australian burrowing, herbivorous marsupials. It doesn't matter. With digital video, you can do it all.

Video Production — Past and Present

Until the coming of MiniDV, the quality of video production was based on the size of your pocketbook. If you wanted good-looking and good-sounding video, you needed expensive equipment — and lots of it. This, of course, also meant you needed lots of qualified people to operate the equipment. Digital video, particularly MiniDV, is changing many of the "givens" associated with video production. MiniDV makes a high-quality video image. And MiniDV equipment is relatively inexpensive and simple to operate.

In video production, anything having to do with quality is relative. Something is perceived as good because it is better than something else. In order for you to properly appreciate MiniDV, you need to see how it compares to other kinds of video production. In this section, you get a little outline of video production.

Starting at the top: The commercial house

Until recently, only the *commercial* production houses (for example, production houses that create television advertising) had the wherewithal to acquire and house the kinds of equipment needed to produce the truly top-notch videos, that is, *film-quality* videos.

Film-quality video is considered best because it produces a video product that is closest to what seems normal to the human eye. Therefore, when making high-end videos, commercial houses sometimes recorded with film — 35mm or 16mm — rather than videotape. The film was later converted to videotape at the conclusion of editing. In addition to shooting with film, commercial houses also used the Betacam SP format. (See Chapter 2 for more on the Betacam SP format.)

Today, many commercial houses have or are converting their equipment to a commercial version of digital video.

Working in industrial video

Traditionally, the next level was *industrial* video production. Industrial video producers customarily used the Betacam SP format. This level of production generally encompassed corporate in-house work, training materials, and some low-end commercial products. Although industrial video needed to look and sound excellent, it usually didn't need to rival film quality. Industrial video production usually didn't have the full-blown budgets enjoyed by commercial houses.

Prosumer: Neither fish nor fowl

Next came prosumer production. This level of video production typically used the S-VHS (Super VHS) format. The term *prosumer* was coined to describe a professional version of the consumer video format standard. (In video production, the *consumer* format standard is VHS or Video Home System — what you play in your home video tape player. But more about the consumer format in just a moment.)

In comparison to commercial and industrial production, you generally produced prosumer video on a more limited budget. Typical examples of prosumer productions included wedding videos and low-budget training videos.

The prosumer video industry is quite large and sales of S-VHS equipment continue at a strong clip. One reason for its popularity is that the S-VHS format was until recently the only really economical solution to meeting the production needs of thousands of small corporations and organizations. For as little as $2,000, you can own a good S-VHS camera and recorder. And for as little as $3,900, you can have a basic editing system — considerably less expensive than commercial and industrial equipment. You may want to check out the Web sites www.duncanvid.com and www.digitalproduct.com for some good examples of S-VHS equipment.

Characterizing a consumer

Next comes the *consumer*. Consumer video uses the VHS format. Consumer doesn't describe people, but, as does prosumer, a level of equipment — in this case, equipment that most people can easily afford. Though you can use VHS to record videos, it's pretty useless for editing them because the videos lose a good bit of quality during the process.

Birthing of the Digital Prosumer

The prosumer of old was near the bottom of the food chain among video professionals. The *digital prosumer,* however, is an entirely different breed. Using MiniDV camcorders and specially-equipped computers, digital prosumers are videographers and editors who achieve image quality that virtually breaks the format chains experienced by consumers, S-VHS prosumers, and industrial production facilities. Digital prosumers are, in fact, a happy group of people with a world of possibilities that rival commercial houses — without the stress or the need for square footage.

Now you can take advantage of this digital revolution. In Chapter 22, I show you an array of affordable digital video equipment. Without changing your profession (or risking financial insolvency), you can own all the right gear to be a digital prosumer.

In this book, you discover that as a digital prosumer, you can write, produce, and shoot video, create graphics and animation, edit, add special effects and music — and deliver it to videotape at broadcast quality. What you produce will exceed consumer and industrial image quality standards. For much less money than you would have to pay for a Beta SP camcorder, you can be a digital videographer and a computer-based editor.

But I haven't finished yet. You can own digital-quality wireless microphones, an audio sweetening bay, and a full-blown professional music library — and don't go looking for a warehouse to put all this in; you can work right in the corner of your room. As a digital prosumer, the only limitations to high-quality digital video production are your own creativity and effectiveness as a producer.

Editing the nonlinear way

As an industry, video production is just less than a couple of decades old. For most of its life, video production depended on *linear* editing. Linear refers to the method of editing where you copy video from one machine to another. Machine-to-machine editing can be performed only sequentially, where you lay one video segment on the record tape, followed by another segment, and so on. If you make a mistake, you must go all the way back to where you made the mistake and start over from that point.

Imagine doing linear editing for hours upon hours, laying one visual sequence after another in a seemingly never-ending row of edits. There is no lower moment than when, after you have sacrificed all personal relationships and semblance of sanity to create the marathon of editing marathons, you hear someone say, "We have to make a change in the middle of the video." In linear editing, this means you have to go back and erase all your work from that edit on!

But it can get even lower than that. You suffer through one more 48-hour stretch to make that little 3-second change only to hear, "I guess I liked it better the other way." Linear editors aren't normal people. They are former people.

Nonlinear editing (computer-based editing) changed all that. *Nonlinear* refers to a completely different way of editing. It doesn't involve multiple machines to perform an edit (see "Creating Multi-Generations," later in this chapter). Instead, thanks to the technology I mentioned at the beginning of this chapter, all the video segments are immediately converted into digitized data that can be stored and used on a single computer as computer files. One machine (your computer) does it all! With nonlinear editing, you can modify a video as many times as you want and in any order you want — not much different from the way you edit on a word processor.

The coming of age of nonlinear editing

Nonlinear editing was born and continues to thrive on the Mac, but, in my opinion, it has come of age on Windows systems. In the mid-1990s, Avid introduced a Windows NT-based version of its lower-level nonlinear editing software called MCXpess. The research and development done by Avid on an NT-based medium-range nonlinear editing system established a credibility link to an otherwise Mac-dominated industry. The Windows platform began to be embraced by growing numbers of users.

In 1998, Adobe Systems, Inc. launched Premiere 5.0, a low-priced, full-fledged nonlinear editing application for Windows 95, Windows 98, Windows NT, and the Mac. The earlier version, Adobe Premiere 4.2, is for all practical purposes, a multimedia-editing program for creating movies for CD-ROM. As you see in Part IV of this book, the 5.1 version of Premiere is a powerful program and one of the major pieces that makes digital video a professional reality for prosumers.

Nonlinear editing is a personal experience

I'll never forget the first time I saw a nonlinear system. The year was 1990. I was in Washington, D.C., producing a pay-per-view national teleconference. I had rented the studios of WETA, the local PBS affiliate. While there, someone suggested that I take a few minutes to see the station's new nonlinear editing system by Avid Technology, Inc. That was the first time I had even heard the words "Avid" and "nonlinear." Like most folks in video production at that time, I came to see the two words as permanently, inextricably, beautifully bound.

I walked into a tiny, overheated cubicle. In front of me sat a staff member in a much-too-small stenographer's chair at a tiny steel desk.

There, on one screen, were a bunch of little pictures. He told me each picture opened at the very moments each of the video clips was stored on the computer. He did something simple on his keyboard, and one of the clips started playing. I can't describe my reaction as I watched the computer play full-screen video on a monitor and with stereo sound to boot!

Next, he showed me how a transition took place on something he called "the timeline" and how he could layer images on top of each other to create special effects. He did a couple of quick edits, some cutting and pasting, and added background sound. As I stood and watched, I knew my professional life as a producer was at a crossroads. Either I would quickly adapt or be left behind. My love affair with the idea of nonlinear computer-based editing began that day in that room.

Things have progressed in nonlinear editing since the early '90s. Avid remains the leader. Its Mac-based Media Composer 9000 remains the gold standard of the industry, but numerous competitors abound. Competition has created lower-priced, scaled-down editing systems. Enormous advancements have occurred in lower-priced systems, and the gulf between the best and the good systems is constantly narrowing.

As a result, today you are able to perform nonlinear editing on a scale and quality that in many ways rivals the high-end commercial big brothers at a fraction of the cost. This is due in part to competitive development of nonlinear software programs, but also to advances in speed and storage capabilities of computers and their operating systems. Part IV of this book is dedicated entirely to helping you become a nonlinear editor.

Digital versus analog

Okay, before beginning this little section, you need to be clear about the difference between analog and digital signals and how they relate to video.

Analog refers to changing the original signal acquired (in a camera) into something that represents the signal — in this case, into a wave form (see Chapter 2 for more on analog and digital signals).

As I mentioned earlier, the term *digital video* means a couple of things. It can refer to video that is shot by a digital camcorder, and it can refer to video that is captured (digitized) on a computer.

The quality and glamour of digital video is that it can *begin* and *remain* digital from camcorder to computer. You accomplish this thanks to a standardized wiring connection, or cable, used between the camcorder and a special card (board) on your computer. This cable and its connections, known by three names — IEEE 1394 (which I generally choose to use), i-link, and Firewire — are some of the most significant factors in the development of the digital prosumer industry because they keep digital video digital. Without an IEEE 1394 connection, the video signal would be degraded into a another format, such as VHS or S-VHS.

The IEEE 1394 connection is the lifeline of the digital prosumer. Because of it, you are able to maintain the digital resolution and audio quality of your video throughout shooting and editing and up to the distribution of your product.

Desktop publishing

And last but not least, an important piece of the puzzle for digital prosumers is state-of-the-art desktop publishing. As shown in Part IV of this book, you can now create high-end graphics, animation, and special effects with very affordable desktop publishing programs. These capabilities are significant to just about anyone in digital video production. Whether your end product is a PowerPoint presentation, AVI or QuickTime files for CD-ROM-based multimedia, full-screen NTSC video, or RealVideo streaming (*streaming* is sending video or sound files — or both — over the Internet so that they begin playing before they finish downloading), you can triple the value of your work with simple-to-create, awesome-to-behold graphics and animation.

In addition to visual tools, you also delve into audio applications in Part IV of this book. The quality of your digital video is directly proportional to the attention you give to your audio. Again, advances in desktop publishing make it possible for you to use audio desktop publishing programs to perform amazing feats with your sound — from repairs to intricate mixes.

I E (0), I E (0), it's off to work we go!

IEEE stands for Institute for Electrical and Electronics Engineers, which sets the standards for electrical and electronic devices and systems. IEEE 1394 is a low-cost digital interface that integrates cameras, recorders, and computers. For example, by connecting the IEEE 1394 cable to your camcorder and your computer's special capture card, you can transmit digital video images from your MiniDV cassette through your capture card to your computer's hard drive.

Creating Multi-Generations

The term "video production" shouldn't intimidate you. Any time you do something to video to make it better, you are performing video production. Until the advent of digital video, the segregating factor in video production came down to the cost of maintaining top-quality resolution. Tack on to that statement, "through the editing process" — because all video production conventionally ended up in the edit bay.

Simply put, the reason people put so much money into their production formats was because the better formats have what's called *multi-generation survival capability.* Say what? In video production, multi-generation means that a finished video has been re-recorded (or edited) a number of times. Before digital video, multi-generations meant multiple machines and multiple stages of recording of a program on videotape.

Prior to being distributed as a final product, a typical video production, whether it was a network broadcast or a corporate training video, was at least three to five generations old. As you might imagine, more expensive recording equipment, such as Betacam SP, maintained the quality of a video image across multiple generations much better than did less expensive recording equipment, such as S-VHS.

Here's a sketch of the generations that videos would go through (see also Figure 1-1):

- **Generation one:** The video is shot using a camera and recorder or a combined unit. The videotape is then placed in a video player.

- **Generation two:** Portions of the video are chosen and edited onto another tape. Sometimes a second player is used where video A dissolves or wipes into video B. (In case you want to know, this A to B transition is called "A/B roll" editing.) Whether one player or two is being used, the resulting recorded tape is still generation number two.

- **Generation three ("program master" or finished product):** Frequently, the video will need additional editing, such as adding background music or a special graphic. The generation two tape is placed in the video player. Now the added graphic or audio is mixed in and taped onto a third tape.

- **Generation four ("duplication master"):** Because of the time and money put into the creation of the generation three tape, a fourth copy is made, and the generation three program master is put in safe keeping.

- **Generation five (duplicated copy):** This generation is all the tapes that are copied from generation four — and is the one purchased by the customer.

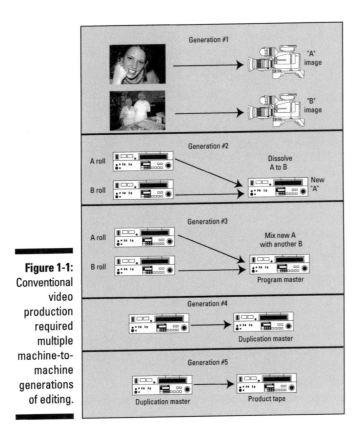

Figure 1-1: Conventional video production required multiple machine-to-machine generations of editing.

As you will see in Chapters 10 and 17, digital video has dramatically changed the method and quality of outcome of multiple generations. Now, using a single computer, you can make 4, 40, or 400 generations of video without losing any image quality. From one digital program master, you can make countless duplicate videos, CD-ROMs, and Web-based movies. And the cost of the equipment is only a fraction of the costs related to conventional multiple-generation video production.

Chapter 2

Where Does Digital Fit into Video?

• •

• •

*P*erhaps I should say right up front that you may want to refer to Chapter 1 before or while reading this chapter. In Chapter 1, I define the term *format* and say that until recently, format dictated everything in video production, with the most costly format producing the best videos.

In Chapter 1, I also indicate how a little connecting cable, called IEEE 1394 (also known as Firewire and i-Link), is changing things. With IEEE 1394 connections, you can send digital video and audio signals from one piece of digital equipment to another. As a result, all kinds of digital equipment — from the least expensive to the most expensive — can now "talk" to each other.

You can now select your equipment more like a wardrobe — what fits *you* best. Without sacrificing image quality, you can set yourself up in a full-fledged video production studio, commit yourself to a special niche for your video products, and create awesome materials — all at a very modest cost. The bottom line is that you are free to make diverse decisions about your professional-quality digital video. Based on what you do and who you do it for, your decisions can be quite expensive or surprisingly economical.

In this chapter, I talk about the digital equipment that you can use to take advantage of these innovations — specifically, equipment based on the mini-digital videotape format (or MiniDV format, which is a miniaturized digital video format) format. In order to explain MiniDV's significance, I compare MiniDV equipment to other professional-quality equipment. And I explain how digital video enables you to create and maintain beautiful video for playing on your television set, on a CD-ROM, or on the Internet.

When you finish this chapter, you will better understand the pieces that make up the whole puzzle of video production, and you'll have a better idea of where you want to fit into digital video. So, after pondering this bit of news, you need to start with the big picture.

Getting a Bead on the Big Picture

Digital video is a way of recording video in binary code (ones and zeros) as opposed to the conventional analog signal (which is recorded in waves). For an explanation of digital video, binary code, and analog signals, see the Chapter 5 sidebar, "Stuff you really don't need to know about digital audio." Digital video creates an image that is resilient to distortion, and, as I mentioned earlier, MiniDV is a miniaturized version of digital video. Don't be too worried if this sounds awfully technical. I'm not going to get into engineering talk in this chapter. All I really want to convey to you is that digital video is something special, you can probably afford it, and you're going to be able to shoot video that rivals video shot with very expensive equipment.

Video production pros are getting into MiniDV because they understand four things: acquisition (or collection), formats, editors, and distribution (AFED — this isn't really an acronym; I just couldn't resist starting a trend). Because you're joining their illustrious ranks, you need to be AFED-aware, too.

Acquiring visual (and audio) signals

Hold on to your chair for some earth-shattering information: A camera and a camcorder are *not* the same thing. A camera *acquires* (collects) a visual image. A camcorder does that and more: It also records.

Sometimes status symbols are a good thing

One of the surest signs that a new product is a good one is that the pros like it. If they're willing to be seen in public with it, you've probably got a winner. With that in mind, you might like to know that video professionals are the largest group of purchasers of MiniDV camcorders — particularly, the Canon XL1. Why? Good question.

Although Sony Corporation is a pioneer in the manufacture of MiniDV camcorders, in my opinion (at least at the time I'm writing this book), the Canon XL1 is unmatched for its price, options, and overall performance, which isn't to say that Sony or some other manufacturer won't leapfrog past Canon. After all, competition *is* the name of the game. For details about camcorders in general and the Canon XL1 in particular, go to Chapter 3.

In professional video production, you'll frequently find "cams" without "corders." An example is live broadcast television. No recording is necessary. With that as the given, you are going to better understand video if you separate the acquisition (collecting) phase from the recording phase. (Also, try to forget about audio for the moment. I bring it in later.)

In video, a camera acquires light and color on chips called *Charge-Coupled Devices,* or CCDs. (In case you're wondering, a *chip* is a tiny electronic circuit that's mass-produced on a pint-size wafer of silicon.) These CCDs collect visual images and convert them into either an analog signal (waves with varying amplitudes) or a digital signal (a series of ones and zeroes).

Most professional cameras have three CCDs (and are referred to as 3-CCD cameras). Light from the camera lens reaches a beam-splitting prism. The prism separates the light into individual color components — red, green, and blue (see Figure 2-1). Each of the components is sent to its own CCD. This process creates highly accurate color reproduction and detail.

Figure 2-1:
A prism splits color into red, green, and blue images.

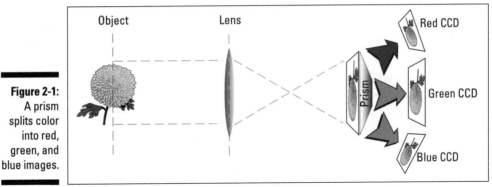

Making a place for digital video

Digital video has changed the relationships among the four elements of video production. Take a look at Figure 2-2, which illustrates those relationships. The Acquisition column shows two groups of camcorders. The top two are digital and the bottom two are analog. The Formats column lists digital and analog recording formats. The Editors column lists kinds of editing systems. The Distribution column lists types of finished video products.

Column One shows four camcorders. For the purpose of this discussion, I'm focusing only on the acquisition capabilities of the camcorders (not the recording capabilities, which comes later). I've selected four models. I Don't list all the kinds available. But these four are sufficient for illustrating formats. Each of these camcorders is a popular representative of its respective format:

JVC GY-X2BU S-VHS

Sony UVW-100B Betacam SP

Canon XL1

Hitachi Z-3000W

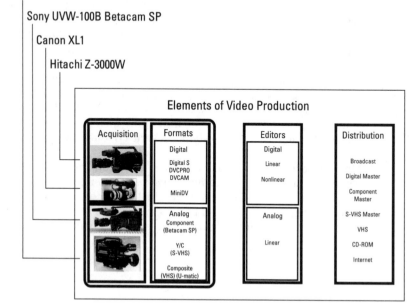

Figure 2-2:
This figure
shows a
snapshot of
the current
state of
video
production.

✔ **Analog prosumer:** The camcorder shown at the bottom of the first column in Figure 2-2 is a JVC GY-X2BU. This camcorder is a 3-CCD high-quality camera and S-VHS format recorder. Until recently, this $7,000 (approximate list price) camcorder was the best you could buy without crossing the technology chasm into the very expensive world of the Betacam SP format.

✔ **Analog industrial/commercial:** The second camcorder from the bottom is the Sony UVW-100B. This is a high-quality 3-CCD camera and Betacam SP recorder. List price for the UVW-100B is approximately $15,800. For quite a few years, Betacam SP has been the standard for professional formats. Other professional formats are out there, but few people use them. Go to any professional sporting event, and you'll notice that nearly all the camcorders used by television stations are based on the Betacam SP format.

✔ **Digital prosumer:** The third camcorder from the bottom is the Canon XL1. The XL1 is also a high-quality 3-CCD camera and MiniDV recorder. It is one of the stars of the MiniDV format, and I discuss it in depth in this book. The list price for the XL1 is approximately $4,700.

✔ **Digital commercial:** The top camcorder in column one is the Hitachi Z-3000W. This cutting edge, very high-quality camera uses three CCDs with advanced all-digital processing. The camera, if used as a camcorder, docks with any of three digital recorders: Sony DVCAM, Panasonic

DVCPRO, or JVC Digital-S. The Hitachi Z-3000W and its companion recorder are considered top-of-the-line. As an example, the list price for the camera with the JVC BR-D40 Digital-S is approximately $28,000.

Why am I telling you all this stuff? I just want you to begin to see where MiniDV fits with the big boys. The Hitachi Z-3000W/JVC BR-D40 digital camcorder is used by network broadcast professionals. The same is true of the Sony UVW-100B. The Canon XL1 (MiniDV format) creates a video and audio signal that is equivalent in quality to the signal produced on camcorders based on the Betacam SP format. As you can see, the digital prosumer format is nestled in with the big hitters.

Audio acquisition

The collection of a visual image is completely separate from the collection of sound. You'll often see a microphone hanging onto or built into a camera. This may leave you with the wrong impression. A camera doesn't acquire audio. For all practical purposes, the camera is merely serving as a convenient carrier for the microphone. That's all. The microphone's signal is acquired by the *recorder,* which may seem a minor point, but it's not.

If you're used to working with a VHS camcorder, you've probably never had a reason to think about sound because most VHS camcorder microphones are built into the unit. You aren't offered alternatives for audio recording. But you need to become very conscious of sound. Good quality sound is worth every bit of effort you can give it. Quite often, a camera-mounted microphone is the last thing you want. If, for example, you're 30 feet away from your subject, your audio is going to include a bunch of stuff you probably don't want. You need to collect the audio you want with a wired or wireless microphone connected to the recorder.

A good recorder on a camcorder offers the option of two channels for acquiring audio. These channels can be the same signal or two separate ones, and they can record audio from another source.

In professional video production, the visual and audio acquisition commonly are performed by two people — something I recommend whenever possible.

Functioning in unfriendly formats

As an overview, video recording formats are either digital or analog (refer to the Formats column in Figure 2-2). Though the various formats nestle into one of two groups, all the formats are basically incompatible with each other. By this, I mean that you can't play a videotape from one format in a machine of another format. Of course, what's a rule without an exception? In this case, you have two exceptions. VHS tape will play on a S-VHS machine (but not vice versa), and a MiniDV tape will play in DVCAM machines (but, again, not vice versa).

Analog formats

The analog recording formats are found everywhere in video production. They've been the only games in town for many years, and video production studios have thousands or hundreds of thousand of dollars invested in their analog recording equipment. For these reasons, analog formats will be around for a long time to come.

Here's a quick rundown of analog formats (refer to Figure 2-2, starting from the bottom of the Formats column):

- ✔ **Composite:** Composite is a video signal containing a combination of all light and color information.

  VHS (a video format that produces composite output) has no real value in video production other than as an end product. As I mention in Chapter 1, the VHS format is pretty useless for editing videos because the videos lose a good bit of quality during the second round of editing. But because VHS is the common format of the video world, almost all recorders have a composite output.

  The ¾-inch U-matic, a 20+-year-old format, is the first commercial-quality format small enough to be carried. Prior to the ¾-inch U-matic, video recording equipment was impossibly large. If you're old enough, you might remember President Nixon's visit to the Great Wall of China in 1972. The video shown of that trip on network television was shot with a ¾-inch U-matic portable recorder. Like VHS, U-matic is also a composite signal. Its signal strength is a little better than VHS because of the video-tape's size. However, U-matic is an outdated technology. The equipment is no longer made and is increasingly difficult to maintain. Even so, many organizations continue to use U-matic because of their initial investment.

- ✔ **S-VHS:** S-VHS is a legitimate professional production format because it can survive relatively well through a couple of generations of editing. The S-VHS signal is different from VHS signal in that light *(luminance)* and color *(chroma)* are kept separated. S-VHS is also referred to as Y/C. Until MiniDV, S-VHS was the only low-cost format option for industrial video production and the virtual domain of the prosumer (see Chapter 1 for more on prosumer). Though not directly competitive with commercial and industrial formats, S-VHS has been successful in numerous applications, such as in-house corporate video and low-end event videography. S-VHS recorders accept VHS tape.

- ✔ **Betacam SP:** Betacam (now Betacam SP) is a component analog format. In this format, not only is color separated from light (as in S-VHS), but colors themselves are also segregated to ensure quality of the signal over multiple generations. In addition, the quality of the resolution of the Betacam format is significantly greater. For all practical purposes, other than both being analog, Betacam SP and S-VHS have little in common.

The component (Betacam SP) format remains the gold standard of the commercial video production industry. Worldwide, professionals buy more Betacam SP camcorders, such as the UVW-100B, than any other format. Even though it is extremely popular, in its purest state, component is restrictively expensive. A fully-equipped, truly component video production studio costs hundreds of thousands of dollars.

Digital video formats

All digital formats have some common traits. For one thing, (as I've mentioned) digital video formats use binary code (signals that are made of series of ones and zeros). The least expensive to the most expensive digital video formats share the enviable capability of unlimited generations (of editing) without a decline in quality.

Analog signals corrupt as you transmit the signal from the camera to the recorder and on to another recorder (editing). This isn't so with digital video. In many ways, digital video recorded to tape is like a word-processor file. No matter how many copies (generations) are created, the files either work or they don't work. There's no in-between. Also, digital video can be converted to analog video. Last, and perhaps most important, all the digital formats have excellent resolution quality.

Resolution quality is the degree of sharpness of an image as measured by the number of pixels (picture elements) across and down on a display screen.

MiniDV format

MiniDV is the "low-cost" brother of the digital formats. Even so, it goes toe to toe with Betacam SP, the video industry standard. The resolution quality of MiniDV and Betacam SP are perceptively similar. But the audio signal of MiniDV is actually better than Betacam SP's. And, as just mentioned, the multi-generation tape-to-tape quality of MiniDV is better than Betacam SP's. MiniDV has some limitations, which I discuss throughout this book. But, compared dollar for dollar with Betacam SP, MiniDV is a technological wonder.

Digital S, DVCPRO, and DVCAM formats

The top three commercial digital formats (shown earlier in the Formats column in Figure 2-2) are offered by JVC, Panasonic, and Sony, respectively. Even though they are all digital, they are not compatible. The comparative value of one over the other is a matter of personal preference. I think JVC Digital S is the best, but a lot of people will say they prefer DVCPRO or DVCAM. As a matter of fact, if you were to put 20 producers in a room to decide which of the digital formats is best, you'd better make sure they first leave their guns, knives, and tripod handles at the door. In any event, one significant difference among the three is that DVCAM equipment accepts video tapes with a MiniDV format.

The three commercial digital formats (top three in Formats column in Figure 2-2) share a digital output standard called Serial Digital Interface (SDI). This format is the way digital-format recorders transmit their digital video to other digital equipment, such as other digital recorders or computers. SDI and MiniDV's IEEE 1394 are distinctly different technologies for accomplishing approximately the same thing.

Editing made easy

Again refer to Figure 2-2, this time to column three (Editors). When it comes to editing, you've got linear and nonlinear editing.

Sometimes there's a little confusion in assuming that digital video formats are always edited in nonlinear systems or that analog video formats are always edited in linear systems. But this isn't so. As you can see in the Editors column in Figure 2-2, you have linear and nonlinear digital editors. Any recording format (digital or analog) can be edited on a digital nonlinear editing system. This is made possible by having the right kind of hardware (capture card) for the format you want to edit on your computer. The same is not true for analog editing systems. Analog editing systems are much more format-dependent. For example, Betacam SP videotape requires Betacam editing equipment.

Linear and nonlinear editing are well-chosen terms. Linear editing doesn't allow cutting and pasting. In linear editing, you must edit videotapes piece by piece, shot by shot, sound byte by sound byte onto a recording tape. Wherever you need to make a correction — at the beginning, in the middle, near the end, wherever — you must re-record from that point forward — piece by piece.

In comparison, in nonlinear editing, you can edit and cut and paste anywhere on the timeline of a video, as many times as you want, without having to start over. Figure 2-3 shows a series of video frames that compare linear and non-linear editing procedures.

In linear editing, removal of frames requires re-editing the video from that point in the timeline. In nonlinear editing, the removal of frames is not a problem — just ripple all subsequent frames to an earlier point on the timeline. To *ripple* means to push all the subsequent edits backward on the timeline, thereby removing the hole.

In editing, the image is usually comprised of what are referred to as A and B rolls. "A" roll is the primary visual (such as an interviewee). "B" roll is additional visual, such as location shots, graphics, or other visual points added for emphasis. Though there is no roll of tape in nonlinear editing, the A/B roll terminology is still used.

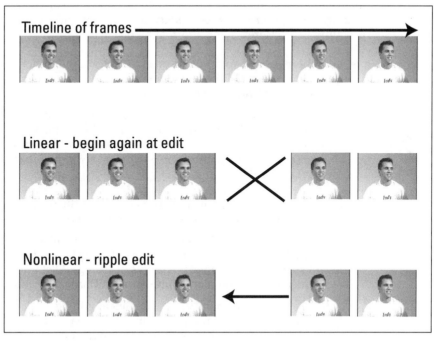

In linear editing (refer to Figure 2-3), a segment of the video's timeline cannot be removed without leaving a hole in the production. There is no way to "ripple" the edits. In nonlinear, everything is groups of digital information — like paragraphs in a word-processing file. Filling a hole is as simple as cutting and pasting.

Both linear and nonlinear editors depend on what's called *time code.* Let me briefly explain this point. In almost all video production, camcorders record individual frames of video, each with its own unique numeric name. Time code is designated in hours, minutes, seconds, and frames. In North America and many other parts of the world, video is made up of 30 frames per second. A typical time code can be 01:02:03:04 (Hour 01 of 24: Minute 02 of 60: Second 03 of 60: and Frame 04 of 30).

Linear editors

Linear editing requires at least two videotape machines — the *source machine* that contains the original video and the *recorder.* All linear editing systems have one thing in common: an *edit controller* that automatically operates the source machine(s) and the recorder. You use the edit controller to search and find specific video segments and then place the segments at specific places on the record tape.

Nonlinear Editors

Nonlinear editors are computer-based. In fact, a nonlinear editing system is basically a computer with special software and a special piece of hardware (a capture card). Here's some information on each:

- ✔ **Computer choice:** Your choice of a computer for your nonlinear editing workstation is one of the most important decisions you make in regard to fitting digital video to your needs.

  The topic of computers is where people get into arguments about the supremacy of the Macintosh or the open architecture of Windows. I think they both are incredible — when selected for the correct reasons, so I guess this isn't much of a tip, is it? I use a Windows-based computer for all of my work. As a matter of fact, all of the graphics and movie files on this book's CD-ROM were made on that PC. The Macintosh G3 is a great computer for digital video production. At the time of this writing, the most recent version comes equipped with a built-in IEEE 1394 port.

  Whether you choose a Macintosh G3 or a Pentium III with Windows 98 or NT 4.0, select your computer with the following in mind: It needs to have lots of speed, lots of memory, and lots of storage. I get into some specific recommendations about computer types in Chapters 8 and 22.

- ✔ **Software:** Among its many values, nonlinear editing is a kind of chapel for the marriage of desktop publishing software programs with video and audio production software programs. What once took numerous specialized suites of an expensive video production studio can now be performed with relative ease at a single computer desktop.

  As an example, I'm writing this book at the same computer workstation where my wife and I also capture video and sound, create graphics and animation, author multimedia applications, develop Web sites, encode streaming video, and output to video tape, CD-ROM, and the Internet.

- ✔ **Special hardware:** The single greatest feature that distinguishes one nonlinear editing system from another is its capture card. Capture cards are built-in or plug-in hardware boards installed on a computer. The capture card is where incoming video is digitized (that is, signals are changed from analog to digital signals, thereby enabling the computer to use the signals) into a computer file. So the capture card is what makes playing video on your computer a possibility. (See Chapter 9 for more on capture cards.)

  Capture cards are often broken into two categories — real-time and rendering. Real-time capture cards are expensive. Rendering capture cards are much less expensive. Basically, *real-time* refers to a nonlinear editing system's capability to make special editing changes (transitions) such as dissolves or wipes at normal speed. *Rendering* refers to a nonlinear editing system's capability to build transitions, frame by frame. (I tell you more about real-time and rendering in just a bit.)

Using Figure 2-4, you can see the difference between real-time and rendering. In the figure, movie clip A (frames shown in top row) is a wedding video of newlyweds kissing at the altar, and movie clip B (frames in bottom row) shows the same couple 10 years later kissing at their anniversary party.

The editor caused a slow dissolve of movie clip A into movie clip B. By *dissolve,* I mean the video smoothly changes from clip A to clip B. In this case, the dissolve happens over a 3-second period.

In video, three seconds equals 90 frames (30 frames per second x 3). The nonlinear editing system calculates and displays each of the 90 frames as they sequentially change from movie clip A to movie clip B. In a dissolve, each frame is an increase in opacity of B and a decrease in opacity of A.

In a real-time nonlinear editing system, the editor can play this transition between the two clips without any wait. A nonlinear system without real-time performs what's called *rendering,* which is a procedure where each of the frames is created at a speed slower than 30 frames in a second. The speed of rendering varies because it depends on the processing speed and memory of the computer and on the resolution quality of the video image.

For this reason, real-time nonlinear editing systems cost more than systems that depend solely on rendering.

Figure 2-4:
In a dissolve, each of the frames is a unique combination of slowly hiding clip A (top row) and slowly revealing clip B (bottom row).

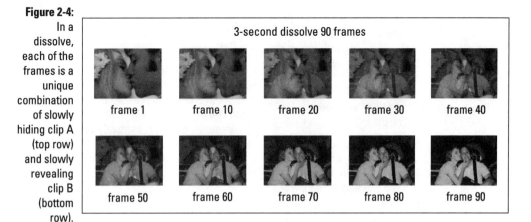

3-second dissolve 90 frames

frame 1 frame 10 frame 20 frame 30 frame 40

frame 50 frame 60 frame 70 frame 80 frame 90

Distributing your video

Distribution refers to the way you give your work to others. You can give it to them on videotape, on the Internet, and on CD-ROM. In this sense, you can think of *distribution* as being what you do with your final product. (Refer to the Distribution column shown earlier in Figure 2-2 for a list of product options.) A typical finished product is a master. In video production, a *master* is a final-edit version of a tape (referred to as generations three and four in Chapter 1).

People usually put the word "tape" after master. But, in addition to, or instead of, a master tape, you can edit video to fit into PowerPoint presentations, to promote a product via CD-ROM, or to stream on the Internet. We cover each of these distribution options in this book. In the future, you also will probably be able to affordably make DVD and MPEG versions of your video.

Your format of choice may aid or conflict with distribution. Case in point, if you intend to create programs with MiniDV, you may want to find someone who is capable of using MiniDV or Sony DVCAM tapes for VHS duplicating machines. Another example is broadcast. Though MiniDV is broadcast quality, many television stations have no way to play digital videotapes.

Where does MiniDV fit?

MiniDV is a superior prosumer format, providing the capability of broadcast-quality video. MiniDV and the IEEE 1394 interface are economical links to full-fledged professional production. Prior to them, most of us were relegated to S-VHS linear editing with almost no graphical capabilities. The only alternative would have been to invest in Betacam SP production equipment and corporate- or industrial-quality nonlinear editing equipment. Until MiniDV, there were no other alternatives.

MiniDV camcorders, such as the Canon XL1 and the Sony and JVC counterparts, provide excellent opportunities to people who want to produce high-quality video and audio. The images and sound they produce are very good and are commercially viable. I use MiniDV successfully in my work.

However, the quality of a MiniDV camcorder does not equal the quality of commercial digital camcorders, such as the Hitachi Z-3000W with the JVC Digital-S recorder. The differences in professional features and overall performance are significant.

But, at the same time, the cost of the 3-CCD MiniDV camcorder is approximately one-sixth that of the 3-CCD digital video camcorder. And when you compare MiniDV images to Betacam SP images, they're perceptively just as good, plus the sound is better. Bottom line — MiniDV is a high-quality prosumer video production medium.

Part II
Shooting Digital Video

The 5th Wave   By Rich Tennant

In this part . . .

Probably the single most important skill you can possess in video production is an understanding of what your digital camcorder can do for you. A lot of space-age technology has been crammed into that little electronic device, and the technology is all there for you to use. You just need to understand what's possible. Part II helps you do just that.

In this part, each of the chapters dwells on a specific subject related to digital video recording. One chapter is about the camera itself. Another chapter shows how to provide the right kind of lighting in your recording environment. One of the chapters walks you through the basics of audio recording. And the last two chapters familiarize you with the art and practice of production planning and direction. All in all, you're in for a full-course video production extravaganza.

Chapter 3

Maximizing Your Digital Video Camcorder

*L*et me say it right up front: This chapter is not exactly "action-packed" and may not be for everybody. Why? Because what follows is a kind of Digital Videography 101. Actually, you don't have to ponder these principles to get a great shot with your camcorder. However, you can greatly increase the quality of your shot if you have a working knowledge of the concepts provided here. So delve into this chapter as little or as much as like; you can always read portions of it and come back later.

In the world of video, the term *production value* refers to a perceived quality of video image and sound. When I hear the term, my first thoughts run back to when I worked in industrial video.

I always used every trick available to maximize the visual and audio quality of my videos. My frustration level ran pretty high because I often saw people using more sophisticated equipment and getting beautiful footage, while I meticulously tried to do something that inevitably ended up of lesser quality.

The tables have turned dramatically. As I mention in Chapters 1 and 2, you can now shoot in a format that rivals broadcast quality. So, I challenge you to go all the way and make the most of what's being offered. By understanding some simple procedures (which you can find in this chapter) and turning them into habits, you'll be able to make your camcorder *sing* as you wish.

Get ready and set to go — because you're about to find out how to get the most out of every shot you take.

Understanding the Basics of the Image

Much of the language and practices of video production have their roots in film production. Terms that were first coined in the era of silver nitrate film and megaphones are still the fundamental lexicon of videography. This rich language continues to exist because video technology has, in many ways, simply improved rather than evolved. Today, when you talk about shutter speeds or wide shots, you're communicating ideas based on the development of a time-honored craft. Your understanding of key concepts can make worlds of difference in the quality of your videos. Explanations of the concepts include these juicy tidbits (more about these fine points in the following sections):

- Aperture and iris
- Focus and depth of focus
- Focal length and perspective

Defining aperture and iris

Say that you have a digital camcorder. You want to do something relevant with it, such as shooting video. But, first, you're overcome with an urge: You check to make sure no one is looking, you point the camcorder at your nose, and you stare into the darkness of the lens.

This may be a very special moment, so I don't want to intrude. But while you and your camcorder bond, you may notice something rather interesting: If you're in a well-lit room with a light background behind you, the lens responds to you as you move the camcorder toward and away from your nose. Hold the camcorder at arm's length and move it toward you. Something is happening inside the lens. You may think it's winking at you (bonding is a wonderful thing). You've just watched your camcorder automatically attempt to adjust aperture with its iris.

In digital video geekspeak, *aperture* refers to the overall amount of light that reaches through the lens to the focal plane inside your camcorder (see the next section "Grasping aperture basics" for more on focal plane). And *iris* is an adjustable opening at the lens.

If you have photographic experience, you probably already know about aperture and iris. The same concepts apply in video (and digital video). If you aren't versed in the subject, this little bit of information is invaluable. By knowing about your options for controlling light, you can greatly affect the composition of your video, technically and aesthetically.

You can begin by taking a look at Figure 3-1, which shows a simplified cross-section of the workings of a 3-CCD camcorder and its lens. (In Chapter 2, I mention that, in video, a camera acquires light and color on chips called *Charge-Coupled Devices,* or CCDs. See Chapter 2 for more details CCDs and 3-CCD cameras). In front of your lens is an object. Your camcorder's job is to translate a high-quality 2-D likeness of the 3-D reality you are shooting. A number of issues affect the success of this mission. The first issue is aperture.

Figure 3-1:
The object's likeness is accurately collected at a specific place called the focal plane.

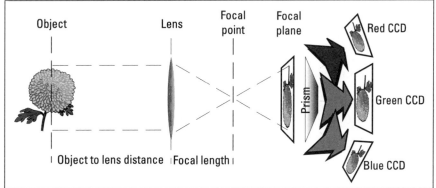

Grasping aperture basics

For the best approach to grasping the basics of aperture, imagine that you have a primitive lens with no zoom capabilities. Now imagine that in front of the lens is an object, such as the chrysanthemum in Figure 3-1.

With that context set, briefly ponder the following principles:

- ✔ **Focal point:** The nature of lenses is that their convex shape (curved outward) bends an image and reduces it to a point, called the focal point.

- ✔ **Focal plane:** The focal plane is the point where the likeness of the object being photographed is in focus and optimized. Specifically, beyond the focal point, the image reverses and enlarges until, at a point equal to the distance between the lens and the focal point, the image is an exact 2-D likeness of the object in the lens. This point (actually a thin plane) is called the focal plane.

- ✔ **Focal length:** The distance between the lens and the focal point is called the lens focal length. (See the section "Checking out focal length and perspective," later in this chapter, for more on this topic.)

- ✔ **Aperture:** Aperture is the opening of a lens that controls the amount of light permitted to reach either film or a collection device in video cameras; that is, aperture controls the amount of light that reaches the focal plane. Aperture is the relationship between two factors: the diameter of the lens opening and the distance from the lens to the focal point.

Technically, aperture equals focal length divided by the diameter of your lens and is referred to as *f-stop*. For example, a 100mm lens with a diameter of 50mm has a maximum aperture (or f-stop) of f/2 (100mm divided by 50mm). See the sidebar "Much ado about f-stops" for more on f-stop and the section "Checking out focal length and perspective" for more on focal length, both later in this chapter.

✔ **Maximum aperture:** Every camera's lens has what's called maximum aperture, which is the widest diameter allowed by the lens for collecting light.

As I said at the beginning of this section about aperture basics, the lens described in the preceding bulleted list is primitive. You probably wouldn't like it because your camcorder would always have to be an exact distance from the flower in order for the image on the focal plane to be focused. And the object would always have to be ideally lit.

If you were to leave the lens unchanged and decrease the distance of the object to the lens, things would change dramatically. As the relationship of the object to the lens shortens, so does the location of the focal plane — this time in front of the CCDs' prism (see Figure 3-2). As a result, the images on the CCDs are unfocused.

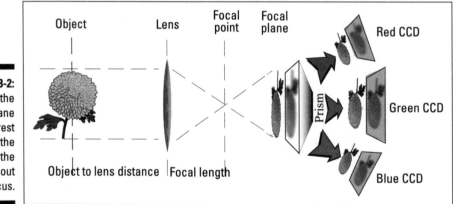

Figure 3-2:
When the focal plane doesn't rest on the prism, the image is out of focus.

As I mentioned earlier, focal length is the distance between the lens and the focal point. When you *focus* an image, you simply make a minor change to the lens's focal length (again, see the section "Checking out focal length and perspective," later in this chapter). In Figure 3-2, I shortened the distance of the object to the lens, which pulled the focal plane away from the prism. In this instance, focusing stretches the focal length until the focal plane intersects with the CCD prism (see Figure 3-3).

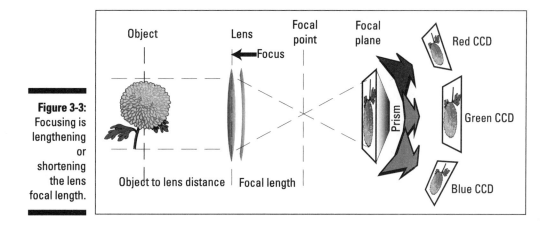

Figure 3-3:
Focusing is
lengthening
or
shortening
the lens
focal length.

Noise — or starving a CCD for light!

Too much light on an object causes the focal plane to lose detail and tend toward *whiteout* (which is a loss of all an image's detail). Too little light causes the electronics of the camcorder to exhibit what's called *video noise*.

A CCD chip typically has 400,000 or more pixels (see Chapter 2 for more on CCD chips). Each of those pixels must receive information in the form of color and light. If the object is underlit, many of the pixels do not receive this information. As a result, the camcorder replaces the missing visual information with jibberish, causing dark colors to appear as though they're covered with dancing specks. These dancing specks are *video noise*.

Videographers are time managers and magicians

Video camcorders don't create light, but they do take full advantage of all available light. This is both good and bad. The good part is that you'll find few situations where a quality camcorder won't get a picture — even in near darkness. The bad part is that you may be tempted to depend too much on your camcorder's low-light features. Here is an excellent axiom for you as a budding digital videographer:

If there is a better way to prepare a shot, do it!

Professional videographers use time for all it's worth. If you have a lot of time to set up a shot, to properly light it, and to ensure quality of sound, use every moment of that time to get the best quality you can and then shoot semi-automatic or totally with manual settings. If you have only a few moments to set up a shot, make sure to position objects in your shot, do all you can for the sound, cross your fingers, and go fully automatic. Of course, reality is most often somewhere in between.

Adjusting your camcorder for light

What if you want to leave the light alone and "ask" your camcorder to adjust to a proper light level on the focal plane? How can you do that? Only two answers exist so far: Either make the lens diameter adjustable or make the focal length adjustable. Both are good answers. The first procedure is *f-stopping,* and the second is *zooming,* and each has its own result.

The place to begin is f-stopping, which you accomplish by adjusting your lens's iris.

You have two very good reasons for adjusting your iris, and thereby the aperture and the amount of light that reaches the focal plane.

- ✔ Narrowing your iris decreases the light hitting your CCDs.
- ✔ Narrowing your iris deepens your depth of field on either side of the focal plane. (I describe depth of field in just a moment.)

The focal plane is a precise 2-D plane cutting through objects as seen in the lens. Everything on either side of the focal plane is out of focus. The higher the f-stop setting, the lower the effect of unfocusing on either side of the focal plane.

If you leave your camcorder's aperture control on automatic, you'll see the aperture setting go from wide to narrow when you point the camcorder at a dark area and then at a well-lit area. Left to its own, a camcorder adjusts aperture as a way to compensate for light levels. As you become increasingly proficient with your camcorder, you'll tend to set the aperture control to manual so that you can manipulate depth of field (a dimension in front of and behind the focal plane where objects appear to be in focus) or light or both.

Much ado about f-stops

F-stop settings vary from one camcorder lens to another. But, in all cases, the *smaller* the f-stop, the *wider* the aperture. As a general rule, each f-stop from the largest number to the smallest allows more light exposure. For example, the Canon XL1 with its 16X lens and automatic and semi-automatic settings allows eight f-stops: f/1.6, f/2.0, f/2.8, f/4.0, f/5.6, f/8.0, f/11, f/16, plus a protective close setting.

By going fully manually, you can adjust the Canon XL1 to even smaller stops. In that case, you have 27 choices: f/1.6, f/1.8, f/2.0, f/2.2, f/2.4, f/2.6, f/2.8, f/3.2, f/3.4, f/3.7, f/4.0, f/4.4, f/4.8, f/5.2, f/5.6, f/6.2, f/6.7, f/7.3, f/8.0, f/8.7, f/9.5, f/10, f/11, f/12, f/14, f/15, f/16, plus close.

For example, you use a manual aperture control to manipulate light when your object is dark and your background is bright. Videographers often compensate for this problem by zooming in to take an up-close shot with the aperture setting at automatic. Once the aperture has adjusted to the dark object, the videographer changes the aperture to manual and zooms out. The result is that the iris setting is based on the dark object (subject of the picture) and not on the overwhelming light background.

Dipping into depth of field

As I mentioned, depth of field is a dimension in front of and behind the focal plane where objects appear to be in focus. One of the basic facts of video production is that the *higher* the F-stop, the *greater* the depth of field.

Figure 3-4 illustrates this principle. In the figure, you see three iris settings. For this figure, assume that the light is adequate for all three settings. The first setting illustrates a nearly wide-open iris, and the last a nearly closed iris. Ideally, if you can control the lighting of a shot, your best f-stops are in the middle, such as f/5.6 (f/5.6 simply means that the f-stop is 5.6), as indicated in this figure.

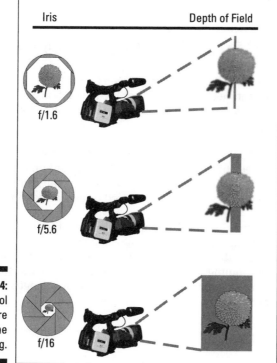

Iris   Depth of Field

f/1.6

f/5.6

f/16

Figure 3-4:
You control
aperture
through the
iris setting.

Videographers like to stay in the middle settings if possible for several reasons:

- A wide open iris is usually undesirable because almost everything in the shot is always out of focus (of course, this may be the effect you're looking for).
- A wide open iris sometimes produces distorted edges to a picture.
- A middle iris setting allows for some play of iris manipulation if the lighting conditions go through subtle changes.
- A middle iris setting usually creates a comfortable feel to the picture by allowing a little of the foreground and background to appear out of focus. This middle setting aids in giving a three-dimensional "feel" to the shot.
- A middle iris setting, if adequately lit, usually produces a comfortable range of brightness and shadow without tending toward starkness.
- A nearly-closed iris setting requires a highly-lit shot where you run the risk of overlit foreheads and nuclear white clothing.
- A nearly-closed iris can create an uncomfortable shot where everything in the foreground and background appears unnaturally in focus — because you don't see three-dimensional reality all in focus (again, of course, this may be exactly the effect you're attempting to accomplish).

Checking out focal length and perspective

You can change the depth of field without changing your f-stop. You can do so via focal length and perspective. Recall that focal length is the distance between the lens and the focal point. By *perspective,* I mean the way objects appear through the lens.

Take a look at Figure 3-5. In this figure, the iris setting remains unchanged and has progressively "dollied" back. (Sorry about that; thought I might sneak in a term while at it. In video production, to *dolly* is to physically move a camera, mounted on a tripod with wheels, toward or away from an object.)

This figure shows something significant happening. Even though the distance between the camcorder and the object is progressively greater, the image size remains the same and the depth of field increases. What's happening? Please don't say we're zooming! That's a non-answer. A hip digital videographer's answer would be that we're changing the lens's focal length. I knew that's what you would say.

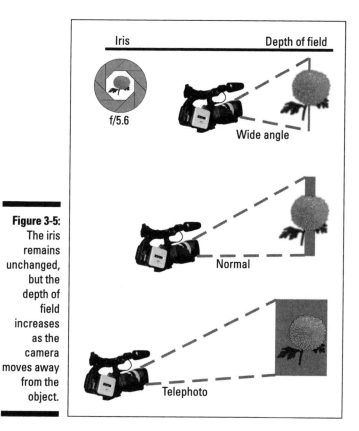

Figure 3-5:
The iris remains unchanged, but the depth of field increases as the camera moves away from the object.

Focal length

A short focal length creates a *wide angle,* allowing the lens to shoot a wide area in a relatively short distance. A long focal length creates a *narrow angle,* causing the lens to capture a narrow area, perhaps in a long distance.

Take a look at Figure 3-6. Focal length affects more than one thing. By increasing focal length (from the top to the bottom image), you narrow the angle of the picture. Imagine standing in a tunnel looking at the tunnel entrance. If you are 100 yards into the tunnel, your view of the outside world is considerably narrower than it is if you stand ten yards from the entrance. The same is true of the effect of focal length.

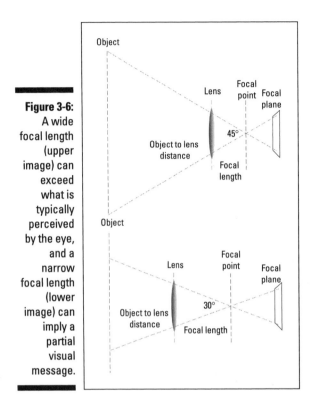

Figure 3-6:
A wide
focal length
(upper
image) can
exceed
what is
typically
perceived
by the eye,
and a
narrow
focal length
(lower
image) can
imply a
partial
visual
message.

Though the increase of focal length reduces the angle of view, the magnification of the image increases. A narrow angle of view creates a *telephoto image* (an image similar to what you might see in a telescope — magnified but narrow). This extension of the focal length also increases the need for light, somewhat like increasing f-stops. The reason for this is simple — the aperture is farther from the focal plane.

Perspective

Recollect that perspective is the way in which objects appear to the eye in respect to their relative positions and distance. In plain English, this means that your eyes are accustomed to judging size and distance of objects by the way the objects spread out or bunch together three-dimensionally. An artist is judged for her abilities to successfully reproduce perspective in the two-dimensional world.

Although it's a rather subjective term, *normal* is the term used in videography when describing angles of view and perspective that seem natural to the eye. Normal angles lie somewhere between wide and telephoto angles.

Normal angles and perspectives display views typical to the human eye. Of course, if you're a budding Hitchcock, you'll know when you want to break from normal to provide a shocking or unnerving perspective or angle. And you'll know how to lull your viewer into a false sense of comfort with preliminary normal shots.

A wide angle exceeds what would usually be seen unaided by normal vision. As a result, wide angle shots tend to seem somewhat grotesque. On the other hand, when focused to infinity, extreme telephoto shots seem to tighten and flatten our perspective to the extent the view can seem close and crowded.

Take a look at Figure 3-7. Depending on your goals, you can use a lens's focal length to convey beauty or pathos. The wide angle shot distorts the vertical plane, implying an inappropriateness, isolation, and abandonment to a building. The wide/normal angle shot communicates a building that has been closed and is awaiting a new owner. The normal angle shot depicts reality — a building that has seen its better days. The telephoto (narrow) angle highlights the architectural uniqueness of the structure, while hiding its glaring blemishes. The extended telephoto takes you to an architectural detail. An extended telephoto is an electronic way of doubling the magnification of the lens. This feature is available in many digital camcorders.

Automatically zooming

Okay. I went and used the term. You aren't going to belittle yourself by using your automatic zoom controls on your camcorder. My only problem with zooming is that you can do so much more with manual controls — if you just practice a little. Zooming does a bunch of things all at the same time, like changing focal length, perspective, aperture, depth of focus, and focus. It's kind of scary when you realize what all is being done automatically.

Just be aware that the better the camcorder (for example, one of my favorites, the Canon XL1), the more manual control you'll have available when you want it.

Frequently, some automatic features of the zoom controls are going to get you into trouble. A perfect example is when you're zooming from a wide angle to a close-up using automatic focus. If your subject is off-center and comprises only a portion of the screen, the automatic focus controls go crazy. Another example is zooming out from a close-up of a human face to a bright wide shot. As you zoom out, the human face darkens if you are in automatic iris. Bottom line — when possible, go manual.

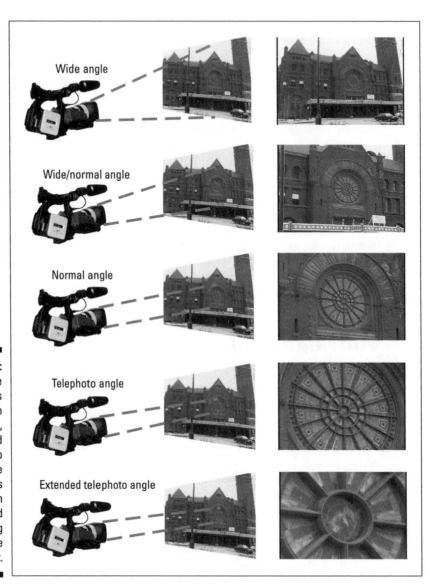

Figure 3-7:
The
differences
between
wide,
normal, and
telephoto
lenses are
obvious
when
compared
by using
the same
subject.

Wide angle

Wide/normal angle

Normal angle

Telephoto angle

Extended telephoto angle

Getting shutter control

Many moons ago, as a way to pay my way through college, I was a motion picture projectionist in a movie theater. Though the pay was good and the movie
watching was free, the work was ridiculously easy and boring. So, in addition
to studying my textbooks, I studied and studied the two 35mm motion picture
projectors in my projection booth. Quite frankly, I was amazed by cinema.
Twenty-four frames per second, film streamed past an intersection of a light
source and the lens.

That was basically all there was to it — except one major problem. Twenty-four frames of film per second should be a blur. How come they are sharp and in focus? The answer is genius simplicity. Twenty-four times a second the film would stop in front of the lens and then continue. During each frame advance, a mechanical fan shutter crossed the lens opening and blocked out light.

So the movement of the film was always in the dark. All you saw on the screen was the stopped frame — 24 times a second. Twenty-eight years later, film projection is basically still the same. In somewhat the same manner, shutter control is used for video production.

Using this description of shutters in film helps explain shutter control in video. Video is shot at 30 frames per second instead of the 24 frames per second used in film production. For a number of complicated reasons, video is actually shot so that you have two fields per frame. Imagine a set of horizontal lines, each with an odd or even number. Fields of video are made up of either all odd or all even lines. The two fields are then interlaced, and the video frame results — 30 times per second.

The default shutter speed per second for video production is 60 (equal to the number of fields per second). Once in awhile, the speed of your subject(s) exceeds the normal collection of visual information. An example is an automobile race. Even though you are replacing 60 fields every second, the movement of the cars are still a blur on the video.

If your digital camcorder is a good one, you can compensate for this blur by manually adjusting the shutter control. For example, on the Canon XL1, you can adjust from $\frac{1}{60}$ second to $\frac{1}{15,000}$ second if needed.

Though you're increasing the shutter speed by doing so, the video is still being shot at 30 frames per second. An increase of shutter speed means that the amount of time your shutter is "closed" increases, while your exposure decreases. In this way, you are taking extremely brief snapshots with increased blacked out time in between each field. The result is that your car's movement is no longer blurry.

When you dial up the shutter speed to the higher numbers, a strobe effect may begin to appear. A flutter strobe effect happens because your eye is beginning to detect the increased black time of the shutter.

Chapter 4

Letting There Be Light

● ●

In This Chapter

▶ Getting correct color correctly

▶ Light comes in many flavors

▶ Recording beautifully in natural light

▶ Controlling your light with studio quality

● ●

A camcorder's best friend and worst enemy is light. Light can illuminate and color, add depth and texture, and provide all the visual information your camcorder needs for acquiring beautiful footage. But light isn't automatically good. It can mess up your shot by silhouetting what you want to highlight, cast nasty shadows on noses, burn foreheads, and all around make you look like a schnook of a videographer. Believe me, I've known the gasps of joy at a well-constructed shot, and the grunts of disgust over a day's wasted footage — all because of my good or poor decisions about lighting.

Light can even hurt your equipment. Accidentally leaving your lens (or viewfinder!) unprotected and pointed at a bright object can cost you hundreds or thousands of dollars. Unfortunately, I know about that one, too.

In this chapter, I tell you how you can use lighting to ensure that your viewers see what you *want* them to see. Of course, you could skip this whole chapter and just depend on your camcorder's automatic settings to handle lighting; 70 percent of the time you'd probably be okay. Sooner or later, though, you are going to need to know how to enhance and hide with light. In fact, experience tells me that you will be faced with some lighting challenges almost as often as you turn on your camcorder.

Properly Interpreting Color with Digital Video

A visual image that looks warm and fuzzy to the eye can appear dramatically different in playback on a video tape recorder. That's because the human eye is connected to this thing called the brain. Without realizing it, your brain is constantly translating what you actually see into what it thinks you should be seeing. Your camcorder isn't nearly so smart.

Try this for a simple example: Close one eye and look around your room. With one eye closed, your brain is taking all the light, shade, color, and shapes that your eye provides and translating this information into three dimensions — even though you're, for the moment, actually seeing two-dimensionally. Camcorders don't have brains quite as developed as that.

Perhaps an even better example is a white sheet of paper in a semi-lit room. You know that, in ordinary light, the paper is the whitest white. So, in a poorly lit room, you see the paper, and your brain tells you it is white. Your eye is actually seeing gray, but memory overrides that information. Again, camcorders do poorly with the same information.

But even your eyes and brain can't keep you out of trouble all the time. A good example of this is when you purchase a garment at a clothing store to color coordinate with another garment at home. You fuss and fuss till you select just the right necktie or scarf. But when you get home, you find the colors don't work together at all. What happened? Well, possibly something altogether different than what you might think.

In the store, you may have seen the scarf under fluorescent light. In your mind's eye, you interpreted the scarf's color coordination with your garment at home. The problem is that your memory of the garment at home comes from looking at it in incandescent light or daylight. The only foolproof way to color coordinate is to look at both garments in the same kind of light.

The problems your eyes and brain get themselves into here have to do with color temperature. *Color temperature* is a standardized measurement for the ways colors appear based on the characteristics of the light in which you see the colors. And, if you're an occasional victim of the affects of color temperature, your camcorder is a sitting off-color duck.

Perceiving color temperature

A camcorder has to be told how to interpret color based on the color temperature of the light source(s) where you are recording. When you record in the sunlight, your camcorder's interpretation of an object's color is entirely different from its interpretation of that same object indoors. Perhaps you've already experienced this.

A typical scenario is when you record video as you follow someone from outdoors to indoors. As you first go indoors, your camcorder goes through all kinds of gyrations trying to adjust the iris (turn back to Chapter 3 for more about the iris). But you may notice that, for a few short moments, everything in the room has a bluish cast. Then things become normal in appearance.

These changes are what's called *white balancing*. The term white balancing originated with the practice of placing a white object in front of a camera lens and telling the camera that the object is white. Today's camcorders have automatic white balancing capabilities. Essentially, using an automatic white balance control, your camcorder reinterprets the color white in order to adjust to a new color temperature. If your camcorder can properly display something that is truly white, then all other colors in the picture will also be correct.

If your camcorder can automatically adjust white balance, why even bother discussing it here? For very good reasons. Your camcorder's automatic white balance function is based on an average color temperature in the room. The problem is that, once in awhile, a predominant color in the room can royally screw up the average so that human skin looks eerily tinted.

So, what do the pros do? Sometimes they trust automatic white balance. Once in awhile, they use the manufacturer's presets. But when in doubt, which is often, they manually adjust the white balance.

Manually white balancing is a fairly simple process; just stroll this way to find out how:

1. **Set your white balance selection to Manual.**

   Using the Canon XL1 as an example, turn the white balance knob toward the white balance button (see Figure 4-1).

2. **Position a piece of white paper at the location where white balance is most critical, such as in front of your subject's face.**

   Doing so ensures that the color temperature at the most important spot is selected as the basis for your white balance.

3. **Press the white balance button on your camcorder.**

   Note: Although I use the Canon XL1 as the model camcorder throughout this book, the white balance options provided by the Canon XL1 are typical of most digital video camcorders.

Balancing white with presets

The indoor and outdoor white balance selections are *presets* that the manufacturer provides. These presets provide you with default white balance settings for recording indoors using artificial light and recording outdoors using daylight. As helpful as these two little options may be, they can also be easily misused.

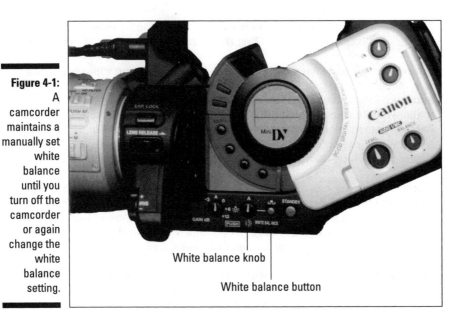

White balance knob

White balance button

Take a look at Table 4-1. The table lists typical color temperatures of various kinds of light sources — from candles to bright sunlight. Presets are for one kind of professional lamp (tungsten) and one time of day. The typical preset color temperatures are for 3200 kelvin (studio-quality lamps) for indoors and 5600 kelvin (midday sun) for outdoors. As you can see, a preset won't help you much if you're using a candle, a standard incandescent, or a fluorescent light indoors. And when outdoors, a preset will mess you up at sunrise and sunset.

Table 4-1	Approximate Color Temperatures of Light Sources
Light Source	*Typical Color Temperatures (measured in kelvin)*
Candle	1,900
Household lamp	2,800
Professional lamp	3,200
Fluorescent light	3,700*
Sunrise and sunset	2,000 to 3,000
Cloudless midday sun	5,600
Hazy day	8,000

*****Note:** Fluorescent light color temperature can vary based on the age of the lamp, coating, filtering, and other factors.

REMEMBER

Basic assumptions about light

Light is the basis for everything you do in video production. Whether you're recording outdoors with available light or indoors with artificial light, you will always be wise to remember some simple axioms:

✔ Light is either satisfying the appetites of all your CCDs' pixels or causing your camcorder to electronically compensate, lowering the quality of your shot.

✔ Your use of light and shadows causes visual hierarchy in your shot — so you and your

light source need to agree about the most to least important elements.

✔ Your use of light and shadows creates a subjective response in the viewer. (I trust that your viewer is laughing because you meant him or her to.)

With light you are setting illusions of relationships in your shot.

Dealing with manual white balance

White balancing tells your camcorder how to interpret the color white. As you practice working with manual white balancing, you'll notice that color temperature problems fade. One thing to avoid whenever possible is *mixed* color temperatures in the same image. The classic mixed-color situation occurs when recording indoors with a window in the shot. If you set white balance for indoor lighting, the outdoor images can have an unpleasant tint. If you can, keep the window out of the shot. But if the shot is important and you don't have control over the lighting, live with your automatic white balance and cross your blue-tinted fingers.

Knowing Your Lighting Options

Unless you have some reason to record video with the lens cover on, you're always either using light or being abused by light in your video production. If you know and use just a few simple facts, you'll be light years ahead in the quality of your work — particularly with digital video. Though entire books are written about proper video lighting techniques, you can accomplish a lot by knowing the lowdown on three processes: setting the primary light, washing with soft light, and using shadows for a good rather than bad effect.

Hitting with hard light

Hard light is a term used in film and video for a direct light source that creates sharply defined shadows. Hard light is dominant; it causes the eye to give priority to highlights. As a rule, the smaller the diameter of the light source, the more distinct and sharp the contrast between the light and the shadow that is created by the hard light. Figure 4-2 illustrates a single hard light source imposed upon a figure. In a studio configuration, hard light can be focused and trimmed so that it illuminates specifically what you want. Outdoors, hard light is usually direct sunlight.

Figure 4-2: As you can see in this figure, hard light accentuates dimension and depth with highlights and shadows.

Suggesting with soft light

Soft light is more subjective than hard light. Soft light washes an area with light and creates comparatively wispy shadows (see Figure 4-3 for an example). Indoors, soft light is created by indirect light sources, such as bouncing a hard light off a white surface. Or an indoor soft light can be a hard light covered with a diffusing cloth or filter. Outdoors, soft light can be achieved on a cloudy day or by working in the shadow of a structure. Sometimes, lighting crews spread silk over an entire scene to cause direct sunlight to diffuse in the silk.

Figure 4-3:
As a converse of the rule of hard light, the larger the diameter of a light source, the less distinct and sharp the contrast of light and shadow created by the soft light.

Controlling shadows

Shadows are the places where light is directly interrupted by an object. How's that for a nice objective definition? Shadows can be good (see Figure 4-4), and they can be very bad. The baddest of the bad is often the shadow caused by a nose. Shadows caused by noses aren't entirely bad. They're bad if they make a person's nose the subject of the video. Believe it or not, you can spend a long time overcoming shadows that make a nose look like an extension of the Adirondack Mountains.

Shadows on an object caused by the object itself are sometimes called *primary shadows*. *Secondary shadows* are those created by a subject and cast upon an adjacent plane, such as a wall. *Tertiary shadows* are those circumstances where an adjacent object casts a shadow on the subject — such as the shadow of a column across the torso of the subject.

Figure 4-4:
Shadows are an important part of a scene because they communicate depth and texture to a scene. Shadows also establish the direction of light source — an important way to establish credibility in a shot.

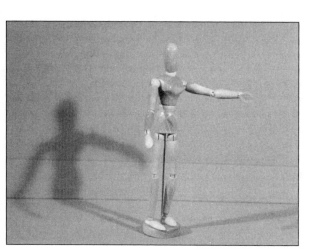

Recording Outdoors

Daylight recording can be some of the most exhilarating and exasperating recording in video production. One of the greatest challenges to outdoor recording is also the elementary one. It's called weather. Changes of weather can virtually ruin the lighting continuity of a video production. Video is seldom shot in what's called *editing order.* That is, you record similar scenes in order, such as all the shots that take place in front of a particular building. Nothing messes up the editing more than to have some shots that were taken in sunlight and others in cloud cover. It's a complete mess.

Not a whole lot can be done about the problems of outdoor recording. But some options exist. For example, you will probably be much more pleased with color quality and texture of scenes that are shot entirely in shade. Cameras love light. But they especially love lots of *indirect* light. Shaded or indirect outdoor lighting is much less susceptible to fluctuations of sunlight.

REMEMBER

Lighting Your Studio

I know you're already thinking megabucks per watt for studio lighting equipment. It's true, lighting equipment can be expensive. But it doesn't have to be. I'm going to show you how to set up some very effective lighting by using only three fixtures. These three lights and some materials purchased at a local hardware store are all you need to create impressive small area shots. Effective lighting is based on the basic principles of key light, fill light, and back light.

Key light (making Aunt Bertha a star)

The primary light of a shot is the *key light*. The key light sets the stage for the shot. By itself, the key light contours and establishes texture and depth of a primary figure. The key light typically comes from a single direction and often is a hard light (see the section "Hitting with hard light," earlier in this chapter). It implies a of principal light source (see Figure 4-5). The key light sets the priority of shadow directions in the scene. All lights are potentially problematic. The key light can create problems by overlighting objects and casting ugly shadows.

Fill light (making Aunt Bertha a young star)

As important as a key light may be, it is usually too stark and unattractive without the compromising wash of *fill light*. For the most part, fill light casts no shadows and lessens some of the harshness of the key light's shadows. As much as the key light establishes a shot, the fill light adds the subjectivity of a livable environment (see Figure 4-6). Just as a key light can harshly overlight a subject, too much fill light can destroy modeling of a figure. Facial contours can disappear. Surfaces can lose their texture.

Direction of light

Figure 4-5:
The key light
establishes
a direction
of light in
the scene.

Figure 4-6:
A fill light
brightens an
overall shot,
including
reducing the
darkness of
key light
shadows.

Back light (giving Aunt Bertha depth)

As I mentioned before, video creates a two-dimensional illusion of three-dimensional reality. One of the basic challenges when recording video is to avoid giving the impression of pasting the subject against the background. The perception of separation from the background is a much more visually comfortable illusion. Separation of the foreground subject from the background is accomplished by using *back light*.

Back light creates a kind of aura on the subject. The highlight lifts the subject from the background (see Figure 4-7). Simply put, back light is pointing a light from the back toward the camera, illuminating the subject from behind.

Figure 4-7:
Back light is
aimed on
the subject
so that it
does not
spill on the
background.

Making a Production out of Lighting

Your digital camcorder is equipped with some amazing features. Left to its own, it can automatically focus, set aperture (refer to Chapter 3 for more on aperture), adjust white balance, and modify shutter speed. All you have to do is try to keep the subject in the center of the shot. Although all these innovations are wonderful, they are seldom totally trustworthy. The more comfortable you become with manual settings, the more you'll like them. One particular environment where automatic settings are especially unnecessary is in the studio.

I use the term "studio" very loosely. Though I have managed professionally-designed dedicated studios for years, I'm often just as comfortable making my living room my studio. For one thing, the coffee pot is a lot closer. By *studio,* I mean an environment where you can control lighting and sound.

You can use your studio for any purpose, from recording canines to canoes. But with a little experience, you'll quickly agree with me — recording a human face is the toughest kind of shot to do right. But it's also the shot you have to be able to perform.

Recording people with pleasure

Though you will sooner or later confront about every kind of video recording situation imaginable, you will always fall back on your fundamental knowledge of lighting the human face.

Making your living room a studio

If you can control outdoor lighting in your living room or any other large room in your house, you've got what it takes for a studio.

✔ **Studio light:** Studio lights, such as the Omni Lights I am proud to own, are a valuable investment. However, regular incandescent lights can do very well, too. The important issue is that your lights need to be portable and powerful. Just remember some basics:

Lights can get very hot. After they've been on a while, you'll probably want to use gloves. Of course, keep the lights away from flammable objects.

Also, you're likely to need some commercial-quality extension cords so that you can move the lights wherever you want and so that you can distribute the power load to more than one circuit in the house if necessary.

✔ **Backdrop:** A nondescript backdrop is essential to studio shots. Here's what I suggest (and, in fact, am using as I write this book — in my living room). Buy some muslin at a fabric store. Paint it a dull, neutral color such as blue-gray. Make a backdrop frame (one that you can easily assemble and break down for carrying in your car). Mine is 8 feet wide by 7 feet high. I simply purchased ¾-inch galvanized pipe at the local hardware store.

To construct a backdrop frame, just go to your favorite hardware store and ask for the following items:

Four 4-feet by ¾-inch threaded galvanized pipe

Two 3-feet by ¾-inch threaded galvanized pipe

Three ¾-inch couples (for putting together the two 7-feet lengths and the 8-feet length)

Two 90 degree elbows (for connecting the sides with the top)

Two Ts (for connecting to the bottom of the 7-feet sides)

Four 1-foot by ¾-inch threaded galvanized nipples (for making the backdrop feet)

Four ¾-inch female caps (for making ends to the feet)

✔ **Alligator clamps:** While you're at the hardware store, buy some spring clamps (six will probably do) for clamping your backdrop to the frame. These clamps are invaluable in video production for a multitude of ingenious purposes.

✔ **Foamcore:** At your local craft or office supply store, you'll probably want to buy some 2 feet x 4 feet white foamcore (¼-inch or ⅜-inch thickness). This board is great for bouncing light as a soft light. Also, you can cut out shapes and slashes and place them in front of a light to create fascinating background patterns. Last, you can use the foamcore in front of a light to flag. *Flagging* is a procedure where you block light to keep it from hitting or spilling into areas of the shot where light isn't wanted.

We're all experts about human heads. Why not? We look at them all the time. To be an expert at recording a human head in video takes some practice though. Subtle nuances of light can either flatter or deride a facial feature.

Corrections in lighting are complex and time consuming. For example, changing a key light usually requires modifying the fill light and possibly even the back light.

Setting the key light

The great challenge of recording the human face comes from the infinite variety of facial shapes and shades. You can't record everyone in the same manner. Of course, the intent of the shot also can dictate the manner in which you want to address a face. For example, lighting a face for a mysterious, eerie scene is entirely different than lighting the face for a causal interview.

Take a look at the images in Figure 4-8.

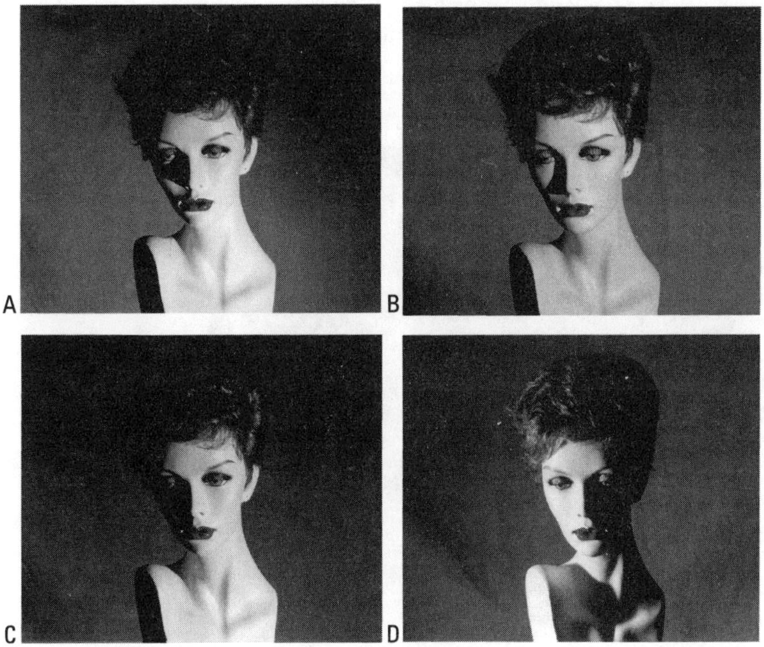

Figure 4-8: The angle of key lighting changes the effect. (A) is an unusual angle, creating a mysterious look; (B) is a natural angle; (C) is also natural but highly-shadowed; (D) is overly bright on the forehead.

In this figure, I adjusted the vertical and horizontal location of the key light in each image to emphasize various features. Using a single facial structure, you can change the angle and the intensity of the key light to create a variety of effects. The effect can be dramatic.

Pulling away from the background

Back light is effective to the degree that it successfully separates the subject from the background. Setting the back light can be fun. The back light isn't as critical as the modeling characteristics of key light or the washing characteristics of fill light. The best way to set a back light is to first turn off the key light and the fill light. You'll find that aiming the light is simpler.

Softening the image

Fill light washes and softens the video image. If you want, you can add a mood with your fill light, while still accomplishing all you need with your key light. The direction of fill light can affect the calmness or the tension of a scene.

Putting it all together

After you set the key light, back light, and fill light, you turn them all on and check them for balance. In Figure 4-9, the key light establishes the direction of the light and creates the depth of the shot without giving a stark appearance. The back light adds a slight aura to the subject. The fill washes the face without destroying the three-dimensional quality of the subject.

Figure 4-9:
The balance of a shot is seldom or never virtually perfect. But your reasonable goal is to compliment and highlight the appearance of your subject.

Chapter 5

Sound Is a Big Deal!

· ·

· ·

*H*ave you ever had to pinch yourself to stay awake while driving on a superhighway? Terrible feeling, right? Well, I sometimes have to pinch myself to stay awake during audio production. Of course, the potential outcomes of falling asleep at the wheel of a car far outweigh the kind of problems you can encounter by lack of vigilance in audio production. Even so, when you realize how benign forgetfulness about audio has ruined your otherwise beautiful video production, the feelings in the pit of your stomach can make you feel like you just crashed into a wall.

The audio content in a video is often as important, and sometimes more important, than the visual content. To prove my point, here are two simple tests. This evening turn on your television, select a program, and mute the audio for a few minutes. During those minutes, develop a summary of the information as it's conveyed. When you're done, do just the opposite. Turn on your audio and position yourself so that you can't see the screen. Again, develop a summary of the information. You may be surprised to find that your comprehension was greater with only the audio content than with only the visual content.

If you're an astute observer, you may have picked up a lot of very different information in each of the two tests. For example, visually, without interference of sound, you may have been more inclined to notice ambiance of the scene, framing of the characters, flow of the edits, and use of light.

In the audio test, without the seduction of visualization, you may have been more keenly aware of the development of the story line, the spatial relationship and proximity of characters through comparisons of their voices, the subjective effect of music (soundtrack), and the use of sound effects such as footsteps, wind, and other embellishments.

You don't always have go to a lot of extra trouble to ensure good audio recording (especially if you're recording with a MiniDV camcorder). Sometimes, such as in the quiet of your living room, you can just point your camcorder in the right direction and press the record button. High-quality audio production can be amazingly simple. Other times though, you need to use every bit of ingenuity you can muster just to get a passable audio signal, such as when interviewing someone next to a busy highway.

This chapter helps you make the most of your digital camcorder's audio production features. With a little reading and just a little practice, you can develop good audio production habits. The pit of your stomach will thank you. In this chapter, I tell you what happens when you record sound, why digital audio is superior to other kinds of audio, and what you can do to get the best sound recording — even in noisy or otherwise difficult circumstances.

Reproducing Reality — Realistically

Here's an admittedly bold statement: The audio you hear on digital video is better than the audio you hear on a CD. In fact, the quality of the audio on digital video equals the quality of the audio on digital audio tape (DAT). Why? Because they are recorded in the same manner. Now, if that answer doesn't quite make sense, don't worry. I explain why in the upcoming section "Audio quality of digital video."

Recorded sound

As I discuss in Chapter 3, the human brain is amazing in its ability to interpret two-dimensional images three dimensionally. In much the same manner, the human brain can do astounding things with a minimum of audio information. Listening to a symphony on an inexpensive car radio illustrates this point. The reality is that your car radio provides you with only a small representation of the fullness, depth, and complexity of the symphony. Yet your mind "fills in the blanks." You can imagine what the symphony must really sound like and lay that over what your ears hear.

Even though your mind pleasantly fabricates what's missing in a reproduction, your mind rejects what is incorrectly reproduced. People are intolerant of recorded voices that are unnaturally *sibilant* (hissing sounds) and of sounds with clipped high notes or overly strong deep resonance. The term for such faulty audio recording is *distortion*.

You cannot fix distorted audio. You can modify it to mask the distortion, but you cannot make it sound completely natural.

You achieve quality audio recording by working within the limitations of your recording equipment. Stay within the limitations of your equipment, and the human brain is happy to make up for a lot of the limits. Step outside the limitations, and the brain rejects the sound — no matter how good it is otherwise. I explain equipment limitations in the section "Sound Production," later in this chapter.

Two kinds of distortion threaten the quality of audio reproduction — distortions caused by *limitations of the recording device* and distortions caused by *misuse of the recording device.* In this section, I discuss the limitations of digital audio recording devices. In the section, "Sound Production," I show you how to properly perform audio recording.

Audio quality of digital video

Take a look at Figure 5-1, which uses a human voice as an example. (I could just as easily have selected a musical instrument or a falling tree.) In this figure, a sound is emitted. The sound is a continuous series of waves traveling through the air and the microphone transforms the waves to electric currents.

Figure 5-1: Sound travels in waves. A microphone collects sound waves and changes the waves into electrical currents.

In Figure 5-1, the waves strike against a vertical surface that is housed within a microphone (mic). The mic translates the waves into *electrical waves,* similar to the waves as they existed in the air. This electrical re-creation of waves results in what is called *analog audio.* The mic wire then transmits the analog waves to a recording device. (See Chapter 2 for more about analog versus digital.)

Take a look at Figure 5-2. This is where the fun starts. Two options appear in the figure. The first option is *analog video and audio recording*. In analog recording, sound waves are processed each time they are moved from one piece of equipment to another. You record the video and audio onto video-tape. In so doing, you lay a bunch of wave information onto the tape.

Next, you play the tape on your tape player. In order to see what you're play-ing, the analog waves are turned into impulses that can be interpreted by your monitor and speakers. This conversion of waves causes them to be somewhat distorted. If you were to take the monitor's signal and pass it onto another tape recorder (a common procedure in editing), you would have fur-ther distortion of the waves, and so on.

Each time the sound waves are processed, they are to some small degree dis-torted. The change is nearly imperceptible in the first generation, but it is still there. Simply put, analog sound loses quality in the normal video produc-tion and playback process (notice how the waves change in the figure).

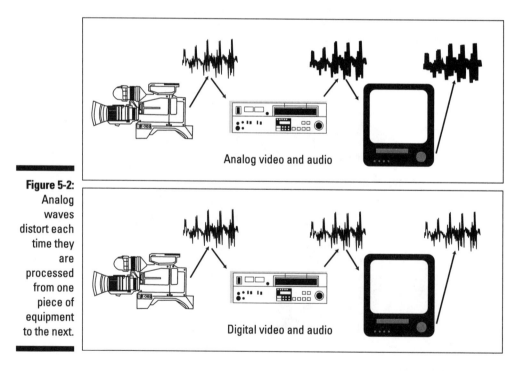

Analog video and audio

Digital video and audio

Figure 5-2:
Analog
waves
distort each
time they
are
processed
from one
piece of
equipment
to the next.

The second option in Figure 5-2 is *digital video and audio recording*. Digital audio doesn't reprocess sound like analog audio does. Once you record sound in a digital format, the sound remains precisely the same throughout its digital life and generations — no matter how many kinds of digital equip-ment you play on and no matter how many times you re-record it.

TECHNICAL STUFF

Stuff you really don't need to know about digital audio

MiniDV camcorders (MiniDV is short for miniaturized digital video format; see Chapter 2 for more on MiniDV) use PCM 16-bit stereo digital audio recording with a sampling rate of 44,100. In PCM audio recording, audio is converted from analog signals to 16-bit stereo digital. The conversion results in audio of such quality that it's dynamic range exceeds the human ear's ability to discern.

If you're still with me, the worst is over because now I'll explain what I just said, beginning with dynamic range.

Dynamic range refers to the outer ranges of a recording instrument. Every recorder, analog or digital, has its own dynamic range.

An audio recorder has minimum and maximum limits in its dynamic range. On some analog recorders, the low range is less sensitive than the human ear. As a result, in very quiet scenes, you might pick up a static noise.

Also, some recorders may have an upper range that is unable to record a richness of sound that satisfies your awareness of what the sound should be like. For example, trombones may seem kind of empty rather than full. In either case, it's possible that you're hearing the limitations of the recording device's dynamic range.

A MiniDV camcorder with its PCM audio recorder has a minimum silence range and a maximum amplitude range (dynamic range) that exceed what can be humanly discerned. Some analog recording devices also have excellent dynamic ranges, but these recorders fall short of 16-bit digital video. Stay with me, because you're about to see why.

The PCM standard is a digital means for transmitting analog information. A PCM signal is binary. (*Binary* is a counting system that uses two digits. Computers count only by twos, and, so, use binary arithmetic.) In binary coding, only two possible states exist — 1 and 0. A bit is the most elemental unit. Each bit is either a 1 or a 0. In 16-bit stereo, that moment is made up of two signals each containing 16 bits of information. For example, as illustrated in the first figure in this sidebar, the analog wave moment can have a value of 0010100111010011 and 0010100111011010.

In the figure, a "moment" of an analog wave signal is being converted to a PCM digital signal. At that moment, the wave has unique characteristics that are being translated into 1s and 0s.

Now one more tidbit (not a technical term), and you'll have a grasp on why digital audio can be so good. No doubt, a 16-bit digital translation of that moment on the wave might be accurate. However, I imagine that you're still demanding the answer to a logical question. How big is that moment on the wave?

Okay. Since you need to know, I have to add just one more term — sampling. *Sampling* is simply how often the PCM standard requires a collection of moment-by-moment information. If, within a second, there were 10 samplings, the 16-bit digital conversion would be a lot less accurate than if there were 100.

Now look at the second figure in this sidebar. As the figure shows, in digital video's PCM audio, 44,100 samplings occur per second. This means that 44,100 times every second a 16-bit digital version of the analog wave is created. The significance is that the accuracy of the digital signal is so precise at its inception that it far exceeds the human ear's ability to discern distortion. And once the digital audio signal is created, it remains digital. So, this very high fidelity is maintained throughout its digital life.

(continued)

(continued)

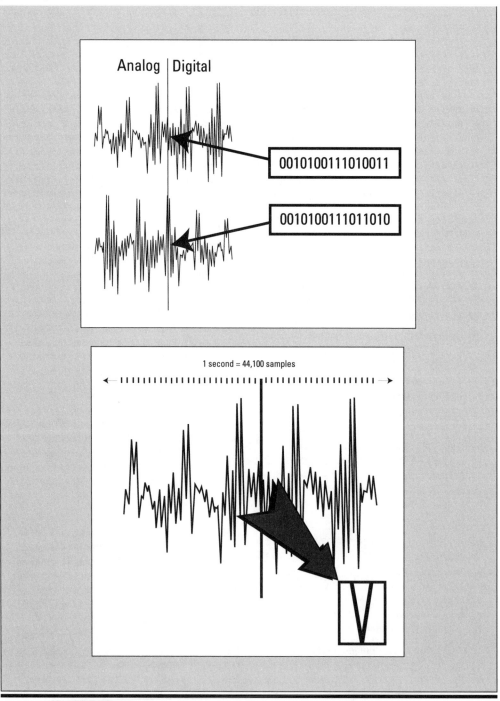

Sound Production

Imagine that you're going to record a wedding. You get to the church early to set up your equipment. You place your tripod where you've been told to. You set up a mic where the vows are to take place. Everything is ready, so you sit back and wait.

The music begins — beautiful, *loud* organ music. The framing of the shot is beautiful, the light is perfect, everything looks great, but your audio volume meter is going berserk.

However, the music stops, and the minister begins to talk. Then the moment comes: The bride responds to her first vow. That is, you think she answers. But the needle on your camcorder's audio meter doesn't budge.

The minister turns to the groom — and the next crisis hits: The groom nearly shouts his "I do." The needles of the audio meter temporarily bury themselves in the red distortion.

This depressing little narrative underscores two basic rules of video production: The time needed to prepare a shot is always slightly less than the time available, and you always allot audio preparation to the portion of time you really don't have.

So what's a digital videographer to do? The following section provides a number of suggestions, much of it quoted to you from my Ph.D. dissertation from the school of hard knocks. I tell you about mics, acoustics, and ways to resolve tough recording problems.

Mics in video production

One of the crazy inconsistencies of video production is that a lens is only useful if it remains connected to its camera body, but a mic is often more useful when it isn't connected to a camera body. Sitting on top of a camcorder, a mic is susceptible to machine noises and inadvertent sounds made by the camera operator and crew (a crew is defined as anybody — who you think will not inadvertently destroy your equipment — that you can blackmail into helping you). Also, especially indoors, a camera-mounted mic tends to be subject to reflective sounds (described in the later section "Planning your recording environment").

Explanations of mic types and their proper placement can quickly become sophisticated and highly technical. In an effort to remain simple and practical, I really only want to describe and recommend a few to you.

TECHNICAL STUFF

Balancing is good for more than checkbooks

If you truly care about your audio, you need to know the difference between balanced and unbalanced circuits.

Balanced circuits: A balanced circuit is an audio-carrying circuit with two active electrical conductors. Both conductors are housed within their own metallic shields. Balanced circuits greatly reduce the pickup of hum and noise in audio system cabling. Balanced circuits use XLR connectors (see the figure in this sidebar). These 3-pin connectors are commonly used in professional audio. The Canon XL1 offers an XLR connector, balanced circuit option.

✔ **Unbalanced circuits:** An unbalanced circuit is a signal-carrying audio circuit with one electrical conductor. Most digital video camcorders provide unbalanced circuits for external mics.

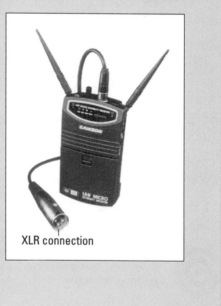

XLR connection

Categorizing mics

Like I said, audio technology is an overwhelmingly complex world of its own. But if you do video, you need to know a little bit about mics. Some mics are excellent for certain uses and lousy for others. Some mics (such as a factory-supplied camcorder mic) are great for general use, but are only minimally acceptable for half of your recording tasks.

REMEMBER

Here are some classifications of mics to keep in mind for your videography needs:

✔ **Omnidirectional — a mic for all directions:** Omnidirectional mics pick up sound in all directions. These mics are typically used when you are confident that all the sound sources within an immediate proximity to the mic are desirable. Your camcorder's factory-supplied mic is probably omnidirectional.

✔ **Unidirectional — a one-person-at-a-time mic:** Just the opposite of omnidirectional, a unidirectional mic collects sound only from the area directly in front of it. Unidirectional mics are especially helpful where you have more than one person wearing a mic and you need to independently control the volume of each person. They are also useful in manufacturing situations where you need to isolate one sound from a bunch of unwanted sounds.

✔ **Shotgun — a long-range mic:** The term "shotgun mic" may be misleading in that it may imply a roaming and haphazard mic. A shotgun mic is just the opposite. You use it for pinpoint isolation of sound. Typically, you use shotgun mics when you cannot place a mic directly in front of a person on camera. A crew member stands off-camera and directs the shotgun mic at the person speaking. The shotgun mic picks up sound only where it is aimed.

Selecting a basic mic

If you're going to record weddings, training, or any other kind of video where the quality of audio reproduction is important, I suggest that you invest in a decent lavalier mic. A *lavalier* is a small mic that can be clipped to a necktie or blouse (see Figure 5-3). Lavaliers are usually omnidirectional, but you can buy unidirectional ones. You typically use unidirectional lavaliers for recording musical instruments.

You may also want a handheld mic. Handheld mics aren't always handheld (they're often on mic stands), but that's not really important. Like lavaliers, most handheld mics are omnidirectional.

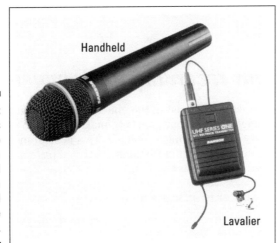

Handheld

Figure 5-3:
A lavalier is easier to mask than a heldheld mic, but a handheld mic is more versatile.

Lavalier

Wired or wireless

Based on your budget and your recording needs, you can use either a wireless mic, transmitter, and receiver or a hard-wired mic. (Hard-wired systems are . . . well, you know, *hard-wired*. You see, you have a mic, and the mic is connected to the recorder by a long audio cable — in some instances, a very long cable.)

In Chapter 22, I describe the UM1 Micro Diversity System, a good wireless system designed especially for use with small digital video camcorders. Manufactured by Samson, Inc., the UM1 Micro Diversity System is inexpensive and ideal for anyone who may need handheld and lavalier configurations.

Though wireless systems are great, they are limited, as follows:

✔ They have a never-ending demand for fresh batteries.

✔ The transmitter is hard to hide on clothing.

✔ Radio interference is occasionally possible.

Hard-wired systems are inexpensive and dependable. Just plug one end into the mic and the other into the recording device. Like wireless systems, wired systems also have limitations:

✔ Dirt and grime can collect (from dragging a wire around on the ground) and can potentially damage equipment or cause signal distortion.

✔ You have the problem of trying to hide wiring when recording.

✔ You may pick up a low hum if you inadvertently run audio wiring in a parallel path with electrical wiring.

Whenever I have a choice, I tend to use a wired system rather than a wireless one. Experience has proven, though, that Murphy's Law requires having both options handy.

Planning your recording environment

In video production, making the most of the challenges in the audio environment is one of your biggest jobs. Your goal is to make the audio on the tape sound like what your ears are hearing in real life. This is seldom an easy task. Here's a simple example (in which I'm assuming that you have a camcorder with a factory-supplied mic available for use).

1. **Set up your camcorder in a large room.**

   If you don't have a large room at home or work, perhaps you can use the foyer of your church or a gymnasium.

2. **Have someone stand approximately 15 feet from your camcorder and begin speaking. Record his or her speech.**

   As you record, note the degree to which the voice sounds normal and proximate. By *normal,* I mean how your ears interpret the resonance of the voice, and by *proximate,* I mean how your ears perceive the relative nearness of the person speaking.

3. Play the tape through a monitor with good speakers.

Note the difference between your memory of the speaker's voice in the real-life situation and on tape. More than likely, the voice now sounds less natural with less resonance and more "echoish." And the recorded voice seems farther away than it did in real life.

What happened? You just ran headlong into the challenge of audio recording — what's called the *reflective audio environment.* Take a look at Figure 5-4. Note that the room causes a multiplication of audio sources. That is, the camcorder's audio recorder is faithfully recording what it is receiving from the mic; however, the omnidirectional camcorder mic is receiving the sum of all the sounds in the immediate environment — not just the speaker's voice.

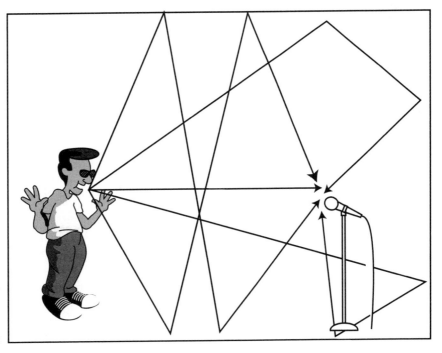

Figure 5-4: Mics don't know what sound to identify as the correct one. So they collect and assign equal priority to all sounds.

Your brain trains your ears to mask all those unneeded sounds. Your camcorder isn't nearly as smart as your brain. On your camcorder, the recorded sound is modified into a sum of information that becomes less resonant and more tinny.

One way to put your mic on a "sound diet" is by modifying or controlling the sound environment around the mic, which leads me to acoustics.

Sounding off about acoustics

Sound is just a bunch of waves. When recording, you can make sound seem more or less realistic by controlling what happens to those waves before they reach your mic. One simple way to improve the realistic nature of audio is to get the mic as close as possible to the source of the sound.

In the example in the preceding section, you could greatly reduce the problem of the reflective sound in the room by using a lavalier mic. The short distance of the lavalier from the source of the sound greatly changes the ratio of the sum of sounds hitting the mic. That is, the reflective sounds remain, but they are proportionately smaller. You want some reflective sound, but only in small doses. The absence of all reflected sound creates what is known as dead sound. A *dead sound* is heavy and causes an unnerving impression of isolation.

Observing audio recording techniques

Here are some tips for increasing your success record with sound recording. You're most likely going to make sound goofs — perfection is an unrealistic goal. But you can definitely achieve a high quality on a regular basis by observing some simple rules.

- **Rule #1:** Buy some earphones and use them. Plug the earphones into the audio monitoring port on your camcorder and wear the earphones for set up and recording. Once you're sure the sound is okay, you can doff the earphones.

- **Rule #2:** You might try turning off your automatic gain control (AGC) on your camcorder. AGC is a normal feature on camcorders that regulates the volume of recording, preventing sound from exceeding the equipment's dynamic range. Try turning it off. Really. I'm not kidding. (Trust the Force, Luke.) I usually use the AGC in only two circumstances: when I don't have the time to care how the audio turns out and when the audio situation is out of control, such as at a loud basketball game. Otherwise, I leave the AGC turned off and keep my fingers poised on the volume control. Why do I turn AGC off? Because AGC is very good at what it is designed to do. It looks for sound and then adjusts the dynamic range of the audio recorder to maximize the sound — even sound I don't want maximized. That can be bad.

  AGC can do other "bad" things, too — for example, when you record in an office building. If you record in an empty office, you may think the room is quiet. AGC will sometimes think otherwise. It may magnify the sound of the furnace blower and the computer fan and the copying machine in the next room to a deafening level. The AGC is only doing its job. Believe it or not, I've had to scrap video footage shot in rooms where the only sound was from the ballast of a fluorescent lamp! In playback, the lamp sound just about drove me crazy. In the real room, I had not even noticed the sound. Thanks, AGC.

✔ **Rule #3:** Sound-check your on-camera person (people). I know this isn't always possible. But whenever you can, get your people to talk naturally on-camera in the location they will speak, adjust your sound level, record, and play back. With a little practice, you can perform this procedure in less than one minute. I promise you, you will enjoy your time shooting video a lot more if you're confident that the audio is laying down properly. As a rule, when I convey my desire to make someone sound and look as good as possible, they usually cheerfully cooperate.

✔ **Rule #4:** Ride the gain. *Riding the gain* is the practice of keeping an eye on the volume meter and finger on the volume (gain) control. With a little practice, you can learn to anticipate moments when a presenter is about to speak loudly or softly. The intent of riding gain isn't to be constantly adjusting the gain control up and down, but to occasionally, subtly adjust the gain to prevent the presenter's voice from distorting or disappearing.

✔ **Rule #5:** Bring some blankets. Seriously, I mean real blankets. You'll find that some rooms are unalterably hot. In audio recording *hot* means too reflective. This condition usually occurs in rooms with tile floors and non-acoustical ceilings. If you're getting an audio signal that's too hot, just toss some blankets around the room (off-camera). Doing so can make a major difference in your audio recording quality.

✔ **Rule #6:** Bring lots of batteries. I promise you, there's a direct relationship between proximity of back-up batteries and battery life. If you don't have a back-up battery available, your mic battery will fail in the middle of an important non-repeatable scene. If you do have a back-up battery nearby, your mic battery will last for days. It's a mystery how it works.

Chapter 6

Plan the Shoot, Shoot the Plan

· ·

In This Chapter

▶ Engaging your viewer with well-crafted shots

▶ Brainstorming with storyboards

▶ Planning and communicating your story with a script

· ·

I am going to make a big assumption: You intend to use your digital video camcorder for more than just shooting some video. Perhaps you want to impress an individual or group of people with an idea. Maybe you want to motivate people to do something by telling them a story. Or you may want to instruct someone in a step-by-step process. Then, again, you may want to document an event, such as a wedding or a football game. Sooner or later, you're very likely to do some or all of the above.

All of these possibilities share a common vital element. With few exceptions, you can't expect to record video that, *unedited,* will meet your goals and expectations. Unedited video is usually boring beyond belief. You've probably sat through some of it (a friend's family vacation, for example) at one time or another, so I won't bother to prove my point.

Bottom line, you have to start with good video — *lots* of good video. The best way to get good video is to know how to use your camcorder as a persuasion tool and to plan (or *script*) the intended outcome.

Persuading with Digital Video

As a craft, video production has a number of time-honored ways of getting the job done. And, as you might expect, a precise technical language exists for about anything you do with a camcorder. Because language is the culture of any affair, you need to become familiar with the vocabulary of video production. Doing so enables you to understand how things are done and how to communicate your ideas effectively. So, always wanting to be helpful, at this point, I describe and illustrate terms associated with the different kinds of video shots.

Naming shots

Figure 6-1 is made up of ten stills. Each of the stills has a name associated with it. These names indicate the proximity of the lens to the subject (the person, item, or event being recorded).

Just as examples, here's a list showing some ways you can use each kind of shot (also check the Cheat Sheet at the beginning of this book for an abbreviated "pocket-size" list):

- ✔ **ELS (extra long-shot):** This shot shows a person within the fullness of an area. Use this shot to effectively establish the environment for opening and closing shots.

- ✔ **LS (long-shot):** The character in this shot occupies one-half to three-quarters of the screen height. Use this shot to clarify the relationship of the character to the overall place.

- ✔ **MLS (medium long-shot):** This shot shows the subject's body plus a little above and below. You often use this shot when the subject is moving.

- ✔ **KNEE (knee shot):** This shot shows a three-quarter shot from the head to the knee. You commonly use this shot to reestablish the relationship of the character to a location or to another character.

- ✔ **MS (medium shot):** This shot shows the top of the head to just below the waist. Use this shot to develop a comfortable, conversational distance between the viewer and another person. The comfort factor can be a negative influence, though, because the viewer can become easily bored. A basic rule of video production is to provide timely visual stimulation. Too much of a comfortable shot can cause the viewer to lose attention.

- ✔ **MCU (medium close-up):** This shot, often called a *bust shot,* cuts from the top of the head to just above the diaphragm. Use this shot as an attention-getting shot because it skirts the edges of the comfort zone of perceived closeness. The shot implies that the character is significant or has something important to say. For this reason, the MCU, mixed with an occasional KNEE shot, is the favorite of the evening news.

- ✔ **CU (close-up):** This shot shows the upper-forehead to the upper-chest. Use this shot for emphasis. But use it sparingly to hit the important phrase in a statement or to establish strong feeling, for example.

- ✔ **BCU (big close-up):** This shot is a full-head shot. Use this shot to elicit a laugh or cynicism, but take care because the shot can appear bizarre.

- ✔ **VCU (very close-up):** This face shot shows the mid-forehead to above the chin. This shot exposes the character in that all motivation and emotion seem to be on the surface. Reserve this shot for dramatic moments.

- ✔ **ECU (extreme close-up):** Use this shot for a very tight face shot or for isolated details. This shot is at the edge of the lens's capability to focus. You use this shot more often for objects than for characters.

ELS

MCU

LS

CU

MLS

BCU

KNEE

VCU

Figure 6-1:
Each shot
causes a
unique
reaction in
the viewer.

MS

ECU

Selecting the length of shot

Even though you can use your camcorder to effectively establish environment or bring a character close or efficiently show movement, you need to use good judgment in selecting the correct mixture of shots. Here are two of the main reasons for changing the perspective of a shot:

- ✔ **Storytelling:** The viewer needs to know relationships as well as details. A wide shot establishes the place and the proximity of other characters. A close-up provides necessary visual details. Changes of perspective are often as important to a story as spoken words.

- ✔ **Editing:** Changes of perspective are essential to good editing. Transitions are much easier to edit when the character perspective changes. A good producer provides the editor (even when they are both the same person) with wide shots and close-ups of the same sequence. This way, the editor can decide when to use the wide shot or the close-up. For example, a narrator talks about the importance of a product's new features. If you have a wide shot of the narrator talking about the feature and close-ups showing the feature's details, you can edit the segment from the wide shot to the close-up whenever necessary to allow the viewer to visually comprehend the significance of the feature.

Be sure to use the right shot at the right moment; otherwise, you may frustrate or misinform your viewers. At the opening of a scene, the viewer wants to know where the action is taking place; a close-up would be disturbing. During an intimate conversation, the viewer wants to be up close, with alternating close-ups of one character and then the other; a wider shot makes the viewer feel left out or like an eavesdropper. But in conversations between two business people, the viewer likes alternating medium close-ups of the two; anything closer seems unnecessarily familiar.

Off-camera action can also be positive or negative, depending on how you use it. You want to use dramatic action off-camera (such as a foot snapping a twig) if your intent is to create tension. Off-camera action is counterproductive if the viewer needs the action to understand the story (such as the emergence of the twig snapper from the edge of the woods).

Video production can be a lot of fun. With a little practice, you can learn how to influence people to feel positively or negatively about a subject simply by how you present the information. At the same time, you can frustrate people when they *want* to feel positive or negative about a subject, but you visually resist them. Universally accepted visual conventions have been developed over the past decades of film and video. If you know these conventions as a producer, you can lead your audience where you want to take them.

Here are some key visual conventions:

- ✔ **Extra long shots:** Use these shots for location, establishing mood, showing relationships, or tracking wide actions.

- ✔ **Long shots:** Use these shots at the start of a scene and, occasionally, at the end of a scene. Long shots are also good for normal movement. The long shot tells the viewer about the location and subjectively establishes an atmosphere.

- ✔ **Medium shots:** Medium shots are the bread and butter of most scenes. Use them for full-body to bust shots. These shots include most of the comfort ranges for the majority of people. Too many wide shots make people feel as though they're merely viewers. Too many close-ups make people feel as though they're intruding.

- ✔ **Closer shots:** Reserve these shots for emphasis and to reveal reaction and detail. Closer shots are very powerful, so use them sparingly.

Using focus as a technique

In Chapter 3, I go into a somewhat technical, although basic and important, discussion of perspective and the workings of the camcorder's lens, including *aperture* and *iris* and their relationship to *depth of focus*. (By the way, if some of these terms are unfamiliar or a little too vague, you may want to turn to Chapter 3 for a quick review.)

As I mention in Chapter 3, aperture equals focal length (or depth of focus) divided by the diameter of your lens. The setting of the aperture is what's referred to as *f-stop.*

In a nutshell, depth of focus directly relates to f-stop. The higher the f-stop, the greater the depth of focus. Therefore, at higher f-stops, the perception of being in focus exists for a substantial distance on either side of the actual plane of focus (focal plane). At the same time, the higher the f-stop, the greater the amount of light needed for the shot.

The opposite is true for depth of focus at lower f-stops. The lower the f-stop, the lower the depth of focus.

This condition means that at lower f-stops, the perception of a shot being in focus is nearly nonexistent on either side of the focal plane. And, at the same time, the lower the f-stop, the lower the amount of light needed for the shot.

You can use these two facts to your digital video advantage when shooting with your camcorder. Take a look at Figure 6-2, which shows two stills. The first still was shot at f/11. The second still was shot at f/2.8. In the first shot, objects in the background are in focus. In the second shot, the background is blurred.

Setting camera height

You can also use the *vertical angle* of a shot to influence a viewer's perception of a character. Take a look at the three stills in Figure 6-3. The first still illustrates the use of a *neutral camera height,* in which the camera's lens is set at chest to eye height. Such shots do not provide a *subjective effect* (that is, they don't influence a viewer's perception of the subject).

In the second shot, the camera height is set above the character's eye height. This angle, which looks down at the character, generally suggests inferiority, weakness, or submission.

In the third shot, the camera height is set waist-high to the character. The subjective message in this shot is one of strength and dominance.

Moving the camera

You can create energy in an otherwise static shot simply by moving your camera. Again, as with the various perspective shots, the technical videographers bestow specific names on each of these camera movements.

Panning and tilting

Panning and tilting are performed with a camcorder resting on the head of a tripod. *Panning* is moving the camera laterally, and *tilting* is moving it vertically on the tripod's head.

Two basic kinds of panning are the *following pan* and the *surveying pan*. In the following pan, the camera operator pans to follow a character, such as into the scene or from one spot to another. The surveying pan looks for a character or an object; for example, the character is already in a scene, and the camera pans to meet him or her.

Tilting is often done simply as a matter of course, such as tilting down to follow an action. However, you can also tilt to achieve a particular effect, such as tilting up or down to denote height or depth.

Figure 6-3:
Camera height places the viewer in a subjective relationship with the character in a shot.

Craning, dollying, and trucking

In addition to moving the camera sideways or up and down from a static position, you can create even greater dynamic energy by moving the camera over, into or out of, and across the scene. Although moving the camera over a scene, called *craning*, may be a bit exotic for your purposes, at least you'll now know the term if and when you hear it. The other two movements — dollying and trucking — are quite achievable and can be very effective.

Dollying refers to moving the camera forward or backward in a scene (see Figure 6-4 for an example of dollying). Although, at first glance, dollying may seem similar to zooming, the two are different in terms of how and why you use them. You dolly by moving the camera, whereas you zoom in and out by adjusting the lens.

Dollying causes the relationship of the character to the overall scene to change. Generally, you must adjust the focus and tilt the camera while you dolly because you are changing the focal depth by moving the camera toward or away from the subject. Foreground objects disappear or appear as the camera moves in or out. Zooming, on the other hand, does not change the spatial relationship between the character and the scene. Rather, it telescopes the lens.

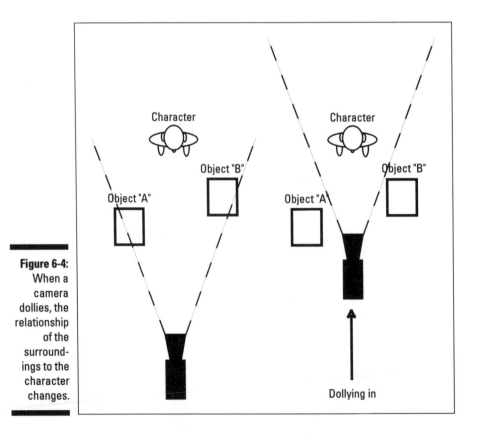

Figure 6-4: When a camera dollies, the relationship of the surroundings to the character changes.

Trucking refers to moving the camera left or right in relationship to a scene (see Figure 6-5 for an example of trucking). When you truck your camcorder, you change the character's background. This movement can make an otherwise dull scene quite stimulating.

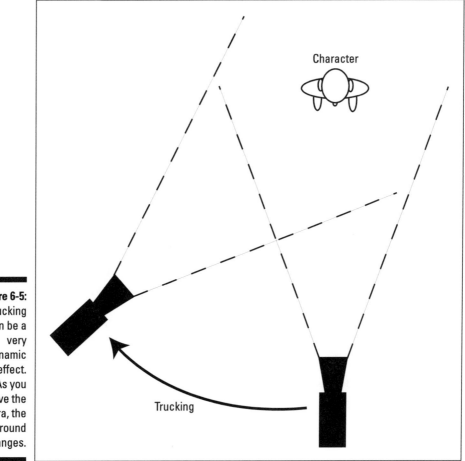

Figure 6-5:
Trucking
can be a
very
dynamic
effect.
As you
move the
camera, the
background
changes.

Though trucking can be interesting, it can also make major changes to the lighting of a character. Sometimes these changes are detrimental. Lighting is usually set based on camera position. To properly light a trucking move, you need to set lights for both ends of the trucking movement. If you don't have enough lights to do so, you may want to reconsider your trucking move.

Composing the picture

One of the fundamental opportunities in shooting persuasive video is the chance to compose your picture. When you *compose,* you prepare the environment where the shooting is to take place. For the sake of discussion, assume that you're shooting on location, say at someone's office.

Here are some points to consider when preparing the environment:

- **Shoot for light.** The one variable with the most obvious impact on the quality of your shot is light, specifically the location and intensity of the light in relationship to your character. Whether natural or artificial, you want the light to give primary significance to your character's face and secondary significance to the scene. If you can't get the sun to cooperate, close the blinds and use artificial light. Don't forget to white balance (see Chapter 4 for information on white balance)!

- **Position the character.** Set the character, sitting or standing, in a dignified manner and location. For example, if the character is sitting, always secure a modest posture for the character. Sometimes, a character isn't aware of how his or her lap is positioned. Also, *always* make a special effort to check out the background. Don't place the character in front of something that inadvertently looks comical. For example (this may seem silly, but it's a real problem), don't let the character sit so that horizontal bookshelves seem to be sprouting out of his or her ears. Believe me, many problems of this kind are avoidable; you simply have to be attentive to prevent them.

- **Dress the shot.** This takes only a moment. But, in the rush of the moment, you may be tempted to forget or ignore it, only to later regret doing so. Not only does this step help ensure a good shot, it's also an act of kindness to your character. For example, if a desk is in the shot, clean the desk and make it look "professional." Avoid ultrawhite or shiny objects in the foreground. Ask the character whether he or she wants family photos in the shot. Also, if possible, dress up the background with a vase of flowers or a book arrangement — anything to avoid a flat background. If you brought along a light kit, throw a colored slash of light across the background (only after you white balance).

Framing the shot

Framing the shot is simply a matter of placing the subject properly in the picture. You don't have much to remember to frame a shot correctly. Basically, you keep three things in mind: safety margins; offset versus symmetrical; and proper head room.

Safety margins

Safety margins are two imaginary rectangles on the outer edges of your picture (see Figure 6-6). Some camcorders actually show these rectangles in their viewfinders. The *outer rectangle* warns that any images or characters outside the rectangle's boundaries may not appear on some monitors. Obviously, vital parts of a scene must be kept inside the outer rectangle. The inner rectangle is the safe area. Within this rectangle, you can safely add images or characters any time during the editing process.

Figure 6-6:
Though safety margins aren't essential in all circum-stances, they are important enough to always consider.

Be sure to keep safety margins in mind while shooting. You don't want to use a shot that's too tight, thereby risking that an editor will later put images or characters on someone's chin or neck rather than across his or her chest. Though you may not have safety margins in your camcorder's viewfinder, you can teach yourself to remember where they would be. An easy way to learn is by using a dry-erase marker (not permanent marker!) on your viewfinder. If necessary, use a crayon.

Offset versus symmetrical

One of the simplest things you can do to add appeal to a shot is to *offset the frame* — that is, you center the character on the third of the frame that is opposite the direction he or she is facing (see Figure 6-7). For example, if the character's shoulders are oriented toward the viewer's right, frame the character on the viewer's left. If the character's shoulders are oriented toward the viewer's left, do the opposite. If the character's shoulders are square with the camera, go with the symmetry by centering the character in the screen.

Figure 6-7:
This still shot illustrates the use of offset framing with a graphic added during editing.

Proper head room

Establishing proper head room is one of the simplest habits to learn — once you've learned the basic idea, you'll set proper head room without thinking about it. Simply remember that a person should not look as though he or she has slipped toward the bottom of the screen (too much head room). Also, a person shouldn't appear crowded into the frame as though his or her head might scrape the top of the screen (too little head room).

After you start practicing these techniques, my guess is that you'll like the look you achieve. And they are especially helpful if you plan to layer text later on — to allow room. Refer again to Figure 6-7, which illustrates the use of offset framing with a graphic added later on in the editing process.

Preproducing Your Digital Video

Preproduction refers to the planning and implementation of the many details that will help you produce a successful video (in the industry, this means that your video winds up with a high production value).

Note: You may find it odd that I bring up the matter of *preproducing* your video *after* telling you how to shoot it. But, trust me, this order is logical. Why? Because of language. In order for you to preproduce your video, you needed to understand some of the vocabulary covered earlier in this chapter.

So, now that you know what preproduction is, let me tell you *how* to do it by storyboarding, scripting, and planning the shooting.

Storyboarding

As the story goes (sorry about that), storyboarding began in the film industry back in the heyday of cartoons, prior to World War II. Animators sketched the actions of the various characters, such as the moment the character turned or was bopped on the head. These pivotal moments, called *key frames,* represented a series of related frames leading up to and away from the action. The key frames were taped or pinned to a board and were the basis for planning a cartoon. In a preproduction meeting, the animation team moved the key frames around on the board, added and subtracted them, and finally arranged the surviving key frames in the order of a cartoon plot. Thus, the name "storyboard."

The process was so successful that it eventually became a way for planning some conventional film productions. And, as the years passed, storyboarding found its way into the boardrooms (sorry about that one, too) of corporate America.

Creating the storyboard

So how do you do it? Crudely and as quickly as possible is probably the best way.

1. **Draw the key events and the scene where the events will take place.**

2. **On the individual sheets, include some basic ideas of what is happening and what is being said.**

3. **Discuss the order of the key events, moving them around, adding and deleting the sheets as needed until you agree on an order for the key events in the story line.**

4. **Name the scenes or segments of scenes for each of the key events.**

Using the segment or scene names, you can develop lists of the elements that need to be prepared prior to video shooting, such as costumes or props.

Planning the shooting

After you develop your storyboard, you need to plan the shooting. You need to assign camera instructions, such as shots and close-ups for the various key events. Of course, you may modify your plans when the time comes to do the actual shooting. But to prevent chaos during shooting, you're wise to have a shooting plan.

One of the most important steps in preproduction is planning your shooting order. *Shooting order* refers to a chronological list of the segments to be shot. By the way, you don't necessarily want to shoot your video in the order of the plot. Doing so can be a waste of time and resources. (See Chapter 4 for more on producing out of order for lighting.)

Scripting

Scripting is a textual plan of all that will be said and performed in a scene. A script usually includes camera instructions, locations in the scene for sound effects, and general instructions to the editor for editing. For some people, like me, scripting is as much fun as the actual production. For other people, just using a word processor is nearly impossible — let alone writing creatively. I don't claim that writing a script is necessarily easy, but I quake to think what might happen in some productions without one.

To understand how a script can help you, you need to first distinguish between two approaches to script writing — subjective and objective.

- ✔ **Subjective:** Subjective scripting is storytelling (see Figure 6-8 for an example of a subjective script). The subjective script depends largely on video to establish the environment (note the video instructions in the left column in Figure 6-8, for example). In subjective scripting, you have characters, a plot, and some kind of dramatic development. Or in a video where you're primarily communicating a feeling (such as a music video), you present a combination of movements and sounds to elicit an emotional response in your viewer.

- ✔ **Objective:** Objective scripting is goal-oriented information or instructions (see Figure 6-9). You want to influence or train your viewer to do or believe what you're presenting. Objective scripts are need-oriented in that they exist to overcome some kind of lack in the viewer.

Subjective scripts tend to be much more complicated than objective ones. Conversely, objective scripts are subject to a tough test — namely, the success or failure of achieving the objective.

VISUAL	AUDIO
(Scene opens. Camera LS. Martha is seated on the left side of her bed. Bed is frame right. She is in her bathrobe. Her long hair is for the first time untied and lying across her shoulders, slightly unkempt. She is staring camera left at nothing.)	
	(The night table telephone rings.)
(Martha reacts with a start.)	
(Camera MCU. Martha stares down left at the phone.)	
(Camera BCU on phone.)	(Second ring.)
(Camera VCU on Martha. The look of worry belies her temptation not to pick up the phone.)	(Third ring.)
(Camera MS on Martha and phone. She suddenly reaches out and snatches it up mid-ring.)	(Fourth ring interrupted by Martha grabbing the phone from the receiver. Martha speaks softly, barely above a whisper.)
	MARTHA: HELLO.
	(Pause. Soft unintelligible voice on phone.)
	MARTHA: YES, YES IT IS . . . THIS IS SHE.
(Martha looks down left again.)	(More soft unintelligible voice on phone.)
(Camera VCU on photograph by the phone. The photo is obviously an old one of a much younger Martha and a much slimmer George.)	(Music softly fades in - the Scene One wedding reception ballad. This time it has an echoish caste. Behind the music, the sound of laughter.)
(Tracking left, Camera frame right CU on Martha, still looking down at picture. Tears are forming.)	
	MARTHA: DID YOU . . . DID YOU . . . FIND HIM?

Figure 6-8: In this example, the audience is led through the experience by the storyteller.

Of course, many scripts are both subjective and objective. A good example is political digital video advertising. You have only 30 seconds to achieve your objective — convincing viewers to vote for your candidate. So you pack the objective message with all kinds of emotion-evoking (subjective), flag-waving tricks to cause viewers to feel positively toward your candidate.

VISUAL	AUDIO
(Camera LS on ACME 200HP riding lawn mower. Mower is frame center, visibly rumbling in neutral. Behind the mower is wide swath of mown lawn, smoke still rising from the turf.)	*(Trainer's voice off camera.)* TRAINER: CAUTION MUST BE USED WHEN APPROACHING THE ACME 200HP LAWN MOWER WHEN IT IS IDLING IN NEUTRAL.
(Surveying pan right to trainer. She is wearing the required flame retardent jump suit and approved safety helmet as described in previous scene.)	TRAINER: IF YOU FOLLOW THESE SIMPLE INSTRUCTIONS, YOU WILL HAVE NO PROBLEM MOUNTING THE UNIT AND PLACING IT BACK IN GEAR.
(Following pan of trainer to mower. Camera MLS. She stops camera right of mowing unit.)	TRAINER: AS I MENTIONED EARLIER, STEEL-TOED SHOES ARE REQUIRED WHEN RIDING THE ACME 200HP RIDING MOWER. THIS IS PARTICULARLY IMPORTANT WHEN APPROACHING THE MOWING UNIT, EVEN IN THE NEUTRAL, UNENGAGED MODE.
(Postproduction. Add dotted line to indicate edge of safety area.)	

Figure 6-9: The writer of the objective script must equip the viewer with enough information to make a decision or perform a function.

Storyboarding

In the preproduction stage, one of the most exciting parts of storyboarding is visualizing the finished product. In your mind's eye, you follow your character's action from scene to scene. You can almost hear the music playing and see the special graphics and animation you will include during the editing process. Within all this excitement though, you need to ask this question: With this storyboard, am I realistically providing the editor (who just might be you) with enough to get the job done? If anything, err toward excess. You may add 15 minutes or an hour to the shooting by taking another shot from a different angle. But, by doing so, you may save hours of headaches in the postproduction stage.

Be sure that you plan more than enough shots for each key event. If your story is complicated or if it involves a lot of speaking, you may also need to create a script.

Chapter 7

Digital Video Production Tips

· ·

· ·

*O*ne of my favorite moments in video production is the deep feeling of satisfaction I get at the end of a good day of shooting. To use a day productively and safely tuck away video clips for later editing is a basic goal of every video producer. Some days are like that. Others don't quite measure up.

What makes some video production projects go well and others poorly? What can you do to better ensure success? What problems lurk out there just waiting to grab you when you least suspect them? Answers to these questions aren't always easy or foolproof and nothing about quality video production is inherently easy. But you can have a completely satisfying experience. As a matter of fact, a large part of the enjoyment you derive from successful video production comes from preventing, facing, and overcoming obstacles.

As I mention in earlier chapters, the breakthrough technology of MiniDV provides you with the opportunity to produce professional-quality video. The emphasis here is on the word "opportunity." You can make beautiful video. Digital video provides you this opportunity, but you still have to work. This chapter is filled with tips for accomplishing successful production. Some of my suggestions are always true in every kind of project. Others are the good-to-know variety for those times when you face special challenges. ***Note:*** Part V of this book covers details for producing specific kinds of video.

Shooting Digital Video with Style

I tend to be overly optimistic. Life's more fun that way — you know, thinking that I'm just one light lunch away from losing those extra pounds. Optimists like me have to work hard at being realists. One carrot and celery lunch won't undo a paunch I worked years to create. The same is true in video production. Optimism is great. Preparing for the unforeseen is better. By knowing and doing certain things, you and others will enjoy the results of your efforts.

I've based this section on two assumptions:

- ✔ You plan to shoot on-location (where something is happening).
- ✔ On-location is no place for optimism. The location is not friendly; it may want to bite you.

Sorry, but on-location production can be downright tough. Just take a look at folks who produce documentaries for public television. You know, those 33-year-old producers who look like they're 70? These people are the ultimate location shooters — producing in the treetops of rain forests and such. Your location shooting may not be quite as exotic, but without special care, you too may start noticing bags under your eyes in your early twenties.

You don't have to go far to be on-location. It may simply be an office on another floor of the same building. Or it may be out in the parking lot. And, of course, it can be on someone else's property. So what is the difficulty of shooting on-location? When you're on-location, you're on someone else's turf, subject to someone else's schedule, and using someone else's resources to get your job done. These variables, when left to their own devices, can often prevent you from getting your job done to your satisfaction — and strain some relationships in the process.

Knowing your legal and safety limitations

Shooting on-location is supposed to be fun and interesting. To keep it enjoyable, I'd suggest refraining from doing things that will put you in jeopardy. Here are a couple of basic rules about using a camcorder on someone else's turf.

Don't take your camcorder anywhere you'd have to hide it to get it in. For example, don't take your camcorder where signs are posted forbidding use of cameras and recording devices. You risk the possibility of your equipment being confiscated or worse.

Don't record individuals on your camcorder without their permission. People can get very upset about this — even to the point of wanting to punch you in the nose. As a basic courtesy, I always ask for permission before I record. The exception to this is at a private event, such as a wedding.

Producing on-location can be dangerous

On-location shooting can be tough — especially on your equipment. For example, in the past two weeks I saw a viewfinder destroyed when its lens was exposed to the sun and a recorder and Steadicam (a device for making hand-held camcorder movement smooth) damaged when they were dropped. These accidents may have been avoidable, but they were all performed by responsible people just making some careless mistakes.

Protecting equipment

Of course, you'll need to shoot video in places where equipment can be damaged or lost. But you can increase the survival rate of your equipment by insisting that you and others develop some simple habits.

The number one culprit of on-location shooting is grime, so make sure that you and others do the following:

- Protect your equipment to and from a shoot by keeping the equipment in cases.

- At the location, keep plastic covering available for protection against wind-blown debris.

- Carry a lens cleaning cloth for your lens and canned air (available at electronics stores) for blowing off your equipment.

- Always wipe your equipment at the conclusion of a shoot. If you have used electrical wiring, take special care to remove grime before storing the wiring with your other equipment.

The number two culprit is theft. I've been victimized a number of times, so I know how it feels. A friend of mine actually had a very expensive camcorder stolen in the lobby of a hotel. The camcorder was at his side on the floor — and then it was gone! Expensive toys attract attention. Don't ever leave your equipment unguarded — even in seemingly safe locations.

Also, because you are attracting attention, your gear is not the only target. So are purses and bags. Unfortunately, my wife has had two purses stolen while shooting on-location.

The third culprit is breakage. Breakage happens two ways. The most obvious way is by dropping. But, more often, breakage happens when untrained people use equipment. In the video production industry, you will find very few pieces of equipment that can withstand forceful abuse. The most common damage occurs when people try to force a piece of equipment to do something it's not meant to do.

Be sure to follow these two good rules of thumb:

✔ If you don't know how to use equipment, ask.

✔ If the equipment doesn't want to do what you are attempting to do, stop. You're probably doing something wrong.

Effects of weather

Weather and temperature can drastically affect video equipment. Simple things can cause big problems. For example, taking a camcorder from a warm environment to a cold one can cause condensation within the equipment — rendering the camcorder unusable for an hour or two. Leaving equipment in the cold can be a problem, too. For example, the fluid in a tripod's head can become thick in cold temperatures, which can make the tripod unusable until it is warmed.

Here are some suggestions:

✔ Don't take electronic equipment from hot to cold environments (or vice versa) without allowing time for the temperature of the equipment to adjust.

✔ Don't leave equipment in your car (including the trunk) overnight in cold climates.

✔ Avoid exposing your equipment to extreme heat.

✔ Avoid using your equipment in extreme high humidity.

Power

Your equipment's on-location electrical demands can be tricky. Here are a couple of recommendations.

✔ **AC outlets:** When using electricity on-location, always, always, always ask for permission before plugging in. I have personally witnessed two occasions where people's computers went down while I was plugged into their electrical outlets. Of course, in both instances, folks immediately blamed me for the outage and lost files! Imagine that.

✔ **Circuit breakers:** If you plan to use lighting on-location, always arrange in advance for restoring a tripped circuit breaker, just in case something happens. Find out where the electrical panel is located and, if possible, identify the circuit you'll use. Again, ask whether you may use the circuit and explain that you might possibly cause an outage. And if you're using your own lighting, avoid any possibility of burns to individuals or property.

✔ **Batteries:** Using batteries on-location can be a shocking experience. Not literally, but almost as bad. Your typical problem is running out of power. Many batteries take longer to charge than they do to expend. Bottom line — have two hours of charged batteries for every hour you plan to shoot. And if you expect a lot of shooting time, recharge the batteries on-location if possible.

If you plan to take your camcorder out of the country, you need to find out in advance what kind of converter you'll need for running your equipment and for recharging your batteries.

Shipping and travel

Shipping video equipment can cause you anguish. Unless your camcorder case is designed for shipping (you can buy such cases, but they're expensive), be sure to take extra precautions when shipping your camcorder. An inexpensive way to ship your camcorder is to wrap it in oodles of bubble packing and put it in oversized boxes. Even so, insure your shipment for its total value. If you're taking your camcorder on a plane, you may want to put the camcorder case in cargo but carry the camcorder on the plane.

If you plan to take your camcorder across national borders, beware! You may not be allowed to take it from one country to another without prior arrangement. I was once prevented from taking a camcorder into Canada! If you are planning to go out of the country, contact your local Customs Service office weeks in advance of your trip to find out what you may need to do.

Characterizing kinds of on-location shoots

You'll typically encounter the following four kinds of on-location shooting (all these terms are coined by yours truly, but me thinks they'll do fine for the purposes of this little discussion):

✔ Spontaneous

✔ Event-style

✔ Formal event

✔ Produced for video

Spontaneous

Spontaneous shooting is the simplest and the chanciest form of on-location shooting. As the name implies, you turn on your camcorder, point, and shoot. In spontaneous shooting, you have little or no way of predicting how your camera's settings and capabilities will match up with the challenges of the circumstances or the environment. Most people with camcorders are experts at spontaneous shooting because that's all they ever do.

Event-style

Event-style shooting is different from spontaneous in subtle but significant ways. Like spontaneous shooting, event-style allows you little or no control of the environment. But in event-style shooting, you can manipulate some of the circumstances.

Say that you're asked to videotape a high school football game. The request gives you license to go places and do things others might not have the freedom to do or explore. You have no control over time and events. But you do have control over the circumstances.

For example, because of the request, you ask to attend the afternoon pep rally to get some introductory shots for the video. At the rally, you select to sit across the gym from the students, where you can use your zoom to capture groups of students as they do the berserk things teenagers do at pep rallies.

You arrive early, judge the best place to sit, and blend in with the crowd. You take some preliminary shots to make sure all the settings are correct and put on your earphones. Then you wait and shoot as you deem appropriate and interesting. In other words, you control certain circumstances.

Later that evening, at the game, you explain to one of the coaches that you are shooting a video for the parents' club. You ask whether you can move about the sidelines during the game. Again, you are controlling the circumstances, as follows:

 ✔ You make conscious decisions about the location of the lens in relationship to the students.

 ✔ You position yourself early to wait for shot opportunities.

 ✔ You ensure that your settings are correct.

 ✔ You wear headphones to hear the events as they unfold.

In an event-style shoot, you have numerous, seemingly unrelated ways to control what is being recorded on tape. You can't tell people what they should wear, and you aren't able to control the environment — such as football games at night. But you are able to have some control over the subject matter (such as going to the pep rally) and the circumstances (such as selecting where you stand at the rally and the game). Your chances for getting some good footage are better with event-style shootings than they are with spontaneous shootings.

Formal events

When shooting formal events, you can have some control over the environment as well as the circumstances. Examples of formal events are weddings and lectures. The distinguishing factor of a formal event is that you are expected to provide a relatively high-quality finished product. You may be doing this for free — for example, for relatives or your church. Or you may be shooting the formal event as an employee or a freelance videographer. Whether you're working for free or for hire, it doesn't matter. You have a customer, and the customer is expecting the video. Though the expectations are higher in formal events, so are the opportunities for accomplishment.

In formal events, your customer usually allows you to prepare for the event. Quite often, the customer even allows you to alter event planning in some little ways to accommodate your shooting needs. Prior to a formal event, you usually do the following:

- ✔ Negotiate with the customer about the location and operation of your video and sound equipment.
- ✔ Resolve your electrical needs (especially if you're planning to provide lights).
- ✔ Plan a list of shots with the customer.

Formal events are often more controllable than spontaneous and event-style videos. Though the action is unstoppable and occurring for reasons totally unrelated to your production needs, you still have some leverage in planning the environment and the circumstances.

A simple example of environmental control occurs at a lecture. For example, the lecturer (your *customer*) stands in front of a live audience and makes a PowerPoint presentation, using a projector and a screen. Normally, the lecturer will want to lower the room lights to enhance the image on the screen. You will need to do some advance negotiation with the lecturer. The two of you will need to work out a lighting compromise between what's best for the screen and what's best for the camcorder.

Produced for video

The fourth type of on-location shooting is "produced for video." In this scenario, you actually get to control the circumstances and the environment of production. Within the limitations of your budget and schedule, you can pull out all the stops necessary to ensure a quality production.

Using Time to Your Advantage

Through my years in video production, I have yet to hear anyone complain about having too much time to complete a video project. Time is the single most precious resource in video production, and it is the hardest to control. So time management is important. But the matter goes deeper than that.

Shooting for editing

When all the dust has cleared, the factor determining the failure or success of your production time-management efforts is whether you created appropriate and sufficient materials for editing. During editing, your video is cropped, embellished, and assembled into a coherent and useful message. But if you left something out or created confusing, unrelated clips, your video will suffer directly, and you'll add many unpleasant hours to the editing process.

Here are some hints for making your editor a grateful fan with no appreciable loss or graying of hair.

Logging your shots

I'm sure at one time or another you've seen a reenactment of a film or video shoot in which someone holds up a strange-looking board with a little board on top of it and says something like "Scene 14, shot 7, take one. Action." Then the person slams down the little board, making a large clacking sound. This scenario may seem like some archaic practice, but in reality, in various ways, the practice is still being performed. What was the person doing? A message was being sent to the editor.

Take a look at Figure 7-1, which illustrates what's often referred to as a *take board.* Though it may look different from one production to the next, the take board usually includes the name of the production, the date, the scene number, and the take number. The term *scene* refers to a series of shots that, when edited, complete a dramatic action or a portion of a message, such as the famous "shower scene" in the movie *Psycho* by Alfred Hitchcock.

A *shot* is a specific segment of a scene. A *take* is a taping of one of the shots in that segment. Frequently, even in simple productions, a shot is taped many times because a word was misstated by the on-camera person, the camera was out of focus, a noise occurred on the set, and so on. The board is clacked to create a sound that's easy for the editor to hear later while she shuttles the video back and forth. While editing, she hears the clack and realizes she is passing over the beginning of a take. She stops the tape, backs it up, or goes forward until she can read the message on the take board.

The take board is only one-fourth of the conventional record-keeping process. The other three parts are the script, time code, and the log. The script is the actual plan of the production, including descriptions of action, camera instructions, instructions to the actor(s) and any dialogue in the scene. The take board's information reflects the names of scenes as listed in the script. Time code is a particular kind of identifying information recorded by the camcorder onto the video tape. Time code makes frame-accurate editing possible. It is the frame-by-frame permanent identification of the video information on the tape.

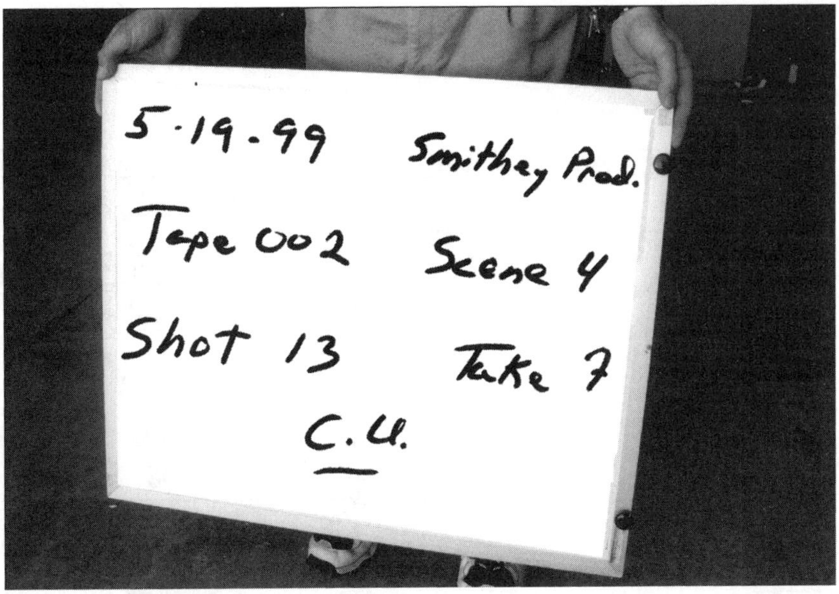

Figure 7-1:
The take board provides all the information the editor will need to identify a given segment of a scene.

All this discussion brings us to the *log*. You can make the most of your time during the production — time on the clock and time code on the tape — through well-disciplined logging. During shooting, someone logs information about each of the takes.

In Figure 7-2, you see the number of the scene and the take and information about the take. By keeping an accurate log during shooting, you ensure that all the planned shots have been taped and that you've written all the information the editor will need to find the good footage. One of the important functions of logging details is to ensure continuity.

Continuity

One time-consuming problem editors face is reconciling missing or visually unrelated sequences. Let me use a common mistake as an example. You can follow along, if you like, by referring to Figure 7-3. Say that in one of your scenes, the presenter points to an object, requiring a close-up. After pointing, the presenter goes on with the narration.

According to the script, you need to shoot a close-up of that object. So you set up for the close-up and have the hand come into the picture and out again. Later on, the editor puts the wide shot of the pointing hand and the close-up of the pointing hand together — only to discover that the hand in the wide shot is the left hand and the hand in the close-up is the right hand.

Aaargh! This lovely little situation is called a *break in continuity*.

| DATE: 5/19/99 | | | | |
| LOCATION: | | | | |
TAPE	SCENE	SHOT	TAKE	COMMENT
001	02	4	1	Bad focus
"	"	"	2	Stumbled words
"	"	"	3	Good!!
"	02	5	1	Good!!
002	02	5	2	Confidence Shot (use #1)
"	"	6	1	Sound of airplane
"	"	"	2	Good!!

Figure 7-2:
The log always contains details about the segment.

In video and film, *continuity* means the proper ordering of the details of a scene. Another common example of a continuity problem is a door that's open in one segment and closed in the next. Another common example is a person holding an object in one shot, but not holding it in the next shot. After your eye becomes trained to continuity, you become aware of the surprising number of times continuity errors occur on network television.

Create editing options

One of the simplest ways to cover yourself in the event of unnoticed production goofs (and you will have many) is to give your editor lots of alternatives.

Here are a couple of easy-to-do examples that illustrate my point:

 ✔ A person is speaking directly into a camera. Imagine that you're the editor of the video. What do you do if you discover while editing that you need to take something out of the speech? A straight cut of video footage will look apparent and bad.

Now switch roles and imagine that you're shooting the video. What can you do during production to anticipate the editor's needs? One simple way is to record the speech twice at different zoom perspectives — say, a medium shot and a medium close-up. In this way, wherever the edit is needed, the editor can cut from a medium shot to a close-up and back to the medium shot. This procedure is one of the oldest and simplest ways to give your editor some leeway. (See Chapter 6 for more on shooting medium and close-up shots.)

✔ Now imagine that you're shooting an ordinary interview, in which the interviewer is sitting off-camera and directly next to it. The person on-camera isn't looking into the lens, but is looking directly at the interviewer. How can you use this style to help your editor help you?

Again, let me give you the simplest and oldest procedure: Take some reaction shots. By *reaction shot,* I mean after the interview is over, turn the camera to the interviewer. If you want, have the interviewer ask the questions on camera. Later, the editor will put the questions and answers together. Even more simple, get lots of reaction shots of the interviewer nodding her head, looking pensive, smiling and laughing, whatever is appropriate for the things said by the person being interviewed. These reaction shots can be used by the editor to shorten the interview and adjust the order of questions and answers as necessary.

Figure 7-3:
The image in the close-up shot (middle image) isn't continuous with the preceding and following shots.

Here are two final tips on helping your editor help you: Be sure to get some reaction shots of the person being interviewed and be sure to shoot ambient sound. *Ambient sound* is silence in the environment where you are shooting. Silence is very different from one location to the next. For example, silence at a computer workstation is filled with the sound of the computer's fan motor. Outdoor silence may include as background the sound of cars on a nearby street. An editor needs ambient sound to properly edit location shoots. Of course, be sure to note ambient sound in your log.

Working with People On and Off Camera

On-location production can involve as few as two crew members or as many as a dozen or so. But no matter the number, two of the most important principles of successful on-location shooting are knowing that the director is the boss and having a director who allows the crew members to do their jobs. In order for a crew to work efficiently, everyone should be clear about his or her role.

The following section provides a classic description of crew roles. These roles are not necessarily held by one person. And one person can have more than one role. The director just needs to make certain people understand the role(s) for which they are responsible.

Roles

First, an important clarification: A video shoot is not a democracy. In video, clear-cut roles are as essential as they are on a football team or in an army platoon.

Second, pecking orders don't exist in video production. There isn't a concept of greatest and least. Everyone simply has a job to do.

Following is a formal description of roles. In real life, the interaction is probably much looser than I describe here. Even so, when push comes to shove, all the crew members realize that this is the skeleton that holds the crew together.

Producer

The *producer* is the person responsible for the overall completion of the project. Frequently, the producer predates everyone else on the crew. The producer negotiated with the customer, set the budget, and signed the contracts (if this a commercial project). The producer will usually be with the project long after the crew dissolves. The producer will work with the editor, arrange for distribution, oversee general administration, and see the project to its conclusion. On location, the producer does all that is necessary to keep the director focused on the production.

If a representative of the customer is at the shoot, the producer is responsible for interacting with the customer and communicating concerns to the director.

Director

The *director* is like the hub of a wheel. The director must understand everyone's role and guide the overall movement of the production. But even more important, the director is the person with the vision. The director knows what the production is supposed to be like and what it is intended to accomplish. The director's first and foremost job is to hold the vision together throughout the production. A good crew keeps the director focused on leading, not problem solving.

Customer/technical consultant

In some productions, especially training, the customer will provide a *technical consultant,* also known as a subject matter expert (SME). The SME is often ultimately responsible for the technical accuracy of what is said and done in front of the camera. The director and the producer frequently depend on the instructions of the SME. But the SME instructs the crew only at the request of the director and only in the specific instances where such action is needed. Otherwise, the production can become a chaotic mess. Also, the SME cannot appear on camera. If he or she does, you need another SME — because once a person appears on camera, you can't depend on his or her objectivity.

Videographer (photographer)

A *videographer* is a camera or camcorder operator. In the world of television news, such people are called "photographers." A good videographer is a humble but confident person. The videographer must follow the director's orders, but must also be able to tell the director if there's a better way to do the job. Usually, directors and videographers develop close professional relationships and learn to read each other's nuances of meaning and mood. One important rule that's seldom, if ever, broken is that no one directs the videographer other than the director.

Sometimes the videographer, depending strictly on the preference of the director, is a kind of assistant director, giving instructions to the other crew members. A director may choose this route when he or she has to give full attention to the person in front of the camera.

Sound technician

The *sound technician* is a bit of an odd role. I've never been able to figure out whether they're sleeping or concentrating on the sound. The sound technician's job is a rather lonely one. It requires listening to the audio with earphones. The sound tech keeps fingers poised on a field mixer, anticipating fluctuations of volume in order to maximize the recorder's dynamic range.

The sound tech must call for a retake whenever an alien sound or a speaking glitch is heard through the earphones. The sound tech usually works with the videographer.

Gaffer

The *gaffer* is the crew member responsible for anything having to do with light and electricity. Typically, the gaffer works directly with the videographer in framing the shot and setting light levels.

Grip

On a small crew a *grip* is primarily an assistant to the gaffer. The grip is responsible for setting up lighting for a shot. Normally, the grip also helps move the camera and tripod and any other gear.

Production assistant

The *production assistant,* affectionately referred to as the PA, is the do-every-thing-else person on the crew. Usually, PAs are the ones who keep the shooting log up to date. The PA typically handles the take board. But the PA also assists in moving equipment as needed. One important note about PAs: They are usually eager to help — sometimes to a fault. Be sure that they know how to use equipment before allowing them to handle it.

In front of the camera

Two kinds of people appear on camera in video productions: talent and real people. *Talent* are professionals who have usually logged many hours in front of a camera. They are fun to direct because they know exactly how to do whatever you ask them. But, unfortunately, there's a cost for such skill. If you have something important that you need to shoot and if the video is heavy on message, try to find the money to hire talent. Because they are so good at what they do, you can cut your shooting time in half.

In videography, *real people* are not trained to speak or perform in front of a camera. Some real people are astonishingly effective — most aren't. The director's biggest job with real people is to set them at ease during production. If a real person is not nervous, he or she will usually look good in front of the camera. The viewers of video aren't turned off by people who lack beauty. They're turned off by people who act incompetently in front of the camera. The two are totally unrelated.

Making people look like people

Because video is an electronic visual medium, real-life colors and clothing combinations may look entirely different through a camera lens than they do in real life. Following are some points designed to help you overcome this problem.

Costume considerations

Avoid dark clothing, particularly in dark scenes or on dark sets. Avoid patterned dresses that may blend into backgrounds. Dress for modesty, especially when sitting. Also, low necklines in close-ups look like the person forgot to wear anything at all. Avoid white and red clothing. White messes up the aperture (the light that reaches the focal plane in your camcorder — see Chapter 3 for more about aperture and focal plane). And red duplicates poorly. Just try to recall the last time you rented a video with lots of red in it. The red expands to the right, which is referred to as *red shift.*

In addition to certain colors, avoid tight stripes and herringbone patterns — camera and video player technologies can't as yet handle close designs. The result on-screen is called *moire* — an unpleasant wavy effect on the fabric.

John Wayne wore makeup

Makeup is often necessary for indoor shooting — not to make a person pretty, but to restore color and hide reflection. Women are usually more open to applying makeup than men are. But even a fairly macho guy will probably cooperate when the director tells him that, without makeup, he may wind up looking pale and clownlike on video. (Directors are great at convincing and schmoozing people.)

Here are some tips for applying makeup:

- ✔ Use a sponge applicator to apply makeup.
- ✔ Always cover clothing with a cape.
- ✔ Use a matte finish, translucent powder to fix shines between takes.
- ✔ Remember that fair skin often needs to look a shade darker.
- ✔ If you need to mask a beard, be sure to use pancake makeup that matches the person's skin.

Part III

Using Your Computer for Digital Video

The 5th Wave   By Rich Tennant

Principal

"I found these two in the multimedia lab morphing faculty members into farm animals."

In this part . . .

A computer is basically unintelligent — complicated but unintelligent. You have to tell it what you want, and you have to arrange it to accomplish the job correctly. Once everything on the computer is arranged correctly, it accomplishes amazing feats. You can't "train" your computer to bring you your newspaper and slippers, but you can get it to capture and edit video. In this part, you find out what's required to ensure that your computer rolls over and does video editing tricks.

Chapter 8

Making Your Computer DV-Ready

*O*nce upon a time when we were lost, my family and I came upon an ingenious little book. We were driving along in the Colorado Rocky Mountains looking for the west entrance to the Rocky Mountain National Park, which was good; but we'd received some poor instructions and didn't have the slightest idea where we were, which was *very* bad.

By chance, we drove around a corner of a winding road and to our delight, discovered a general store. We stopped and asked the proprietor if she knew how to get to the park. She laughed and told us it was right around the corner. I asked if she had a map to direct us through the park. She handed me a little book with the directions.

The book had two beginnings. Either way was the *correct* way to begin. One way started at the east entrance of the Rocky Mountain Park, and the other started where we were, the west entrance. As we worked our way through the book, we eventually came to the middle page, which happened to be the middle of the park. We then flipped the book upside down and continued to the other end (which was actually another beginning).

Are you wondering what all this has to do with digital video? Well, the book you're holding in your hands could have been designed in the same way (if only I could have convinced my publisher, that is!). The book could have had two beginnings — because people come at digital video from two directions. Some people are more familiar with cameras than they are with computers, so they start with a camera and make their way to the computer side of digital video production. Other people are more familiar with computers, so they start at the opposite end. Well, just so you'll know where you are — because this book is on the former route (camera to computer), you are, right now, smack dab in the middle of the digital video park. This chapter is the "You Are Here" place, where you turn everything upside down to continue. (Whoa! I'm typing standing on my head!)

In this chapter, you see how digital video production merges with nonlinear editing. You don't hear any more about aperture and focal lengths, gaffers and grips (ahhh . . . did I hear a sigh of relief from some of you?). Now, it's megabytes and processing speed, digital compression, and rendering times (oops . . . did I hear a groan from the rest of you?).

Your existing computer may be almost all the hardware you'll need for editing digital video; then again, it might not fill the bill at all. How can you know? And if you're considering plunking down some major change for a computer, how can you be sure you'll get the right one for editing digital video? These are both good questions. This chapter provides you with many of the answers. And the chapter explains a number of things you may not have thought to ask about.

Nonlinear Editing (NLE) with a PC

Editing video on a PC is called *nonlinear editing.* (You'll probably find it no big surprise that you can use a personal computer, or PC, to do things like edit video for television — after all, you can do almost anything else with a PC, so why not? But, the truth is, I'm still amazed.)

I introduce nonlinear editing in Chapters 1 and 2, but the short story is that nonlinear editing is based on computer software programs that enable you to shorten, combine, and modify video clips. Nonlinear editing equipment includes the software tools you need for adding music, sound effects, special visual effects, and more. And nonlinear editing enables you do all these things without overwriting the original video clip.

As I mention in Chapter 2, affordable nonlinear editing has been around for a few years. But unless you had some very expensive video production gear, such as Betacam SP cameras and recorders, your editing suffered because of the limited formats of the initial video, namely video based on the VHS and S-VHS formats.

VHS, S-VHS, and Betacam SP are all analog formats. An analog format represents video and audio signals as waves. Waves recorded via the less expensive formats wind up with distortions. For this reason, the great promises offered by nonlinear editing were originally limited to only those who used equipment based on the more expensive format. However, as I explain in Chapters 1 and 2, the MiniDV format and IEEE 1394 changed that forever.

Because of the innovation of low-cost, professional-quality digital camcorders and because of their lossless connectivity to PCs via the IEEE 1394 cable, you can now affordably record and capture high-quality video. (*Lossy* means that some data is lost in transmission. *Lossless* means the digital video signal is virtually the same in the computer as it was on the MiniDV tape.)

And since November 1998, you have been able to edit that high-quality video by using an excellent and affordable nonlinear editing software program. At that time, all the pieces finally came together to make it possible for affordable, professional-quality digital video nonlinear editing. In that month, Adobe Systems certified the first IEEE 1394 capture card that was compatible with Adobe Premiere 5.1. (***Note:*** Capture cards change video signals from your camcorder into digital computer files.) With this certification, it was now possible to put all the pieces together to make an affordable, fully digital MiniDV-based nonlinear editing system.

Now many individuals and small corporations are flocking to this broadcast-quality opportunity. In the rest of this chapter, I show you how this all comes together, and I show you how you can purchase what you'll need to join the digital flock. Excuse me while I take a break. I'm going out for some quackers.

Weighing In Your NLE Needs

To determine your nonlinear editor needs, the place to begin is with *you* — not, as you might think, with computers or software programs or capture cards or any of that stuff. Begin by asking what you already know about using a computer.

I have the privilege of talking to budding digital video enthusiasts every day. They come in all ages and have an endless range of reasons why they want to get into digital video editing. The striking difference among them, though, is their diverse levels of knowledge about computers and video production.

- Some know little about either video production or computers.
- Others are familiar with computers but don't know video production.
- Some have been in video production for years but know nothing to little about computers.
- And, of course, a few know a lot about both.

Which of these four categories best fits you?

- Are you a virtual novice to video production? If so, this chapter and Chapter 9 will answer many of your basic questions about computers and nonlinear editing.

✔ Are you a raw recruit at using a computer? Do you know what a mouse (computer mouse) is? Do you want to ask what Windows is but are afraid somebody might laugh?

If this describes you, I suggest you latch on to Dan Gookin's excellent book, *PCs For Dummies,* 7th Edition, published by IDG Books Worldwide, Inc. Read it or a book like it, and you'll be ready to march right into this chapter and Chapter 9.

✔ Do you have a little working knowledge about PCs? Do you know how to open a program and save a file and stuff like that? If so, you are probably ready to launch into nonlinear editing on a PC. Honest! You could be making art in just a little while.

Starting with the software

If you're going to assemble a nonlinear editing system, you should begin with the software. Strange place to begin? Not really — because your editing software determines how your entire nonlinear editing adventure will work. For that reason, don't outfit a computer and then go out to buy your software — and risk finding out that your computer doesn't support the software you need and want.

So what kind of software do you want for your nonlinear editing? First you need to determine whether you want to go proprietary or nonproprietary. Huh?

Proprietary NLEs

A *proprietary* nonlinear editing system is a closed-box kind of program and computer (that is, the editing software isn't compatible with computer platforms other than its own). Few of these systems are out there. Casablanca, manufactured by Draco Corporation, comes to mind.

What is a nonlinear editor?

A nonlinear editing *application* is software, such as Adobe Premiere 5.1. A nonlinear editing *system* is the combination of software and hardware (computer, boards, monitors, and so on) that are required to do the work as commanded by the software. Just think of the software as the brains and the hardware as the body. The brains and the body have to be a match or very weird things can happen. Even Dr. Frankenstein would get chills and goose bumps. By the way, a nonlinear *editor* is you (or soon you will be)!

People who own proprietary systems swear by (I hope not at) them. They are designed specifically to perform the job for which they are intended — in this case, capturing and editing video. The software and the hardware system are sold as a unit and often are not capable of handling additional off-the-shelf computer applications. If you'd like to know more about Casablanca, check out the Draco Web site at www.draco.com.

Nonproprietary NLEs

A nonproprietary nonlinear editing system is open-ended (that is, the editing software works on Mac or PC computer platforms). Nonproprietary nonlinear editors are a little more complicated to set up than proprietary ones. But to their advantage, they can share files with other off-the-shelf computer hardware and software.

Specifically, the nonproprietary nonlinear editing software program showcased in this book is Adobe Premiere 5.1. Adobe has come a long way in its research and development of nonlinear editor software. The previous version, Adobe Premiere 4.2, was for years considered a good multimedia editing program. See the following sidebar "Adobe Premiere has come a long way!" for a bit more on these programs.

By the way, folks overuse the word *multimedia* — and mean many different things when they use it. When I refer to multimedia in this book, I'm talking about interactive CD-ROM applications that include video, audio, and animation.

Adobe Premiere has come a long way!

Adobe Premiere 4.2 was great for capturing video at up to 720 x 486 resolution. You could use it to integrate audio and animation files with video files to create short movies that could then be imported into multimedia authoring programs such as Macromedia Director or Aimtech Icon Author. The strength of Adobe Premiere 4.2 was that it was great for selecting the right kind of resolution and compression/decompression (codec) for any kind of multimedia use. A number of companies developed capture boards for use with Adobe Premiere 4.2.

It was a good program. I used it for years in my work in multimedia authoring. But Adobe Premiere 4.2 was not suitable for full-fledged video nonlinear editing.

In March of 1998, Adobe Systems launched Adobe Premiere 5.0, which quickly became Adobe Premiere 5.1. The difference between Premiere 4.2 and 5.1 was (please excuse my excitement) extraordinary. The many features of the program are discussed throughout this book. So, let me simply say for now that Premiere 5.1 is a full-fledged nonlinear editing application that is capable of performing many of the functions previously found only in very expensive applications.

Sizing up the computer operating system

Do you like reading the backs of cereal boxes? Then you're a natural for assembling a nonlinear editing system. The place to start is reading the back of the box of Adobe Premiere 5.1. (Don't worry, I'm not going to ask you to pour milk on the contents.) If you don't happen to have one of those boxes around, go to the Adobe Web site at `www.adobe.com/prodindex/premiere/prodinfo.html`. Press the hyperlink System Requirements or scroll to the bottom of the page. (I'm beginning to think the back of the box is easier to find.) On that Web page, you can find the nifty information you're looking for. But to make life easier, I list Adobe's minimum and recommended system requirements in this section.

Why are minimum and recommended system requirements so important? Because nonlinear editing is not your normal computer venture. Your computer must equal or exceed the nonlinear editing hardware specifications or you will have all kinds of ugly problems that you don't even want to think about.

At the Adobe site, you see that the requirements are for both Windows-based and Power Macintosh computers. But to keep things simple here, I provide only the info for Windows-based computers. Be sure to notice that you have a "Minimum" and a "Recommended" choice. Here's where the fun starts.

Minimum

Before beginning, here's a bit of advice: To varying degrees, the term "minimum" may be a cause for caution. In my opinion, minimum requirements are nice to know, but to avoid as much as possible. A minimum requirement is like low-octane gasoline — you'll be able to make it up hills, but, once in a while, you'll feel like you're about to start rolling back down the hill. With that said, allow me to walk you through the following specifications:

✔ **Intel Pentium processor:** The big thing to notice here is that your old 486 processor isn't going to cut it; it really won't work for Adobe Premiere 5.1. And a Pentium II or a Pentium III processor performs noticeably better than a basic Pentium. I don't recommend less than a Pentium II 300 MHz (megahertz) processor.

✔ **Microsoft Windows 95, 98, or NT 4.0, or later operating system:** Sorry, but Windows 3.1 doesn't work. If you plan to purchase a new computer, I suggest you go with the Windows NT 4.0 or later approach rather than Windows 95 or Windows 98. Doing so isn't critical, but you'll find that the NT version of Windows is more robust (less prone to crashing) and more capable of handling multitasking (running more than one application at the same time).

✔ **32MB RAM:** I'm sorry, but the Adobe minimum on this one is pretty scary. These days, you can hardly play Solitaire with 32MB RAM. (*RAM is the memory on an operating system.*) The amount of RAM you have directly affects your graphics and video playing capabilities. For minimums, let's talk 128MB RAM. Maybe 32MB would work, but I doubt you'd have much fun.

✔ **60MB hard disk space for installation (30MB for storage):** Sixty megabytes is sufficient only if you're creating tiny multimedia files, as in postage stamp variety. Unfortunately, if you intend to use your computer for digital video, 30MB is approximately 12 seconds. Da ta dee, da da. Oops. I'm sorry we've run out of space. Again, in my opinion, the *true* minimum should be in the order of 200 to 300MB (and that is only a minimalistically minimal minimum). For example, 300MB of MiniDV quality digital video equals about two minutes.

As I mention in Chapter 9, you really need at least 2GB (1 gigabyte equals 1,000 megabytes) for holding all your audio and video files. Common hard drive sizes for storage of audio and video files are 9GB or18GB.

✔ **256-color video display adapter:** This minimum is legitimate, but not for you. This VGA 256-color adapter is for people who might be developing something for multimedia applications. You need a full-fledged graphics card with its own built-in memory. One that comes to mind is Matrox Millennium G200. This one would be a good minimum. It offers you true color (necessary for a nonlinear editor) and speed. For more information, check out the Matrox Web site at `www.matrox.com/mga`.

✔ **CD-ROM drive:** Yup. They nailed this one.

Recommended

Now we're getting into some stuff that runs from absolutely necessary to wouldn't it be nice.

✔ **MMX processor or multiprocessor system:** An MMX processor adds some quality and speed to your graphics. A multiprocessor is very nice, particularly for nonlinear editing systems that are real-time. *Real-time* refers to a computer capture board's capability to cause transitions, such as wipes and dissolves to happen as you watch, rather than through rendering. *Rendering* is a frame-by-frame procedure of building transitions. I mention rendering in Chapter 11. For the moment, let me simply say that a multiprocessor system for an IEEE 1394-based capture board is not an absolute necessity, but it sure is nice. Multiprocessing is great for creating special effects (discussed in length in Chapter 14) and for increasing rendering speed in editing.

✔ **Large capacity hard disk or disk array:** You can say that again. Actually, if you have Windows NT, you *want* to say that again because you would be much better served having two 9GB (gigabyte) hard drives rather than one 18GB hard drive. Windows NT permits *striping,* which is a way to have two drives receive information simultaneously from a single processor. Striped disks increase the effectiveness of a nonlinear editing system. In any event, with Windows 95, Windows 98, or Windows NT, I recommend a minimum of 18GB of storage space. In digital video, 18GB equals a little over 86 minutes of video. Also, the drive for your video *must* be captured and stored on a separate drive from your software. Your software drive (called a *system drive*) can have as little as 2GB capacity, but I suggest at least 4GB.

✔ **Microsoft Video for Windows-compatible or QuickTime for Windows-compatible video capture card:** If the nonlinear editing software is the brains of the system, the video capture card is its heart. The capture card is like a pump that receives, processes, and sends the lifeblood of the system — da video! The capture card needs a lot of discussion, so I dedicate the next section to it.

✔ **Sound card:** No special sound card is needed. You simply need one.

✔ **Modem:** Since we're talking about power and efficiency, you need to have at least a 28.8K modem internal or external (56K modem is recommended).

Choosing the capture card

As I've said (more than once), nonlinear editing software is the brains of the operation. For that reason, you have to look to the software for guidance about acceptable capture cards (the hardware that captures and plays video). The reasoning for this may seem obscure at first, but you'll quickly get the idea. Here's how it works (kinda):

1. **The computer listens to the brains (Premiere 5.1).**

2. **Premiere 5.1 tells the capture card that it's time to capture some video from the IEEE 1394 input.**

3. **The capture card has its own software that obeys Premiere and operates the card and the recorder/player.**

4. **The video is captured and turned into a computer file.**

5. **Premiere closes the capture card's software and goes back to the editing process.**

Obviously, Premiere 5.1 and the capture card have a chummy relationship. For that reason, Adobe lists the cards that are certified to work with Premiere 5.1. You can find an up-to-date list by going to www.adobe.com/prodindex/premiere/main.html and clicking the hyperlink Capture Cards. Figure 8-1, which shows the information that you find at the Web site, is accurate at the time I'm writing this book.

The relationship between Premiere 5.1 and the capture card is critical. If the relationship works well, you're going to have a blast. If it doesn't, well . . . let's just say you won't be very happy.

Premiere 5.1			
Capture Board	Vendor	Platform	Driver Version
Bravado DV 2000	Truevision	Windows 95/98/NT	v1.4
Buz	Iomega	Macintosh	v1.0
Digisuite LE	Matrox	Windows NT	v3.0
Digisuite	Matrox	Windows NT	v3.0
Dynamo VideoPump	ViewGraphics	Windows NT	v1.1.15
FireMax "C"	ProMax	Macintosh	v1.4
Fuse	Aurora Design	Macintosh	v1.5
Media 100qx	Media 100	Macintosh	v5.1
Media 100qx	Media 100	Windows NT	v5.0
miroMotion DC30plus	Pinnacle Systems	Macintosh	v1.2
miroVIDEO DC30plus	Pinnacle Systems	Windows 95/98/NT	v1.32
miroVIDEO DC30pro	Pinnacle Systems	Windows 95/98/NT	v1.32
miroVIDEO DC50	Pinnacle Systems	Windows 95/98/NT	v1.32
miroVIDEO DV200	Pinnacle Systems	Windows 95/98/NT	v1.6
miroVIDEO DV300	Pinnacle Systems	Windows 95/98/NT	v1.6
MotoDV	Digital Origin	Windows 95	v1.1.3
MotoDV	Digital Origin	Macintosh	v1.1.3
MotoDV Studio 1.0	Digital Origin	Macintosh	v1.4.1
MotoDV Studio 2.0	Digital Origin	Windows 95/98/NT	v2.0
Perception Video Recorder	DPS	Windows NT	v2.58
Power Macintosh 8500	Apple	Macintosh	OS v7.5.5 or greater
Power Macintosh 8600	Apple	Macintosh	OS v7.5.5 or greater
Reeltime	Pinnacle	Windows NT 4.0	v2.0
SDxstream	ViewGraphics	Windows NT	v1.1.15
TARGA 1000/TARGA 100 Pro	Truevision	Windows NT (Quicktime only)	v3.0.0.0, 1C5
TARGA 2000 DDR	Truevision	Windows NT	v1.0
TARGA 2000 Pro/RTX/DTX	Truevision	Windows NT (Quicktime only)	v3.1.0.0.1

Figure 8-1:
Choose from Adobe's list of certified capture cards. Uncertified capture cards aren't worth the risk.

Of the more than 30 capture cards (or _boards_) listed in Figure 8-1, only a few are IEEE 1394 cards, such as the miroVIDEO DV300 by Pinnacle Systems. The majority are analog cards. What?! Isn't this all supposed to be digital editing. Well, yes. The capture card digitizes video. But only the IEEE 1394 cards are intended for working with video that _began_ as digital video. Most of the cards listed are for _converting_ analog video into digital video.

In Figure 8-1, notice that Adobe lists the name of the card (board), the company that makes it (vendor), the platform (Windows or Macintosh) the card is compliant with, and the version of the drivers that are certified to work with Adobe Premiere 5.1.

A couple of notes about all the information in Figure 8-1. First, notice that capture cards are designated as Windows or Macintosh compatible. Some of these cards actually work on both platforms, but are certified only for Premiere 5.1 on one of the platforms. Be careful about this. Second, you may have the right card, but the wrong drivers. Drivers are what make the card recognizable to the computer's operating system and to the software application. If you have the wrong driver, access the vendor's Web site to download an updated version.

Chapter 9

Capturing Digital Video

· ·

· ·

*F*ifteen years ago if someone had told me that a single computer would someday replace the equipment of a conventional postproduction house, I would have probably believed it. But if they had also told me that the cost for such a computer would be less than the cost of a single industrial videotape recorder, I would not have believed it. I could imagine many computers taking over video postproduction houses — big, imposing, complex computers. I was totally unprepared for the opposite — a single, small, user-friendly, understandable, and affordable computer.

This chapter focuses on an example of the hardware and software you need to capture and play your digital video. In later chapters, you get to actually use sample software programs to try out nonlinear editing, graphics, and animation. Unfortunately, because the capture and playback processes are hardware-based, I can't provide you a tryout experience in this chapter. What I do provide is a basic description of the installation and use of a capture card and its software. This information may help you to better understand nonlinear editing and to make wise purchases.

Setting Up Your Computer for MiniDV

One of the amazing aspects of preparing your computer for capturing is that you aren't dedicating your computer to an exclusive function. On the same computer, you can do word processing, surf the Internet, and balance your checkbook. You just need to load some software, add a simple piece of hardware, and follow some straightforward instructions to prepare for capturing.

In Chapter 10 and throughout the remainder of this book, I show you the basics for using nonlinear editing (NLE) software (for example, Adobe Premiere 5.1). But now I need to share some basic information about NLE software and plug-ins.

Plugging in your capture card's software

Windows-based and Mac-based NLE software programs are *nonproprietary*, which means that they can operate on and (perhaps) share files with other software programs on the same computer.

Many capture software programs are designed to work within Adobe Premiere 5.1 (the NLE discussed throughout the latter chapters of this book). These capture software programs "plug in," making it possible for your capture card software to work properly with Adobe Premiere 5.1. Without the plug-in, you probably wouldn't be able to capture and edit video. See Chapter 8 for more about NLE and capture card compatibility.

Selecting and adding the capture card

This book is about digital video from start to finish. Many people don't have digital camcorders but would like to perform nonlinear editing. In their cases, if they own an analog camcorder (such as one based on a VHS or S-VHS format), the capture card is where the digital conversion begins. Many capture cards are made for analog video formats (presently more than are available for MiniDV).

What I am about to cover will probably help you whether you are using a MiniDV or analog format. But, in order to remain consistent in this book, I use as my example a capture card specifically designed for the MiniDV, the Pinnacle Systems digital miroVIDEO DV300 capture card. (Go to www.adobe. com/prodindex/premiere/main.html for a list of all Premiere 5.1 compatible capture cards.)

Your capture card requires that your computer comply with some minimum system requirements.

Some capture cards simply won't work with certain computer hardware. Before you purchase a capture card, you should see whether any reports exist that indicate a compatibility problem with your computer system. Pinnacle Systems provides such reports at www.pinnaclesys.com/dv300/.

Of course, you may be planning to purchase a new computer with a capture card already installed. In Chapter 22, I provide an example of a fully configured computer.

Here are the minimum specifications for the miroVIDEO DV300. (You can also find the compatibility report for miroVIDEO DV300 at www.pinnaclesys.com/dv300/.) If this information flies technically over your head, don't be concerned. You just need to ask your computer dealer to make sure that the capture card's minimum requirements are met or exceeded by your computer. For example, if you don't know what a PCI-slot is, not to worry. Just tell your computer dealer that your computer needs to have an available bus mastering 1x32 PCI 2.1 slot.

✔ **Your computer's speed — 200 MHz Pentium processor or faster:** If you're planning to buy a new computer for nonlinear editing, I suggest at least a Pentium II 300 MHz (megahertz). They're not much more expensive than a 200 MHz Pentium, and they're much faster.

✔ **Capture card slot — 32-bit PCI 2.1 slot with bus mastering:** Make sure your computer has an unobstructed PCI (Peripheral Component Interconnect) bus mastering slot available. You can usually identify the PCI slots because most of them are ivory-colored or white.

✔ **64MB RAM (more recommended):** This is the minimum RAM (Random-Access Memory) recommended by Pinnacle for this capture card. However, I recommend at least 128MB RAM for your NLE and capture card.

✔ **50MB free hard disk space:** Your system's hard drive (normally the C drive on your computer) must be capable of storing a number of software programs. The digital video300 software needs 50MB of disk space.

✔ **2GB video audio visual hard disk space:** Though 2GB (gigabytes — 2GB is 2,000 megabytes) sounds like a lot, it isn't. At least for digital video, it's not much space. Two gigabytes stores only 9½ minutes of video. A reasonable amount of audio video storage is 18GB.

As you can see from the preceding minimum requirements, you must know a bit about your computer before choosing your capture card. You may also have to upgrade your computer's power, memory, and storage capacity to meet these requirements. And as I said at the beginning of this section, help is as close as your computer dealer if you need it.

Installing the capture card software

Properly installing a capture card into your computer is relatively easy *if* you're an experienced computer user; however, doing so may be a little intimidating if you're a bit of a novice. Here's my recommendation: If you're familiar with the term *bus mastering PCI slot* and if you can install SCSI connectors (SCSI stands for Small Computer Systems Interface, a high-speed, standardized means for connecting hard drives, CD-ROM drives, and peripheral devices to a computer), you probably know enough to install the capture card yourself. Otherwise, save yourself some stress-related headaches and ask someone else with technical know-how to do it for you.

As recommended by the capture card manufacturer, you'll most likely need to have the NLE software and the capture card installed on your hard drive before you install the capture card software (the plug-in). When you run the setup utility for your capture card software, the utility goes looking for your NLE program to which it adds the plug-in. Of course, the best procedure is to read the installation instructions that come with the capture card and its software.

Connecting MiniDV Devices

After you install the NLE software, the capture card, and the capture card software, you're ready to connect and check out your digital video system. You can hook up your camcorder and monitor and begin to find out what all this MiniDV hoopla is all about.

Connecting the IEEE 1394 cable

All my talk about the wonders of IEEE 1394 in Chapters 1 and 2 simply boil down to plugging one end of the cable into your camcorder and the other end into your capture card. I wish it was more highfalutin than that, but it's not. Figure 9-1 shows you how to connect the IEEE 1394 cable to the digital video connection on your camcorder.

IEEE 1394 connection   MiniDV camcorder

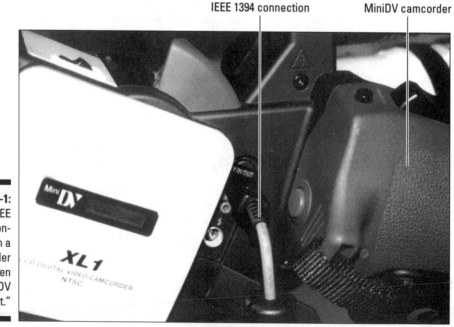

Figure 9-1: The IEEE 1394 connection on a camcorder is often called "DV In/Out."

IEEE stands for Institute for Electrical and Electronics Engineers, which sets the standards for electrical and electronic devices and systems. IEEE 1394 is a low-cost digital interface that integrates cameras, recorders, and computers. For example, by connecting the IEEE 1394 cable to your camcorder and your computer's special capture card, you can transmit digital video images from your MiniDV cassette through your capture card to your computer's hard drive.

Connecting a monitor for playback

Many digital video camcorders (such as the Canon XL1) have composite (VHS) and S-VHS outputs. Figure 9-2 shows an example of composite and S-VHS outputs. Depending on the inputs of your monitor, you can use either of the outputs for viewing your video. After you connect your monitor, just turn your camcorder to VTR mode (the setting for using your camcorder as a video tape recorder) and play your recorded MiniDV tape.

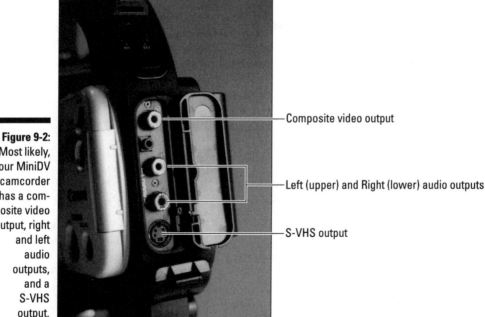

Figure 9-2:
Most likely, your MiniDV camcorder has a composite video output, right and left audio outputs, and a S-VHS output.

Composite video output

Left (upper) and Right (lower) audio outputs

S-VHS output

The IEEE 1394 serial bus cable provides full control of your camcorder's video-tape recorder from your computer through the cable to your computer. From your computer, you can play your camcorder and watch the tape play on your monitor. Not only that, as you see in Chapter 17, you can edit in Premiere 5.1 and watch a full-screen video playback of your edited piece — just as though the camcorder's videotape recorder were part of the computer. In the next section, you find a little info on how the playback system works.

Using Your Capture Card to Play Video

So your capture card and its software are installed. Your camcorder and monitor are set up and connected to each other and to the computer. You're ready to boogie. All you have to do now is find out how to operate the capture software. Fortunately, running capture software couldn't be too much simpler.

When you open the miroVIDEO DV300 capture software (named miroVIDEO DVTools), the first thing you probably notice is the simple design of the program's interface (see Figure 9-3). The interface consists of three columns. The far-left column lists names of tapes. Each of these names contains a database of clips. The middle column is the Capture Gallery. You place clips in the Capture Gallery in order to capture them to your computer. The third column, the one to the far right, is the Tools column. The tools available to you are, from top to bottom, Scan Digital Video Tape, Capture, Edit, and Print to Digital Video Tape.

Scanning a MiniDV tape

The Scan Digital Video Tape tool (refer to Figure 9-3) doesn't capture your video, but it does something equally amazing. When you click the tool, the capture software takes over the operation of your camcorder and searches the entire tape loaded in your video tape recorder. The Scan Digital Video Tape tool creates and saves a library of thumbnails showing the first frame of each clip (see Figure 9-4). Each thumbnail displays the opening frame of a clip and its time code. This library is a useful way of logging all your shots on a tape.

Print to DV Tape

Edit

Capture

Scan DV Tape

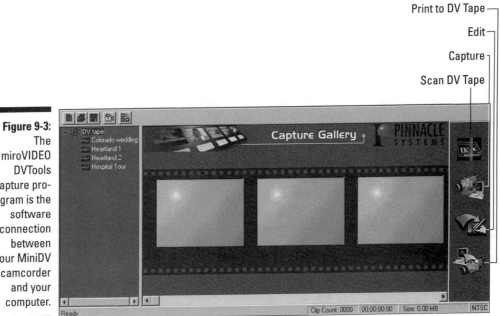

Figure 9-3:
The miroVIDEO DVTools capture program is the software connection between your MiniDV camcorder and your computer.

Time code

Figure 9-4:
The MiroVIDEO program creates a thumbnail library of all the recorded segments residing on your digital videotape.

Running the MiniDV device control

One of the functions of the miroVIDEO DV300 software is the DV Device Control. The digital video Device Control handles the video tape recorder on your camcorder.

Simply double-click any of the thumbnails in the loaded tape's library, and the digital video Device Control automatically advances or rewinds the tape in your camcorder to the clip's opening frame. Your camcorder displays the clip on your monitor. You are ready to play the clip. Figure 9-5 shows a monitor playing the digital video tape recorder clip as it has just been double-clicked in its thumbnail form on the computer. If you want, you can run the MiniDV device control without first scanning the tape.

Figure 9-5:
The digital video device control runs your video tape recorder via the IEEE 1394 cable.

Capturing video clips to your computer

Capturing video to your computer is easy with the miroVIDEO DV300 software. For example, the utility is useful for automatically capturing any number of clips in any order. Using your tape's thumbnail library, you drag your selections to the Capture Gallery. (Figure 9-6 shows the Capture Gallery.) When you are satisfied with your choices, just press the Capture tool (see Figure 9-6). The Capture Gallery begins the capture process.

Capture tool

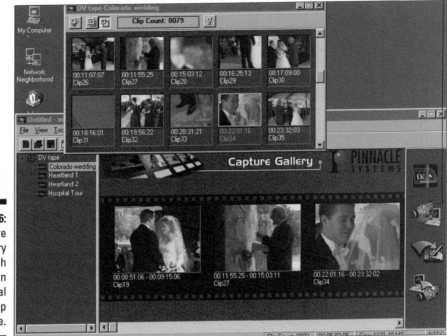

Figure 9-6:
The Capture
Gallery
saves each
clip as an
individual
movie clip
file.

Part IV
Editing Digital Video with Your Computer

The 5th Wave   By Rich Tennant

"IT'S THE BREAK WE'VE BEEN WAITING FOR, LIEUTENANT.
THE THIEVES FIGURED OUT HOW TO TURN ON ONE OF THE
STOLEN VIDEO-CONFERENCING MONITORS."

In this part . . .

Seldom does a human being have an excuse for having
as much fun as you're about to experience. Imagine
learning a software program and loudly exclaiming "Wow!"
at the same time. Doesn't seem possible, does it? If you're
of the opinion that learning a software program and being
excited are mutually exclusive, you're about to change
your mind.

This part has chapters that introduce you to Adobe
Premiere 5.1 (a nonlinear editing program), Adobe
Illustrator 8.0 (a draw program), Adobe Photoshop 5.0 (a
paint program), and Adobe After Effects 4.0 (a 2-D animation program). You're going to use these programs with
some real graphics, audio files, and movie files. And you
will perform some astounding digital video feats.

But, ahem, you're not supposed to be having fun, you're
supposed to be aquiring knowledge about some computer
software programs. Well, maybe just to be on the safe
side, you should to keep a pillow nearby in case you need
to stifle an occasional "Wow!"

Chapter 10

Building a Nonlinear Project with Adobe Premiere

Selecting the right nonlinear editor (NLE) is important. You want a system that meets all your current needs, but one that can also grow to meet needs you haven't even thought of yet. That's why I'm so hot about Adobe Premiere 5.1. Not only is Premiere the very best NLE for its cost, but also because it's part of the Adobe Dynamic Media suite, Premiere opens the door to the unlimited, affordable nonlinear editing options.

In this chapter, I introduce you to the Adobe Dynamic Media suite and to the nonlinear editor Adobe Premiere 5.1, via the Adobe Premiere 5.0 Tryout version that comes on the CD at the back of this book. Premiere 5.0 is the same size as the for-real, full-size version, Premiere 5.1 — about 30MB. When the program loads, it automatically installs an uninstall utility so that you can remove the program whenever you like.

The tryout version does everything the for-real version does *except* capture and save video. But don't worry, I have put plenty of sample stuff on the CD so that you can create a video project in this chapter. The sample files are approximately 21MB and can be easily deleted from you hard drive when you're done. If you want, you can access the sample files from the CD without placing them on your hard disk. But I don't recommend that because the files won't run as well.

In this chapter, I help you set up Premiere and operate it. And, as I said, you get to use sample files to create your own project. You're going to have a blast. Behind its ease of use, Premiere hides incredible power and versatility. But rather than spouting off about it, why don't I just show you. First, though, take a look at the Dynamic Media suite.

Using the Adobe Dynamic Media Suite

Adobe Systems, long known for its many desktop publishing, print-oriented software programs, created the Adobe Dynamic Media suite as a user-friendly way to integrate its various products into a cohesive work environment. With Adobe Premiere 5.1 as the hub of the suite's wheel, you can work with Adobe Illustrator 8.0, Adobe Photoshop 5.0, and Adobe After Effects 4.0. As is true of most Adobe products, the Dynamic Media suite is available in both Mac and Windows versions.

Because these three applications work so well with Premiere, they are, for all practical purposes, extensions of your NLE. I've dedicated a chapter to each of them, and I think you'll be glad I did.

- **Adobe Illustrator 8.0:** In Chapter 12, I show you how you can easily create illustrations in Adobe Illustrator and import them into the NLE, Adobe Premiere. Then I show you how to use the NLE to do some neat things with the illustrations.

- **Adobe Photoshop 5.0:** In Chapter 13, I introduce you to Adobe Photoshop and show you some ways to modify and glorify images for use in Premiere.

- **Adobe After Effects 4.0:** In Chapter 14, you get to pull out the stops and make some amazing animation for video. Then, in the same chapter, you bring animation into Premiere.

One of the reasons that I'm an Adobe groupie is that each of these programs is interdependent. By *interdependent,* I mean that each one stands on its own merits with features and capabilities that reach far beyond what you'll need for making video. Yet, each one completely integrates with the others. You can use Premiere for a long time without adding any of the other three. Then, as your interests and budget allow, you can add them in about any order (the only exception being that you probably will want to purchase After Effects last because you can't do much in the program without first using Photoshop, Illustrator, and/or Premiere).

Getting Ready for Nonlinear Editing

In the first nine chapters in this book, I tell you all kinds of wonderful stories about the glories of nonlinear editing (NLE). Now you get to see for yourself how easy and how exciting computer-based video editing can be.

Installing Adobe Premiere 5.0 and sample files

Before jumping in, you need to install the tryout version of Premiere 5.0 that's on the CD that comes with this book (unless you already have Premiere installed on your computer, of course). For steps on installing Premiere, turn to Appendix B.

You also need to download the Chapter 10 sample files from the CD-ROM at the back of this book. These sample files are stored on the CD-ROM in a sub-folder named CHAP10, which is located in a folder named CLIPS. Turn to Appendix B for steps on copying the Chapter 10 sample files to your hard drive.

When you complete this chapter, you can delete the sample files from your hard drive to save space.

Installing QuickTime

Some of the movies you will be watching and using in this chapter and throughout the remainder of the book are made to play using QuickTime for Windows. If you don't already have QuickTime for Windows version 4.0 or later, you can install a free copy by going to www.apple.com/quicktime on the Web. On this Web page, you will find easy-to-follow steps for downloading and installing your own free version of QuickTime.

Introducing Adobe Premiere

After you install Premiere, you're ready for the great moment.

To start the program, go to your desktop, click Start, and select Programs⇨ Adobe⇨Adobe 5.0 Tryout⇨Adobe Premiere 5.0 Tryout. Whew! There's got to be a better way!

You see a little box that offers you the opportunity to buy the program. Go for it if you want. Or click OK for now. Next you see the New Project Settings dialog box, which isn't all that fascinating (see Figure 10-1). But it's necessary. Pondering Figure 10-1, you see that the General Settings category is selected. Which is good because, before you begin working in the Premiere window, I want you to change a couple of settings so that you can use the sample files on this book's CD-ROM. Your Current Settings information may be different than what you see in the figure, but don't worry about that. Here's what you need to do:

Figure 10-1:
Use these
settings to
begin
creating a
nonlinear
editing
project.

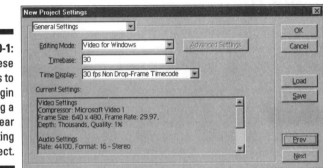

1. **Click the Timebase drop-down box and select 30.**

   Just in case it comes up at the next cocktail party you attend, in the world of broadcast video, there's a little term known as "drop-frame," which refers to the Timebase setting, 29.97. You don't really need to understand all this right now, other than to know that because of some crazy engineering issues, 30-frames per second in television is actually 29.97 frames per second. Because you're not going to create a project for broadcast, 30 frames per second will work better for your current purposes.

2. **Click the Next button.**

   You now see the New Project Settings dialog box with the Video Settings category selected (see Figure 10-2). Here you set the Frame Size and Frame Rate.

3. **Click the arrow beside the Frame Size drop-down box and change the width to 240.**

   If the Aspect button is checked, the height automatically changes to 180.

4. **Click the arrow beside the Frame Rate box and change the Frame Rate to 15.**

   Fifteen is the common frame rate for multimedia files.

   You've made all the changes necessary to play with the sample files.

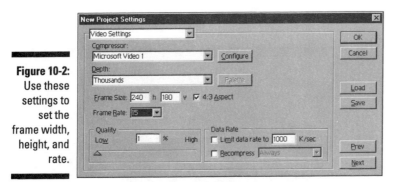

Figure 10-2:
Use these
settings to
set the
frame width,
height, and
rate.

5. Click OK.

The numbers in the Frame Size boxes are pixel counts. A *pixel* is short
for "picture element," the smallest unit of a picture on a monitor's
screen. You make the frame size smaller when you reduce the pixels.
Leave Aspect checked because a television monitor and a computer
monitor have 4:3 aspect ratios. Even though you make the frames
smaller than full-screen size, you want to maintain the width and height
ratio for the examples in this chapter.

Welcome to the Adobe Premiere window

Now you turn to the Adobe Premiere window, which you can set up any way
you like. The main thing is to have access to the Monitor, Timeline, and
Project windows. In this section, you find out how to prepare your screen for
editing. By the way, I don't discuss the Monitor window until the later section
"Laying clips on the Timeline."

If your monitor's resolution is set at 800 x 600 or 640 x 480, you'll find the
Premiere window a little crowded because Adobe Premiere packs a lot on the
screen (see Figure 10-3). For now, you can do the following to help "clean up"
the window:

1. Go to the Adobe Premiere menu and select Window➪Hide T**ransitions**
and Window➪Hide **N**avigator.

These actions temporarily hide a couple of windows.

Next, you do some more housekeeping to reduce the Project window's size.

2. Click the lower-right corner of the Project window and continuing to
press the mouse button, drag the window up until you shorten the
window by about half.

Project window   Monitor window   Transitions palette

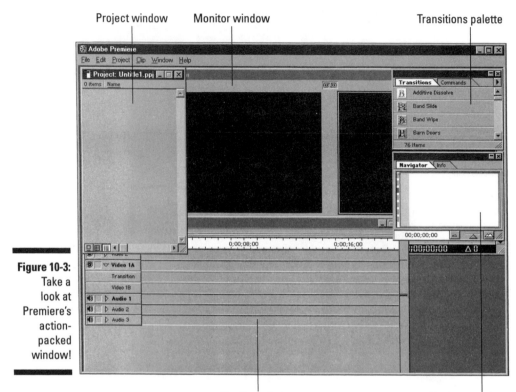

Figure 10-3:
Take a
look at
Premiere's
action-
packed
window!

Timeline window   Navigator palette

3. **Click the highlighted portion of the window and drag the window to the lower-right corner of the screen.**

4. **Next, click anywhere in the Timeline window to highlight it and drag the Timeline window up until you can see the lower-right corner.**

5. **Click the lower-right corner of the Timeline window and continuing to press the mouse button, drag and reduce the Timeline window vertically until its bottom is just below the Audio 2 channel.**

6. **Again, select the top of the Timeline window and drag the resized window down until it abuts the lower-left side of the screen.**

   Your screen should now look something like the one in Figure 10-4.

Figure 10-4:
You can set up your Premiere window any way you like. The main thing is to have easy access to the Monitor, Timeline, and Project windows.

Creating a Project in Premiere

Watch out! You're about to become infatuated with the nonlinear editor Adobe Premiere. Well, actually, you won't have a crush on the program itself, but you'll love what you can do with it. You'll want to show everybody what you can make — your friends and neighbors, your boss and your cat. The only hitch with the tryout program that you installed from this book's CD-ROM is that it doesn't allow you to save the finished product (after all, Adobe wants you to buy the full program). Ah love! So passionate, and yet so fleeting.

Now it's time to build your project. Of course, if this were a real-life project, you would have already shot and captured your video. But for the sake of this introductory project, you get to use clips that I provide.

To accommodate your computer's memory and hard drive, I turned some full-screen video into smaller-sized versions. I shot the original clips using a Canon XL1 camcorder and captured the video into my computer using an IEEE 1394 capture card, thereby turning the video into computer files. Then I imported the files into Premiere and reduced their pixel size and frames per second. I also compressed the video files so that they could more easily play from a hard drive or a CD-ROM. (See Chapter 9 for more on capturing digital video and Chapter 16 for more on frames and compression/decompression.)

Importing and Working with Assets (a.k.a. Clips)

I could have called this section "Importing and Working with clips," but then you wouldn't have been nearly as impressed. In the crazy world of nonlinear editing, video clips, audio files, graphics, and animation are affectionately referred to as *assets*. Such warmth. Some people also call video clips "media."

Now for some project building. Because assets need to be listed in the Project window in order to be edited in Premiere, you begin by importing some clips. Sorry, assets.

1. **Double-click the Project window.**

2. **From the Import File window, find the Clips folder that you copied from this book's CD-ROM and open the Chapter 10 folder.**

3. **Click to highlight the file girl1.mov.**

4. **Pressing the Shift key, click to highlight the file jars1.mov.**

5. **Click Open.**

   These two clip files (assets) now appear in the Project window (see Figure 10-5).

Laying clips on the Timeline

Now is a good time to briefly introduce, and in some cases reintroduce, you to the windows on the Premiere screen. You can follow along by referring to Figures 10-3 and 10-4, if you like. At the top is the Monitor window. Farther down and to the left of the Project window is the Timeline window. As is true of most good nonlinear editing programs, Premiere often offers you more than one way to do your work. Advanced editors often work almost exclusively in the Monitor window. Novices and intermediates usually feel more

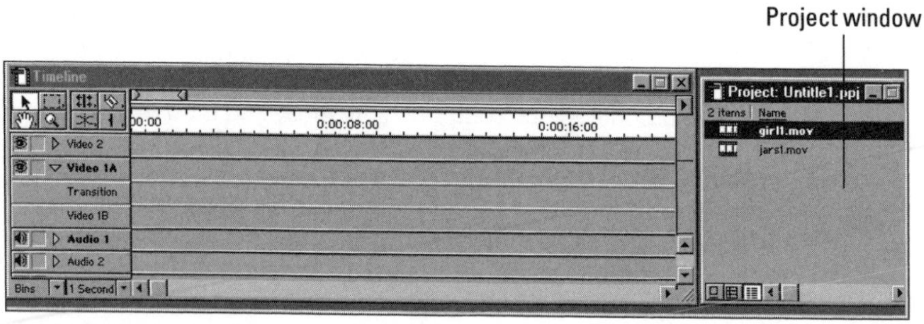

Project window

Figure 10-5:
The Project window lets you import, organize, and store references to clips.

comfortable moving back and forth between the Timeline Window and the Monitor window, which is what I have you do here.

1. **Go to the Project window and highlight the girl1.mov and jars1.mov files.**

   To highlight both files, click the first file and press Shift plus the down arrow key.

2. **Place your cursor over the highlighted files. (The arrow cursor becomes a hand.) Click and drag the two files into the Timeline window and lay them in the Video 1A row. Release the mouse.**

   The two clips appear in the Timeline, and the opening frame of the first clip appears on the right side of the Monitor window (in the Program monitor).

   Way to go. Your screen should look something like the one in Figure 10-6.

The monitor that is showing in the first frame of the clip (the small monitor on the right in the Monitor window) is the Program monitor. The blank monitor (on the left in the Monitor window) is the Source monitor. You use the Source monitor a little later on. (You use the Program monitor to review and modify an assembled project. You use the Source monitor to review and modify a single clip.)

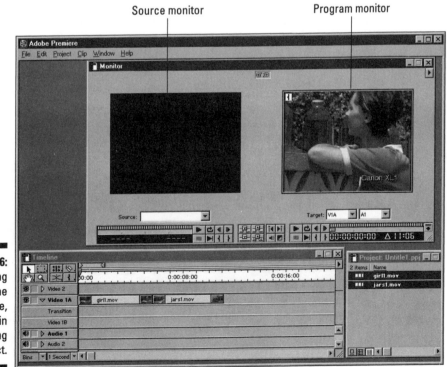

Figure 10-6: By placing clips on the Timeline, you begin assembling a project.

Now try playing the two clips, as follows:

1. **Click anywhere in the Timeline window to highlight it.**

2. **Press the spacebar.**

    The clips on the Timeline begin to play in the Program monitor.

You toggle between stop and restart in the project by pressing your spacebar. If you want to go back to the opening frame, simply press the letter "a" on your keyboard. You're starting to become an editor!

Editing a clip from the Timeline

Your little two-clip project is, so far, unedited. Your job now is to create a simple little segment where the young lady looks down the row of jars, and, in doing so, you'll edit to show all the jars.

The challenge of this little editing excursion is that the woman doesn't appear in the wide shot. Man. Where was the logging sheet? Where was the production assistant? Where was the continuity? (See Chapters 6 and 7 for more on logging sheets, assistants, and so on.) No wonder editors don't smile very much. Well, they may not smile, but they're magicians. Let me show you what I mean. But first, back up a little in your editing process.

1. **Click the jars1.mov clip in the Timeline window to highlight it.**

2. **Press the Delete key.**

    The jars1.mov clip is no longer in the Timeline window, but it's still in the Project window.

When assets are imported into Premiere, nothing is actually done to the source assets. By this, I mean that you can make a zillion changes to a clip in Premiere, but you're not modifying the actual clip. Premiere is a kind of grand database program that stores all kinds of information about how to use an asset without affecting the asset itself.

Now you're going to work with the girl1.mov clip in the Source monitor (the monitor at the left in the main Monitor window).

1. **Double-click the girl1.mov clip in the Timeline window.**

    The clip now appears in the Source monitor (see Figure 10-7). In case you're wondering, "girl1.mov 0:00:00:00," which you see in the Source clip information box, identifies the clip and its place on the Timeline. The zeroes are saying that the clip is resting at the beginning of the hour, at the beginning of the first minute, at the beginning of the first second, at the beginning of the first frame of the project.

In point

Out point

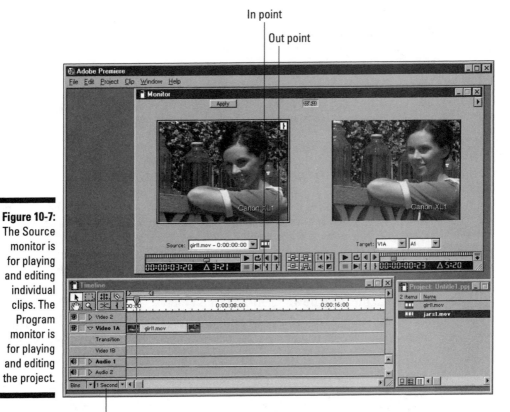

Figure 10-7:
The Source
monitor is
for playing
and editing
individual
clips. The
Program
monitor is
for playing
and editing
the project.

Time unit

2. **Click in the Source monitor to activate it.**

3. **Type a to set the clip at the opening frame.**

   The time code at the bottom of the monitor should now read 00:00:00:00 (see Chapter 6 for more about time code). Following the time code is a triangle followed by the number 5:20, which indicates that the next edit will be at 5 seconds 20 frames.

4. **Click and drag the slider just above the time code until the time code reading is 00:00:03:20.**

5. **Click the out point button at the bottom of the Source monitor (refer to Figure 10-7).**

   This will be the new out point for the clip. An *out point* represents the last frame of an edited clip.

6. **Click Apply at the top of the Source monitor.**

   The clip is now 3 seconds 20 frames long. Note that changing the out point of the clip in the Source monitor also changes the out point in the Timeline window.

You've trimmed one of the clips. Play it, if you want, by clicking anywhere in the Timeline window to highlight the window and pressing the spacebar. The clip is a little long yet, but you're going to use it for something in a moment.

Adjusting units of time

The next thing you need to do requires a little more accuracy in time than the Timeline currently allows. So you must change the scale of time measurement to 8 frames from the current 1 second.

1. **Click the Time Unit menu in the lower-left corner of the Timeline window (see Figure 10-8).**

2. **From the drop-down menu, select 8 Frames.**

   The Timeline changes to an 8-frame unit measurement. Note that changing the Timeline window scale of time doesn't change the length of clips on the Timeline.

Editing clips from the Project window

Next you trim the jars1.mov clip, but you do it a little differently this time. You trim it before you place it on the Timeline.

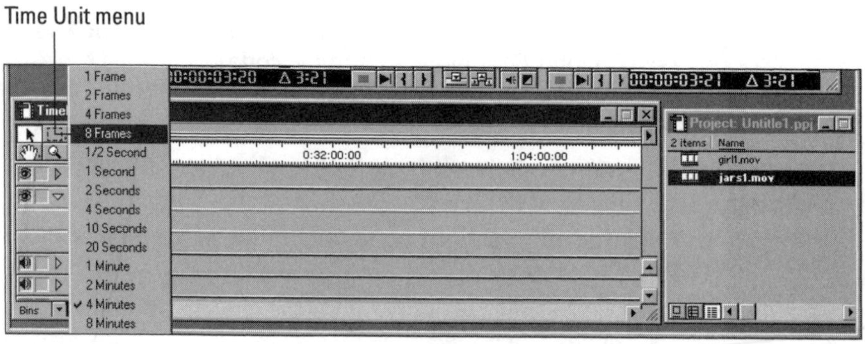

Time Unit menu

Figure 10-8:
The Time Unit menu allows you to zoom in and out in the Timeline window.

1. **Click the jars1.mov clip, hold down the mouse button, and drag the clip to the Source monitor.**

   The jars1.mov clip replaces the girl1.mov clip.

2. **Click and drag the slider just above the time code until the time code reading is 00:00:03:08.**

3. **Click the in point button at the bottom of the Source monitor.**

   You just edited a clip before it is dragged into the Timeline window (see Figure 10-9). As you can see, an in point appears in the upper-left corner of the Source monitor. An *in point* represents the first frame of an edited clip.

In point

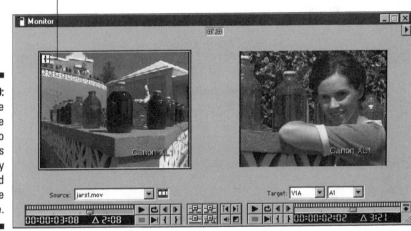

Figure 10-9:
Use the
Source
monitor to
edit clips
before they
are placed
on the
Timeline.

Creating and previewing transitions

Now you edit the change from one clip to another. Rather than butting the clips together, though, you make what's called a transition. By *transition,* I mean change over time from one clip to the other. Here's where Premiere really starts being fun.

1. **Drag the jars1.mov clip from the Project window into the Timeline window.**

2. **Lay the clip in the Video 1B row and overlap the girl1.mov by about a second (see Figure 10-10).**

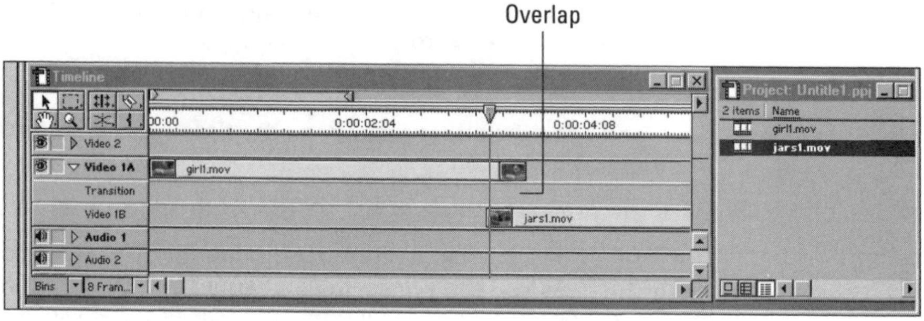

Overlap

Figure 10-10:
The time of
overlap
between
clips is the
time in
which the
transition
takes place.

Now you can add a transition. First, you'll need to show the Transitions window.

3. From the Premiere main menu, select Window⇨Show Transitions.

The Transitions window appears. Adobe packages Premiere with oodles and scads of transition effects.

4. Scroll down the Transitions window until you come to Cross Dissolve.

5. Click, hold down the mouse button, and drag the Cross Dissolve transition to the Transition row in the Timeline window.

6. Position the transition so that it fills the overlap between Video 1A and Video 1B, and release the mouse.

You just set a transition (see Figure 10-11). The transition acts as a visually pleasing way to change from one clip to the next.

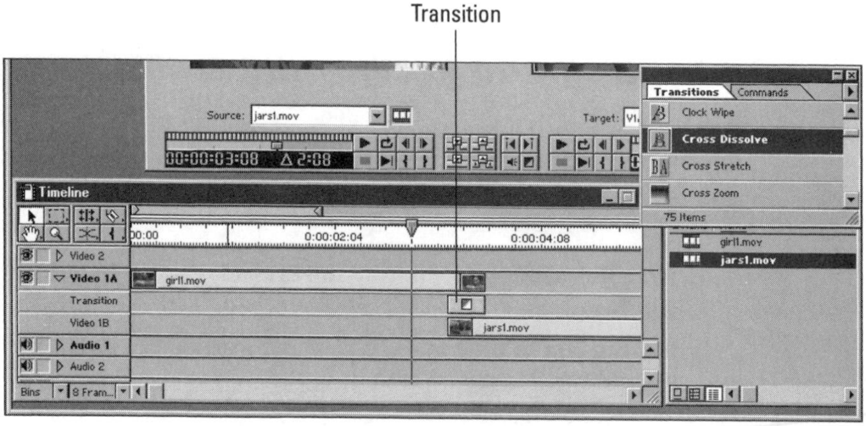

Transition

Figure 10-11:
The
transition
automatically fills the
space of the
overlap
between the
two clips.

Now you're ready to see the fruits of your work. You're going to preview a work area of the project. To set the work area for the preview, you adjust the work area slider (see Figure 10-12).

1. **Using the Time Unit menu, change the time units from 8 frames to one-half second.**

2. **Click and drag the blue work area slider over the area of the transition.**

3. **Drag the left and right edges of the work area until it covers all of the clips.**

4. **Press the Enter key.**

   Premiere builds the preview and then runs it in your Program monitor (see Figure 10-12).

Work area slider

Figure 10-12:
The work area slider sets the limits for what you build in your preview.

Congratulations! You've created a segment of two edited clips with a transition. If you like, delete the transition and replace it with others just to see the various effects available to you. Oh yeah. When you're done with this chapter, feel free to delete the sample files from your hard drive. But keep the Adobe Premiere 5.0 Tryout version installed if you intend to read later chapters of this book.

Chapter 11

Making Sound Decisions with Adobe Premiere

I'm surely not telling you anything you don't already know when I say that audio can completely change the energy and the message of video. Well-produced audio is the least expensive and most versatile tool of video.

Actually, in video production, you have two major categories of audio: audio that is recorded at the time of video recording and audio that is added later. This chapter focuses on the latter — adding audio to video. One of the most powerful tools for editing audio in video is the very same one used for editing visual images — Adobe Premiere.

Like Chapter 10, this chapter is about nonlinear editing. You can consider this chapter a "partner chapter" to its neighbor one number up the street. So you'll probably find this chapter a lot more enjoyable if you already have a little experience with Adobe Premiere as provided throughout Chapter 10.

In this chapter, you take pieces of video and graphics and turn them into a connected whole — largely because of your use of sound. You do a couple of intricate procedures with a song in your heart and on the computer's speakers. Oh, that reminds me. For this chapter, I'm assuming you have a sound card in your computer.

TECHNICAL STUFF

Introducing . . . special files

Adobe Premiere recognizes a large number of file types created by other programs. Premiere can open and use most types of graphics files, sound files, and video files.

In this chapter, you find files using the .bmp, .mov, and .wav extensions.

A .bmp file is a graphics file created in Adobe Photoshop. These files have a 256-color palette.

A .mov file is a video file either captured via a video capture card (see Chapter 9) or created in a nonlinear editing program such as Adobe Premiere. Files with the extension .mov can be video only or both video and audio files. The .mov file extension is recognized by the QuickTime video player.

A .wav file is an audio file created in an audio recording software program. You see how Adobe Premiere can use .wav files for creating background music and "voice-over" narration.

Getting Ready for Audio Nonlinear Editing

ON THE CD

You're about to perform some amazing audio feats that turn ho-hum video into something special. For starters, you need to install Adobe Premiere 5.0 from the CD-ROM at the back of this book. You also need to download the Chapter 11 sample files. These sample files are stored on the CD-ROM in a subfolder named CHAP11, which is located in a folder named CLIPS.

Turn to Appendix B for steps on doing both tasks. To view the movie files in this chapter, you may need to install QuickTime version 4.0 or later, as described in Chapter 10.

When you complete this chapter, you can delete these sample files from your hard drive to save space.

You're now ready to begin working with audio files in Adobe Premiere. To start Premiere:

1. **Go to your desktop, click Start, and select** **P**rograms⇨Adobe⇨ **Adobe 5.0 Tryout⇨Adobe Premiere 5.0 Tryout.**

   The New Project Settings dialog box appears.

   Your Timebase should still be 30. In your video settings, your Frame Size should still be 240 x 180, and your Frame Rate should still be 15. If they're not for some reason, go to the section "Introducing Adobe Premiere," in Chapter 10 and follow the instructions.

2. Click OK.

You are at the main interface for Adobe Premiere.

The last thing you need to do to get ready for audio editing is to bring in the Chapter 11 sample files. In the following examples, you play with an interesting mixture of video and graphics in conjunction with your audio files. This stuff is interesting.

1. **Select File⇨Import⇨File or press Ctrl+I (where ≈stands for Import).**

   The Import dialog box appears. The unique attribute of the Adobe Import dialog box is that whatever you select goes straight into the Adobe Premiere Project window. Watch what happens.

2. **Find and open the Clips folder on your hard drive and then open the Chapter 11 folder that you copied from the CD-ROM.**

3. **Pressing the Shift key, select the files jetski3.mov, natural1.wav, shore.mov, shorestill.bmp, and versatile.wav; then click Open.**

   The files now appear in the Project window.

Putting down the music

A lot of editors like to lay a background music track down in the Timeline window (see Chapter 10 for more on the Timeline window) before doing anything else. You're going to do that, too. But before you lay anything down, you need to vertically enlarge the Timeline window a little because the audio tracks are at the bottom of the Timeline window, and you are about to expand those tracks.

To vertically enlarge the Timeline window, follow these steps:

1. **Click anywhere in the Timeline window to highlight it.**

2. **Drag the Timeline window up a little and then click the bottom border of the Timeline window and drag it down a little.**

   Continue dragging the Timeline window down until the bottom of the window touches the bottom of the screen.

With the Timeline window in place, you're ready to lay down a music track. Laying down a music track is a one-step process. Just click and drag the natural1.wav clip from the Project window to the Audio 2 row in the Timeline window. The Timeline window should now look like Figure 11-1. If you'd like to hear the music, highlight the Timeline window and press the spacebar. Audio files play just like video files.

Figure 11-1:
A .wav file is an audio-only file. This file is different from a .mov or an .ai file, which can be a combination of video and audio.

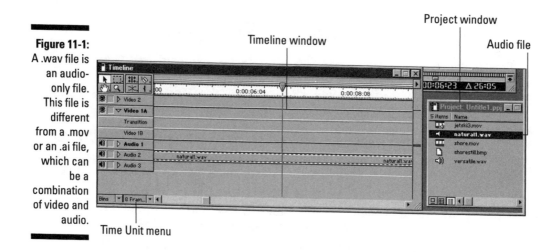

Project window

Timeline window

Audio file

Time Unit menu

Adding video to sound

Adobe Premiere enables you to combine up to 99 audio and video tracks.

Because of this, you can do some fascinating compositing of clips and audio files. You'll do some of that right now.

In Premiere, click and drag shore.mov from the Project window to the Video 1A row in the Timeline window. You've now added a video segment to an audio background. If you'd like, highlight the Timeline window and press the spacebar to see how the video looks with the audio.

Now you add a video file that has its own audio to the Timeline. To make this process easier, first change the scale of time to one second using the Time Unit menu. To access the Time Unit menu, do the following:

1. **Click the Time Unit menu in the lower-left corner of the screen (refer to Figure 11-1).**

   The time units are currently set at 8 frames (as set in Chapter 10).

2. **From the times in the drop-down box, select 1 Second.**

Now it's time to add video to the Timeline.

1. **Click and drag the jetski3.mov clip from the Project window to the Video 1A row in the Timeline window.**

   Notice that the jetski3 video clip brought the audio with it and laid it on the Audio 1 track. When a video clip has audio, the clip appears both on a video track and on an audio track, both showing the name of the clip (see Figure 11-2).

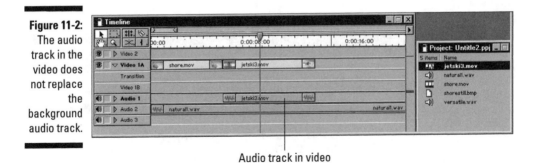

Figure 11-2:
The audio
track in the
video does
not replace
the
background
audio track.

Audio track in video

2. **Click the Timeline window to highlight it and then press the spacebar.**

   As you can hear, the audio from the video clip lays over the audio from the music track and creates a general mess. You'll fix that in a little while. But first you do a couple more things.

Adding narration to video

One of the most common editing tasks you'll perform is mixing narration with video. Adding voice over video is a powerful way to focus a message and clarify the importance of your video presentation. It may be as simple and poignant as the voice of a family patriarch or matriarch over photos from the past or it may be as cutting and high-tech as an announcer's voice in a 30-second action-packed commercial. Whatever the challenge, nonlinear editing (NLE) is one of the best ways to get the job done.

To add a narration to this little project, do the following:

1. **Click and drag the versatile.wav clip from the Project window onto the Audio 3 track of the Timeline window.**

2. **Click the far-right, right-pointing arrow just below the Timeline window title bar.**

   A Timeline window menu appears.

3. **Click the checked Snap to Edges option (see Figure 11-3).**

   This deactivates the Snap to Edges option in the Timeline. You use the Snap to Edges option to line up edges of adjacent clips and to properly set transitions. Premiere has the Snap to Edges option turned on by default. (Transitions are described in Chapter 10.)

   You can now easily drag clips anywhere on a track without the clips trying to attach to the beginning or endings of nearby clips (a feature you normally want to leave on).

Snap to Edges option

4. **Drag the versatile.wav clip slightly to the right on the timeline, leaving about a second between its in point and the jetski3.mov clip out point.**

   (An *in point* represents the first frame of an edited clip, and — guess what? — an *out point* represents the last frame of an edited clip. Turn to Chapter 10 for more on in points and out points.)

   Now you can easily drag the clip.

5. **Click the Timeline window options button in the upper-right corner of the Timeline window again and turn the Snap to Edges option back on by clicking it.**

You've placed almost all the raw materials on the Timeline window. The thing missing is video after the jetski3.mov clip. Shortage of video to match the length of a sound clip is a common problem in video postproduction (editing phase), which I cover in some detail in Chapters 12 and 13. For the time being, let me show you a common solution — stretching video to cover audio.

Stretching video for audio

Because one of the most common editing functions is adding voice to video, it only follows that one of the other most common functions of editing is finding video to cover audio. Sometimes you simply have more to say than to see — you see what I'm saying? Ahem. Anyway, editors are always scratching their haven't-seen-the-sun-in-weeks foreheads to find something to put over audio. One of the ways to do so is to steal a frame from video and streeeeeeeeetch it. You do that in this project.

If you haven't already done so, highlight the Timeline window, press the spacebar, and listen to the versatile.wav clip. You need something appropriate to cover this narration and background music. Hmmm. Take a look at your Timeline. Not a lot to choose from. Welcome to the real world of NLE! Probably the best you can do with what you've got is to take the final frame of shore.mov and stretch it over the audio at the end. Here's how you do that:

1. **Click and drag the shore.mov clip from the Project window into the Source monitor.**

   The blank monitor (on the left in the large Monitor window) is the Source monitor (see Chapter 10 for more on the Source monitor).

2. **Click the Source monitor to highlight it and press the spacebar. Play the clip to its end.**

3. **Select File⇨Export⇨Frame (or press Ctrl+Shift+M).**

Premiere will kick sand in your face and scoff at you and accuse you of trying to save a file in this tryout version. Don't be disturbed. You've got the last laugh. I've saved this frame for you for later use. Ha! I just wanted to take you to this step to show you how you can easily create a still frame from a clip. You'll do this many, many times. So, after you've gotten the sand out of your hair, move on, pretending as though you've just saved a still frame. By the way, you called it shorestill.bmp. Pretty name. You've got a knack.

Normally, you import the file once you save it. Because I saved it for you, you imported the file at the beginning of this chapter. Now you can use the file by doing the following:

1. **Click and drag the shorestill.bmp graphic from the Project window onto the Video 1B track in the Timeline window.**

2. **Drag the shorestill.bmp graphic so that its out point lines up with the out point of the jetski3.mov file.**

   This creates an overlap for a transition. The duration of a still graphic is, by default, 30 frames (1 second). So the shorestill.bmp in point overlaps the end of jetski3.mov by 30 frames.

   Now that you've placed the still frame at its in point, you need to change its duration. *Duration* means the length of the clip in minutes, seconds, and frames.

3. **Position your mouse over the out point of the shorestill.bmp graphic.**

   The cursor changes from an up-and-left-pointed arrow to two vertical lines with arrows pointing in each direction.

4. **Click and drag the out point of the clip to the right until it matches the out point of the natural1.wav graphic.**

Way to go! You've just covered audio by stretching video. Take a look at Figure 11-4 to see how the timeline should look. Why don't you type the letter **a** to start from the beginning and play through to the end. Not bad.

As I said, you're going to put a simple transition in this project. To do so, you first must show the Transitions window, if it's hidden.

1. **Select Window⇨Show Transitions in the main menu.**

   The Transitions window appears.

2. **Click and drag any of the transitions (I chose Band Slide) from the Transitions window to the Transition track in the Timeline window.**

3. **Using the Snap to Edges option, position the transition in the overlap between the jetski3.mov clip and the shorestill.bmp graphic.**

4. **Drag the work area slider over the transition (see Figure 11-5).**

   The location of the work area slider tells Premiere what you want to see rendered. Your screen should look like the one in Figure 11-5.

5. **Press Enter.**

   Premiere makes a preview movie of your work area and plays your transition in the Program monitor.

Now you're ready to set the audio levels and create fades. (*Fades* are a type of audio edit that cause an audio track to increase or decrease in volume over time.) Speaking of time, now is a good time to close (hide) the Transitions window again.

You may notice a black box in the previewed area. Just disregard this box. Premiere is simply reminding you that this is a trial version of the software program.

Transition track

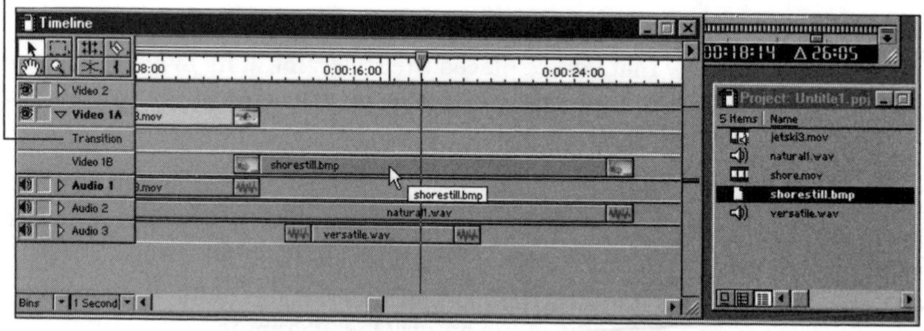

Figure 11-4:
Premiere makes the default duration of a still image one second (30 frames).

Preview in Program monitor

Figure 11-5:
A Preview is
made only
for the area
you have
chosen with
the work
area slider.

Work area slider

Fading and Cross-Fading

If you haven't yet done so, play the entire Timeline a couple of times in order to hear the current status of the audio. You have some work to do. You need to do the following:

- ✔ Fade out the background music during the jet ski sequence.
- ✔ Work a little on the mix of the narration and the background music.
- ✔ Get rid of a couple of audio glitches.

Now jump right into it. You begin by expanding the audio tracks. Look at the far-left side of the Timeline window. You see right-pointing arrows next to Audio 1, Audio 2, and Audio 3. Click each of the arrows. They now point down as the tracks are expanded (see Figure 11-6). If you need to, vertically stretch the Timeline window to fully show all the audio tracks. Now you can see each of the tracks in all of their glory, as shown in Figure 11-6. Note that the fully expanded audio tracks reveal waveforms of the sound.

Expanded arrow

Closed arrow

Figure 11-6:
To conserve
room on the
screen,
Adobe
Premiere
keeps
tracks
closed until
you need
them.

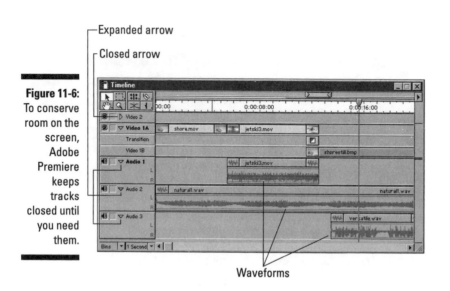

Waveforms

With the tracks fully expanded, start your audio work by fading out the
background music during the jet ski sequence. To make your work easier,
why don't you change the Timeline frame units to one-half second? Scroll
the Timeline until all the jet ski sequence is visible.

1. **Place your cursor over the red line on the Audio 2 track below the
   in point of the jetski3.mov clip and click once.**

   A red handle appears on the volume fader bar (see Figure 11-7).

   By the way, the red line is called a *rubber band*. In reality, this rubber
   band is a volume fader bar. Moving the bar up or down increases or
   decreases volume. You use a red handle to increase or decrease volume.
   If you want to move only a portion of the rubber band, add another red
   handle.

2. **Slightly to the left of red handle, click one more time.**

   You now have two red handles.

3. **Repeat the process below the out point (end) of the jetski3.mov clip.**

   You should now have four red handles on the rubber band.

4. **Drag the inside handles to the bottom of the Audio 2 track.**

   You just faded out the background music during the jet ski sequence.
   The rubber band indicates the level of audio (see Figure 11-7).

Figure 11-7:
The shape
of the
rubber band
is a visual
representation
of volume at
any given
time on
the audio
track's
Timeline.

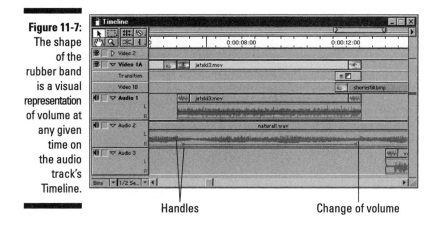

Handles   Change of volume

Press the spacebar to listen to the changed levels. Now, on your own, do
the same thing to lower the music background level during the narration.
You don't have to take the music all the way out this time, just lower it.

Last, fix those annoying little clicks at the end of the narration and at the end
of the music background. Do this by positioning your cursor over the end of
each segment and dragging them ever so slightly to the left to shorten the
segment. These steps will remove the clicks.

You performed masterfully. You can edit audio!

Chapter 12

Adding Illustrations to Your Video with Adobe Illustrator

In This Chapter

▶ Getting around in Illustrator

▶ Using illustrations in Premiere

▶ Adding motion to illustrations

*O*ne of the greatest advantages of a nonlinear editing system (NLE) is the ability it gives you to embellish your video with beautiful drawings, photos, and animation — all with incredible ease.

In this chapter, you find out how to use Adobe Illustrator to create great illustrations for use in Adobe Premiere. In Illustrator, I show you how you can easily draw fancy shapes and great looking text. Then you take these shapes and text into Premiere and make them come alive.

You'll need to have Premiere installed on your computer to do many of the things described in this chapter. For information on installing the Premiere 5.0 Tryout version that is on the CD that comes with this book, turn to Appendix B. Also, if you've skipped some chapters while reading this book, you may not have read Chapter 10. If so, you may want to turn back to that chapter before continuing, because Chapter 10 shows you how to use Premiere.

To view the movie files in this chapter, you may need to install QuickTime version 4.0 or later as described in Chapter 10.

Getting Ready to Illustrate

If you're familiar with Premiere (see Chapter 10), you're probably ready to create some special effects with illustrations created in Adobe Illustrator.

We're getting into some exciting stuff here, so I'd suggest cutting back on sugar and caffeine for a little while — you want to be able to sleep tonight.

First, you need to install the tryout version of Adobe Illustrator that's on the CD at the back of this book. You also need to download the Chapter 12 sample files from the CD. These sample files are stored on the CD in a sub-folder named CHAP12, which is located in a folder named CLIPS. For steps on doing both, turn to Appendix B.

When you complete this chapter, you can delete these sample files from your hard drive to save space.

Opening and previewing Illustrator "at work"

With Illustrator installed on your computer, you open the program by clicking the Start button on the Windows desktop. Then select Programs⇨Adobe⇨ Adobe Illustrator 8.0⇨Adobe Illustrator 8.0 Tryout. The program opens.

You're ready to make art. But before you put on your tam and position your canvas (monitor) for north light, I want to walk you through a finished version of what you're about to make.

1. **Open the Premiere 5.0 Tryout program by going to your Windows desktop, clicking Start, and selecting Programs⇨Adobe⇨Adobe 5.0 Tryout⇨Adobe Premiere 5.0 Tryout.**

2. **Select File⇨Open from the main menu or press Ctrl+O.**

   The Open dialog box appears. Find the Clips folder and then, within this folder, locate the Chapter 12 folder.

3. **Select the illusend.mov clip and click the Open button.**

   Premiere loads the clip into the Source monitor, which located in the Premiere Monitor window.

   In Premiere, the monitor on the left is the Source monitor. See Chapter 10 for more information about the Source monitor. But, in a nutshell, you use the Source monitor to review and modify a single clip.

   (This step is different from the one you perform in Chapters 10 and 11. In those chapters, you import files, rather than open them. When you import files, Premiere places the files in the Project window.)

4. **Click the Source monitor and press the spacebar on you keyboard.**

The Source monitor plays a short clip that includes a seashore graphic plus foreground art created in Illustrator. In this chapter, I show you how to do the same thing. By creating this simple sequence, you learn a lot about Illustrator and how it works with Premiere. If you want, you can close Premiere for now. You'll be coming back to it later in the chapter.

Introducing Adobe Illustrator

People sometimes wonder about the difference between Adobe Illustrator and Adobe Photoshop. Adobe Illustrator is a draw program. Adobe Photoshop is a paint program. Adobe Illustrator is a *vector-based program*. Adobe Photoshop is *raster-based*. For more on vector and raster programs, see the following sidebar "Computer graphics come in two flavors." With Adobe Illustrator, you can easily add and modify draw lines, curves, and shapes, including text. With Adobe Photoshop, you can easily change existing images or paint new ones.

As you look at the Illustrator screen, you see a group of boxes, each with a specific purpose.

Illustrator's whole work area is 227 inches by 227 inches. By default, the page layout is 8½ inches by 11 inches, much like a sheet of paper. You can draw anywhere within the 227-inch by 227-inch work area.

To help you fit your work to a *workable* size, though, Illustrator provides the page, or work area, as three rectangles (as shown in Figure 12-1). The area

Computer graphics come in two flavors

Computer graphics fall into two main categories: vector graphics and raster images.

Adobe Illustrator makes vector graphics, made of lines and curves defined by mathematical objects called *vectors*. Vectors describe graphics according to their geometric characteristics. You can move, resize, or change the color of the vector graphic without reducing its quality. Vector graphics are commonly used for drawing shapes and for laying text into images.

Adobe Photoshop generates raster images. Raster images use a grid (also known as a bitmap or *raster*) of small squares (pixels). Each pixel in a raster image has a unique location and color value assigned to it. When working with bitmap images, you edit pixels rather than objects or shapes. Raster images are the most common computer-based medium for photos or images made in paint programs.

within the inner rectangle is the "imageable area," which is the area that a printer can safely print. Outside the inner rectangle is the "nonimageable area." This is the nonprintable margin of a page.

The second rectangle represents the edge of a page. Outside the second rectangle is scratch area — where you can make things without messing up the art in the imageable area.

This is all important information, but it doesn't have a direct relationship to the project at hand — creating an illustration for video. For one thing, you aren't creating something for printing. And a piece of paper is taller than it is wide. A video screen is wider than it is tall.

On the far left, is the toolbox. The toolbox provides tools (buttons) that you can click to choose certain functions quickly and easily, such as functions for drawing lines, creating boxes, rotating objects, and so on. You use the toolbox in just a moment.

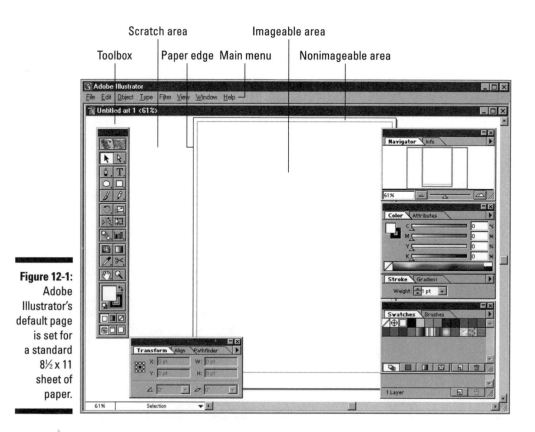

Figure 12-1:
Adobe
Illustrator's
default page
is set for
a standard
8½ x 11
sheet of
paper.

The palette at the lower-left has three tabs — Transform, Align, and Pathfinder. You use these functions to make detailed changes to objects you create. You don't use this palette in this chapter, so I suggest you hide it by clicking the X in its upper-right corner.

The palette at the upper-right is the Navigator\Info palette. You use this palette to move around in large objects when you are zoomed in close. And you use the palette to determine your exact location on the screen. Again, you don't need this palette in this chapter. So go ahead and hide the Navigator\Info palette by clicking the X in its upper-right corner.

You use the Color\Attributes palette to select colors of lines, curves, and shapes and to set their sizes. You use this palette in this chapter, so leave it showing.

The Stroke\Gradient palette is for, respectively, adjusting the width of a line and filling an object with a blend of colors.

The Swatches\Brushes palette is for selecting special color effects and for setting brush characteristics for drawing. You don't need this palette right now. So hide the Swatches\Brushes palette by clicking the X in its upper-right corner.

Click on the lower area of the bottom palette, and you discover that you have clicked on a partially hidden palette. This is the Layers\Actions\Links palette. You use the Layers tab of the Layers\Actions\Links palette in this chapter. You use the Layers tab to make and manage multiple, independent layers of your illustration. Leave it open.

Setting Illustrator to Draw for Video

As I mentioned earlier, the default Illustrator work area is for a document size of 8½ inches by 11 inches — the size of a standard piece of paper. This default dimension is vertical — the opposite of what you need for video. Video is wider than it is tall. The relationship of width to height is called *aspect ratio*. Video has an aspect ratio of 4 to 3 (denoted 4:3), meaning that for every four units horizontal, there are three units vertical. You want to change the aspect ratio of the work area box in order to work with video. See the following sidebar, "Aspect ratio," for more details.

So, the first thing you do is change your work area's document size.

Aspect ratio

Aspect ratio is the ratio of an image's width to its height. For example, a conventional video display has an aspect ratio of 4:3 (4 picture elements in width for every 3 picture elements in height). An HDTV (High Definition Television) video display has an aspect ratio of 16:9.

Typically, video aspect ratio is measured in pixels (picture elements). Examples of 4:3 aspect ratios in pixels include 240 x 180, 320 x 240, 640 x 480, and 800 x 600.

Changing document size

Adobe Illustrator is a powerful draw program of unlimited potential. I'm showing only how you may want to use Illustrator for video. You need to make a couple of changes to the Illustrator document setup utility to coordinate Illustrator to Adobe Premiere's display environment — the environment of video. You need to change the size and orientation of the document within the work area.

1. **Select File⇨Document Setup (in the main menu at the top of the screen) or press Ctrl+Alt+P.**

   The Document Setup dialog box appears, as shown in Figure 12-2.

2. **In the Artboard section, change Width to 240 and Height to 180.**

   As I mention in the Aspect Ratio sidebar, 240 x 180 is a 4:3 aspect ratio. The Artboard units are points rather than pixels. That doesn't matter to Adobe Premiere as long as the aspect ratio is correct.

   You don't need to change anything else in the Document Setup dialog box.

3. **Click OK to close the Document Setup dialog box and to modify the document size and orientation.**

   The document size changes to a small, horizontal (landscaped) box.

The changed document size may seem very small on your screen. For example, my computer monitor is set at 800 x 600 resolution. A 240 x 180 image looks quite small on the screen. In Illustrator, image size is relative. You can easily increase the document size on your screen.

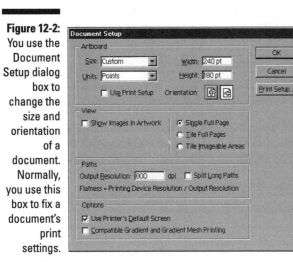

Figure 12-2:
You use the
Document
Setup dialog
box to
change the
size and
orientation
of a
document.
Normally,
you use this
box to fix a
document's
print
settings.

At the top of the Illustrator window and in the lower-left corner of the status bar (at the bottom of the window — refer to Figure 12-1), notice that the document view is a number with a percent sign. Mine is 61%. This is a good time for you to adjust the size of the document on your screen. You can choose from among four ways to zoom the document to full-screen. Three of the ways are using the Zoom feature in View on your menu bar, using the Zoom tool (magnifying glass) in the toolbox, and changing the zoom percentage in the status bar. But here is the fourth, and easiest, way:

1. **Press Ctrl+0 to zoom the document to full-screen size.**

    The document is now zoomed to 270%. Can't get simpler than that!

Creating a document background

To maintain your illustration aspect ratio in Premiere, you first have to create a document background equaling the document size. You do that by making a simple box.

1. **In the toolbox (refer to Figure 12-1), select the Rectangle tool (right column, third row).**

    The cursor changes to a cross-hair shape.

2. **Beginning in the upper-left corner of the document's outer edge, click and drag to the lower-right corner of the document's outer edge.**

You can move the Layers\Actions\Links palette out of the way, but it isn't necessary to do so. You've now created a box.

3. **To more easily see your box, click any color in the rainbow of colors in the Color\Attributes palette.**

    If you choose green as I did, your document will look like the one in Figure 12-3.

4. **Change the color back to white by going to the Color\Attributes palette and clicking the little white box at the far-right of the rainbow of colors.**

5. **Change the box edge color to white by going to the toolbox and clicking the Stroke tool (refer to Figure 12-3) and then clicking the white box at the far-right of the rainbow of colors.**

    Your box is now outlined and filled with the color white.

Stroke tool palette

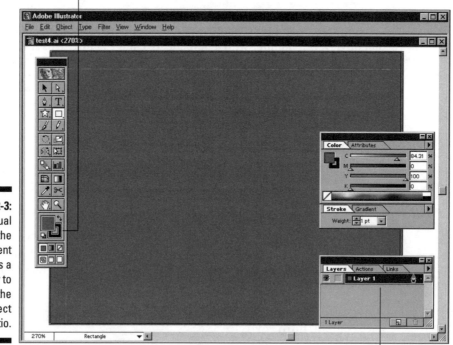

Figure 12-3:
A box equal in size to the document provides a way to maintain the 4:3 aspect ratio.

Layers palette

Making Illustrations for Use in Premiere

As I mentioned earlier, Adobe Premiere is a powerful nonlinear editing program. Part of Premiere's power is its capability of using images created in other programs. Adobe Illustrator is such a program. In this section, you use Illustrator to draw an object and type some text for use in Premiere. In making these two objects, you get a good introductory feel for the potential of this draw program.

In drawing an object, you get to use some of the great features of the Illustrator toolbox, and you fill the object with gradient colors. Working with text, you get a chance to select fonts and set attributes.

But whether drawing an object or creating text, you first need to understand Adobe Illustrator's Layers feature (called a *palette*). With layers, you can independently work on one object or text without affecting others.

Working in layers

The Layers palette enables you to work independently on an infinite number of objects without any of them affecting each other. You are now going to create layers on top of the colored box you drew in the previous section. So far, things don't look all that impressive. But that will quickly change.

Now you will draw a sun for your Premiere shoreline image. To do so, you start using layers. First, you need to lock the layer (that is, prevent any modification of objects on that layer) you created in the previous section.

Locking a layer

Looking at the Layers palette (refer to Figure 12-3), you see that the palette has only one layer in it. You'll change that in moment.

You lock the layer by clicking in the layer's second box from the left. A pencil with a red line drawn through it appears in the box. If you move your cursor over the work area, you notice that it's now a pencil with a line drawn through it. This means that you will be unable to do anything else in this layer or to this layer.

Naming a layer

For sanity's sake, you may want to name layers as you create them (other than their generic name, such as Layer 1), especially if you have a number of layers.

1. **Double click Layer 1 in the Layers palette (refer to Figure 12-3).**

2. **In the Name text box, type** White background.

3. **Click OK.**

   The layer should now read "White background."

Making new layers

Now you're ready to make a new layer that you name "sun."

1. **Click the right-pointing arrow at the far-right of the tabs in the Layers\Actions\Links palette (refer to Figure 12-3).**

   A selection box appears.

2. **Click New Layer.**

   The Layer Options dialog box appears.

3. **In the Name text box, type** Sun.

4. **Click OK.**

   The Layers\Actions\Links palette should now look like the one in Figure 12-4.

Figure 12-4:
In Adobe
Illustrator,
objects can
remain inde-
pendent of
one another
on separate
layers.

Making an object

Now the fun begins. You're ready to create an object — the sun. Begin by restoring the Stroke color to black. Stroke is the width attribute of a linear object, such as the outer edge of a box. Stroke color is the color of the linear object.

Click the black box at the right of the rainbow of colors in the Color\Attributes palette. The stroke color is now black.

Now you're going to create an eight-pointed star with curved rays. You start by selecting the proper tool: the Star tool.

1. **Click and hold your mouse on the Circle tool in toolbox (third row, left column).**

   The Circle tool expands to show four tools (see Figure 12-5).

   Thought you might like to know that any tool with a little right-pointing arrow in its lower-right corner has other tools behind it.

2. **Click the Star tool to replace the circle as the drawing tool in this box of the toolbox.**

With the Star tool selected, you are able to create the object.

1. **Click and drag the Star tool until you have a star about one-third the size of the document. Twirl the star any direction you like by dragging the mouse. Release the mouse.**

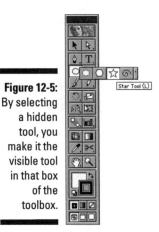

Figure 12-5:
By selecting a hidden tool, you make it the visible tool in that box of the toolbox.

Don't worry about getting the size or location exactly correct. You do that in a moment. If necessary, you can drag the Color\Attributes palette out of your way.

2. **Click anywhere in the star or on its edge.**

   The Star Options box appears.

3. **In the Points text box, change 5 to 8.**

4. **Click OK.**

   A new eight-pointed star appears.

5. **Click the Selection tool (the arrow in the upper-left corner of the toolbox).**

A border appears around the star. This border is called a *bounding box*. The bounding box creates a temporary border around a selected object. The bounding box defines the outer limits of an object.

6. **Click anywhere on the outer edge of the star and drag the star to the upper-right corner of the document area.**

   If necessary, resize the star by pressing Shift on your keyboard and by grabbing and dragging one of the corners of the bounding box around the star.

   Using the Shift key preserves the proportions of the object while you resize.

7. **Using your Selection tool, click the original star and press Delete.**

   The original star is deleted (see Figure 12-6).

You have two more things to do to the star object. You need to color it and modify its shape.

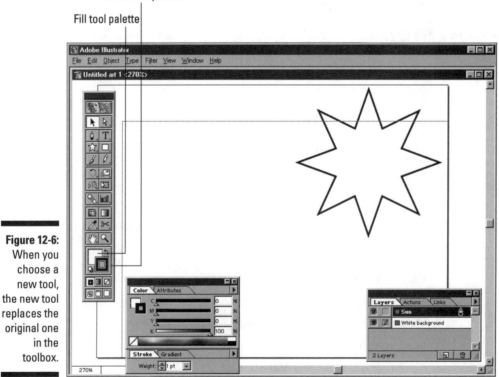

Stroke tool palette

Fill tool palette

Figure 12-6:
When you choose a new tool, the new tool replaces the original one in the toolbox.

1. **Using the Selection tool, select the star.**

   The bounding box appears again around the star object.

2. **Select <u>W</u>indow⇨Show <u>S</u>watches from the main menu.**

   The Swatches palette appears. If necessary, move it so that it doesn't cover the star.

3. **Click the Yellow and Orange Radial (second row, eighth box from the left).**

   You'll know you have the right one by holding your cursor over the box. An information box appears saying this is the Yellow and Orange Radial.

   Your star is now filled with a band of color merging from yellow to orange. You can hide the Swatches box by clicking the X in its upper-right corner.

4. **On the toolbox, click the Stroke tool to ensure that it's activated.**

5. **Click the None color box (the white box with the red diagonal line just below the Fill and Stroke tools palettes, shown in Figure 12-6) to remove color from the star's outside edge.**

   The Star's outside edge disappears.

6. **In the toolbox, click and hold down the Rotate tool (fifth row, left column of the toolbox).**

   Two new tools appear.

7. **Select the Twirl tool, the tool to the right of the Rotate tool.**

8. **Using the Twirl tool, drag to the right or left until you twirl the sun object to your satisfaction.**

9. **Click the Selection tool and then click anywhere away from the star to deselect the star object.**

   You've made an eight-pointed, radial-colored, twirled sun (see Figure 12-7).

Creating text

Last, you need some logo text. To create the words "Wind Tours" on its own layer and using an exotic font, follow these steps:

1. **Create a new layer named Wind Tours.**

   If you don't remember how to create a new layer, see "Making new layers," earlier in this chapter.

2. **In the toolbox, click the Type tool (second row, right column).**

3. **Click anywhere in the document.**

Notice that the Fill and Stroke colors change. The Fill is black, and the Stroke is None color.

4. **Type** Wind Tours.

5. **Click the Selection tool.**

   A bounding box appears around the text.

6. **From the main menu, select Type➪Font➪Braggadocio.**

   The font changes from the default Helvetica to Braggadocio.

7. **From the main menu, select Type➪Size➪24 pt.**

   The type size changes from the default 12 pt to 24 pt.

8. **Drag the Wind Tours object to the low-center of the document area.**

   If necessary, move the Color\Attributes and the Layers\Actions\Links palettes out of the way.

9. **Click anywhere outside the logo text and the sun to deselect all the objects.**

   You just created the logo object and finished your work in Illustrator. You can check out your handiwork in Figure 12-8. Congratulations!

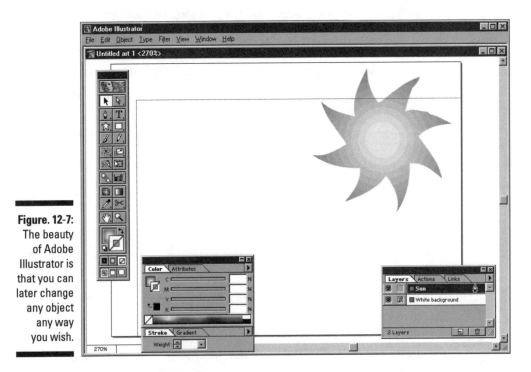

Figure. 12-7:
The beauty
of Adobe
Illustrator is
that you can
later change
any object
any way
you wish.

Because you're using a tryout version of Illustrator (and, so, cannot save files), I've saved your Illustrator files for you. One is called sun.ai and the other is called logo.ai. You can now exit Illustrator and uninstall it if you want.

Making multiple illustrations

One last thing. Simply by making layers visible or invisible, you can use a single multilayered Adobe Illustrator file to make more than one illustration for use in Premiere.

To make an illustration visible or invisible, click the Visibility toggle on any layer. The Visibility toggle is the little eye at the left of each layer.

A layer cannot be saved as an illustration for Premiere if the illustration isn't visible.

I'm going to show you what I mean in Premiere.

Figure 12-8:
You can easily change a font or type size merely by selecting the type.

Using Illustrations in Premiere

Another great Adobe Premiere feature is its capability to turn still images into exciting moving ones. You now get to make the sun move in the sky and to cause text to appear at just the right moment on the screen.

If you closed Premiere earlier, it's time to open it again. This time make one little change to the New Project Settings dialog box.

1. **In the New Project Settings dialog box, click the Next button until you arrive at Audio Settings dialog box.**

2. **In the Audio Settings dialog box, if necessary change Rate to 44 kHz in the drop-down box.**

3. **Change Format to 16-Bit Stereo.**

4. **Click OK to enter the project.**

After you open Premiere, you need to import five files. Two of them are samples of Illustrator files that are identical to the illustrations you just made. A third file is a still frame image taken from a video file used in the previous chapter. One is an audio background. The last one is a finished movie showing you what you are about to make.

1. **Press Ctrl+I to import the files.**

2. **If you aren't already there, find your Chapter 12 folder in the Clips folder on your computer's hard drive.**

3. **Click illusend.mov, and pressing the Shift key, select all the files through wind tours.ai.**

4. **Click Open.**

    Premiere imports illusend.mov, sailing.wav, shorestill.bmp, sun.ai, and windtours.ai into the Project window.

    You find the Project window in the lower-right corner of the Premiere main window (see Chapter 10 for more on the Project window).

You probably would like to look again at what you're about to make. To do so, head this way:

1. **Double-click illusend.mov.**

    The movie loads into the Source monitor. (See Chapter 10 for more information about the Source monitor.)

2. **Click the Source monitor and press the spacebar on your keyboard.**

    The movie plays for you. Watching the movie, observe that you are going to have four elements:

- **Musical background:** If you're really observant, you'll notice that movements correspond with the music.
- **Graphic still background:** The background is a still frame taken from one of the clips in the Chapter 11.
- **Moving sun:** The moving sun is an illustration.
- **Moving text:** The moving text is also an illustration.

Building a Timeline

You need to do two things before you bring the Illustrator sun and text into the Timeline: Lay down the music and establish a background for your illustrations.

1. **In the Project window, click the shorestill.bmp image and drag it to the beginning of the Video 1A track in the Timeline window.**

   For more information on laying down music and images files in the Timeline window, turn back to Chapters 10 and 11.

2. **Click the sailing.wav music file and lay it on the Audio 1 track in the Timeline window.**

   The Timeline window should look like the one in Figure 12-9. If you want, you can play the Timeline to get used to the music. Click in the Timeline and press the spacebar on your keyboard. The music will provide the cues for how to treat the sun and the logo. Note that in video editing, audio is often used to cue video sequences.

Modifying duration

The extent of a clip's time on the Timeline is referred to as the clip's *duration*. Assets, such as video and audio, obviously have varying duration. One of the basic functions of nonlinear editing is to reconcile duration of clips by either reducing or adding to their individual duration. The default length of a still image is 1 second (30 frames). One method of editing is figuring out the duration of background music and then changing the other clips' duration to conform to the music. Another method is to determine the other clips' duration and then change the music's duration to conform to the clips.

Adobe uses nasty little ways to remind you that you're using a tryout version of Premiere. One way is by adding a black box to an image as it's being previewed. To get an idea how your project would look in the real-life version of Premiere, you can replay illusend.mov once in a while in the Source monitor.

To change the duration of sailing.wav, do the following:

1. **Click the sailing.wav clip on the Audio 1 track in the Timeline window.**

   A marquee highlight appears around the clip.

2. **From the main menu, select Clip⊅Duration or press Ctrl+R.**

   The Clip Duration dialog box appears. Notice that the clip's time code is currently 3 seconds, 1 frame in length. You need to cut it down a little.

3. **Type 3:00 in the Enter New Duration text box (see Figure 12-10).**

   Premiere knows it needs to fill in the other time code numbers.

4. **Click OK.**

   You just trimmed the audio track by one frame. By the way, changing duration of a clip on the Timeline does not change the actual clip file.

To make the tracks equal length, just do the following:

1. **Follow Steps 1 through 4 in the preceding set of steps to change the duration of shorestill.bmp.**

   Now the video and audio tracks have the same duration.

Figure 12-10:
Adobe
Premiere
displays
duration in
time code
hours,
minutes,
seconds,
and frames.

2. **Extend the work area (the blue bar at the top of the Timeline window) to match the lengths of the clips on the track by dragging one of its ends to the left or right.**

3. **Press Enter to preview the project.**

Making transparencies

In Premiere, you make multiple layers of a video by using the transparency feature. You make parts of an image transparent by telling Premiere to i-nterpret a specific color as "color none" (like you did in Illustrator). The terms used for this function can become a bit exotic, such as chroma keying and alpha channel. But I'll bypass the terminology and go right to the job.

1. **Go to the Project window (lower-right corner of Premiere window) and click and drag the sun.ai clip to the Video 2 track in the Timeline window.**

2. **Change the duration of sun.ai to 00:00:03:00.**

3. **Press Enter.**

   The Program monitor plays the sequence showing the sun on a white background. You're about to make the white background transparent.

4. **Right-click the sun.ai clip.**

   A selection box appears.

5. **Select Video⇨Transparency.**

   The Transparency Settings dialog box appears (see Figure 12-11).

6. **In the Key Type selection box, choose Chroma.**

   You just told Premiere that you are going to choose a color in the image as your transparency.

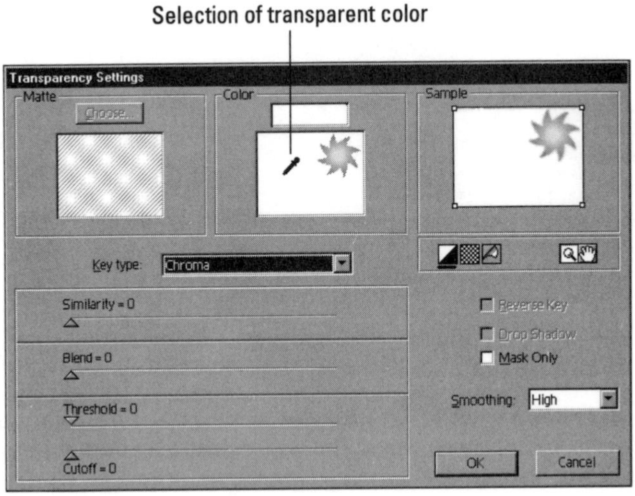

Selection of transparent color

Figure 12-11:
The Transparency Settings dialog box allows you to set the conditions for compositing one image over another.

7. **Hold the cursor over the Color window (the middle window at the top of the Transparency Settings dialog box).**

The cursor turns into an eyedropper, as shown in Figure 12-11. The eyedropper takes whatever color you click.

8. **Click anywhere within the white area of the Color window.**

You just told Premiere that white is now "color none."

9. **In the Smoothing selection box, select High.**

You can see a preview of how your transparency will look by clicking the third button from the right below the sample window (the button that looks like a page being turned back).

10. **Click OK.**

Premiere is ready to build the composited image, showing the sun in the sky.

11. **Press Enter to build the Preview of the project.**

The Preview shows the transparent layer, exposing the background image.

Moving illustrations

Now comes more fun. Premiere has a wide variety of special features. One of them allows you to move clips. You're going to move the sun based on a cue from the music. Play the clip in the Program monitor again. You'll notice a descending sound at the beginning of the audio clip. This falling sound will be the beginning and ending (in point and out point) of the sun's movement.

1. **Right-click the sun.ai clip.**

   A selection box appears.

2. **Select Video⇨Motion.**

   The Motions Settings dialog box appears (see Figure 12-12).

   In the middle of the window is a Time bar, which you use to set beginning, intermediate, and end points for motion (called *key frames*). By default, you already have two key frames — the beginning and ending frames.

3. **Add a key frame by clicking one-third from the left on the bar labeled "Time."**

   You just told Premiere that an action will happen at this frame of the video (thus the name "key frame").

4. **Click the Start key frame (shown at the far-left in Figure 12-12) on the Time bar.**

   This step tells Premiere that you want to adjust motion settings at this frame.

5. **Using your mouse, click and grab the Start box in the upper-right window and drag the sun image until it is above and out of the gray frame and toward the left corner.**

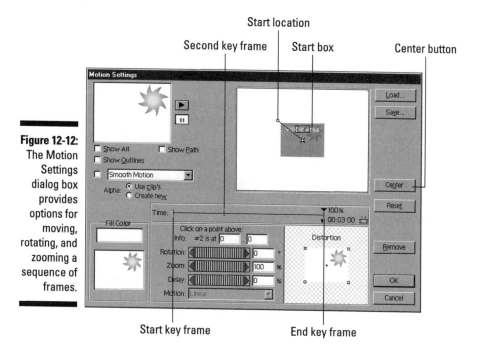

Figure 12-12:
The Motion
Settings
dialog box
provides
options for
moving,
rotating, and
zooming a
sequence of
frames.

You just told Premiere that the illustration's in point is outside the viewing area.

6. **Click the second key frame (the one you created).**

You just told Premiere that you're about to set motion commands for this frame.

7. **Click the Center button, located on the right side of the Motion Settings dialog box.**

Premiere now knows that the sun will move from the outside viewing area to the place where the sun was originally drawn in the illustration; the illustration will be centered in the viewing area. Premiere doesn't need to be told what to do with the intervening frames. It figures that out automatically.

8. **Click the far-right frame (the end key frame).**

9. **Click the Center button.**

By choosing the same setting for the end key frame as you did for the second key frame, you told Premiere that no motion will take place after the middle motion is complete.

10. **Click OK.**

Premiere is ready to build your motion sequence.

11. **Press Enter.**

Premiere builds and runs the motion sequence.

Adding tracks to the Timeline

Premiere allows you to have up to 99 video and audio tracks, which probably doesn't mean a whole lot unless you add a track to see what can happen. You get to do that now. You create a video track and use it to superimpose an illustration with its own motion settings. You begin by adding the video track.

1. **Click the right-pointing arrow in the upper-right corner of the Timeline window (refer to Figure 12-9).**

A selection box appears.

2. **Select Track Options.**

The Track Options dialog box appears.

3. **Click the Add button.**

The Add Tracks dialog box appears.

4. **Type 1 in the Video Tracks box and type 0 in the Audio Tracks box.**

5. **Click OK in the Add Tracks dialog box.**

6. **Click <u>O</u>K in the Track Options dialog box.**

   You just added a video track to the project.

Time for freelancing

Now that you've created another video track, you're ready to add wind tours.ai to the Timeline window. Use the steps in this chapter for setting duration, creating transparency, and setting motions. Have fun and experiment. If you'd like to do it the way I did, play the illusend.mov clip to watch the action of the Wind Tours logo.

Chapter 13

Adding Graphics to Your Video with Adobe Photoshop

*V*ideo consists of edited visual images and sounds stretched over a period of time (that is, a timeline). As an editor, you either keep or lose your audience by how effectively you use images and sound in time. And, although you may think that constantly moving, quick action video is the best way to use the video timeline, that's not always the case. Sometimes, your viewer needs to dwell on a picture or text to catch the significance of a message or to respond with a particular emotion. Sometimes, nothing gets the job done better than a well-developed graphic image.

In this chapter, you create graphics and text for video. And to get the job done, you use one of the most powerful graphics tools available — Adobe Photoshop.

You must have Premiere installed on your computer to do many of the things described in this chapter. For information on installing the Premiere 5.0 Tryout version that is on the CD that comes with this book, turn to Appendix B. You may also want to turn back to Chapter 10 if you need a brush-up on using Premiere. To view the movie files in this chapter, you may need to install QuickTime version 4.0 or later as described in Chapter 10.

Installing Adobe Photoshop and the Sample Files

Much like the tryout version of Adobe Premiere, you have a tryout version of Adobe Photoshop waiting for you on the CD at the back of this book. Also, like the tryout version of Premiere, you won't be able to save anything you make in the chapter. But, not to worry. I've got you covered. I've prepared finished copies of what you need to use in Premiere.

You need to install the tryout version of Adobe Photoshop. You also need to download the Chapter 13 sample files from the CD-ROM. These sample files are stored on the CD-ROM in a subfolder named CHAP13, which is located in a folder named CLIPS.

For steps on installing both, turn to Appendix B.

When you complete this chapter, you can delete the sample files from your hard drive to save space.

Introducing Adobe Photoshop

As I mention in Chapter 12, Photoshop is a paint program that you can use to easily change existing images or to paint new ones. Adobe Photoshop makes raster images. *Raster images* use a grid of small squares (pixels). Each pixel in a raster image has a unique location and color value assigned to it. When working with raster images, you edit pixels rather than objects or shapes.

In this section, you find out how to make some subtle but powerful changes to four photos so that you can use them in a video. But, for fun, start by seeing the end result — how they look when combined in a video.

1. **Open Premiere and select File⇨Open in the main menu or press Ctrl+O.**

   The Open dialog box appears.

2. **Open the Chapter 13 folder you copied from the CD-ROM.**

3. **Double-click the file colorado.avi to open it.**

4. **To play the colorado.avi file, click the Source monitor and press the spacebar on your keyboard.**

   In the Premiere window, the monitor on the left is the Source monitor. See Chapter 10 for more information about the Source monitor.

Although the movie is simple, it's a visually effective treatment of four photos. The four photos have been taken through a series of corrections, improvements, and changes to make them work within this Premiere movie clip.

You can exit Premiere for now. You'll come back to it later in this chapter. Now it's your turn to build the pieces for this movie. In doing so, you get to see and play with some of the powerful features of Adobe Photoshop.

Open the Adobe Photoshop 5.0 Tryout version by clicking the Windows Start button. Select Programs⇨Adobe⇨Adobe Photoshop 5.0⇨Adobe Photoshop 5.0 Tryout. The program opens.

When you open Photoshop, you see the Adobe Photoshop title bar at the top of the window, the main menu immediately under the title bar, and the toolbox at the far-left (see Figure 13-1). At the right are four palettes — Navigator\Info\Options, Colors\Swatches\Brushes, History\Actions, and Layers\Channels\Paths. I explain the functions of many of these palettes throughout the chapter.

Toolbox Title bar Menu bar   Palettes

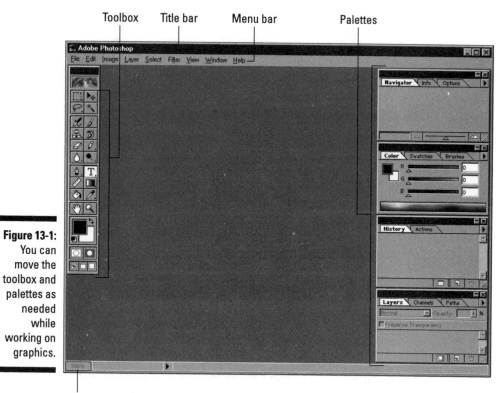

Figure 13-1:
You can move the toolbox and palettes as needed while working on graphics.

Zoom percentage box

Working with Images

The project for your little adventure with Photoshop and its relationship to Premiere is to create a photo gallery of a Colorado vacation trip. You're going to work with four photos.

1. **Select <u>F</u>ile⇨<u>O</u>pen in the main menu or press Ctrl+O.**

   The Open dialog box appears. Find the Chapter 13 Clips folder that you copied from the CD-ROM.

2. **Click the colo1.tif file, hold down the Shift key on your keyboard, and click colo4.tif.**

   Now colo1.tif through colo4.tif are highlighted.

3. **Click Open.**

   The files load into Photoshop, each in its own window (jump ahead to Figure 13-2 to see the files).

Photoshop restricts each file to its own window, which enables you to make changes to an image without affecting the others.

You're going to prepare the four photos according to each photo's needs. The first thing you do is repair a scratch in colo1.tif.

Fixing imperfections

If you look at this image, you can see that the girl has a scratch on her leg. Actually, the photo's scratched, not her leg. In either case, you're the Photoshop doctor. Time to get rid of that nasty imperfection. You do that by using the Zoom and Rubber Stamp tools. Adobe has to come up with more romantic sounding names.

1. **Click the Zoom tool in the toolbox (it's the spyglass — tenth row, right column).**

   The cursor turns into a spyglass with a + inside it.

   Now you need to draw a square around and slightly larger than the scratched area.

2. **Click just above and to the left of the scratch. Pressing the mouse, drag diagonally over the scratch, creating a box. Release the mouse.**

   The image magnifies to a close-up of the scratched area (see Figure 13-2). If you want to know where you are on the photo, look up at the Navigator palette at the upper-right side of the screen. A red box represents the close-up area. As a matter of fact, look all around the screen.

Photoshop is coming alive. The status bar in the lower-left corner records the magnification percentage. The various windows on the right have a bunch of information about your work. I discuss the relevance of some of this information throughout the chapter.

You fix this scratch by taking color and brightness from adjoining pixels. Though such a procedure seems like it would be complex and time consuming, the procedure is actually easy and fun. All you do is use the Photoshop Rubber Stamp tool. Do you see the blend of colors caused by shadowing on the leg? The Rubber Stamp tool helps you match this blend. As a result, your skin doctoring will be a total cure and not a bandage. To do this doctoring, just follow these steps:

1. **Click the Rubber Stamp tool in the toolbox (fourth row, left column).**

   As you pass the cursor over the image, its shape becomes a rubber stamp. Before you use the Rubber Stamp tool, you need to do one more thing. You need to select the right brush size for your work. For something this small, you need a small brush.

2. **Click the Brushes tab in the Colors\Swatches\Brushes palette on the right.**

   A selection of brush sizes appears (see Figure 13-3).

Navigator palette

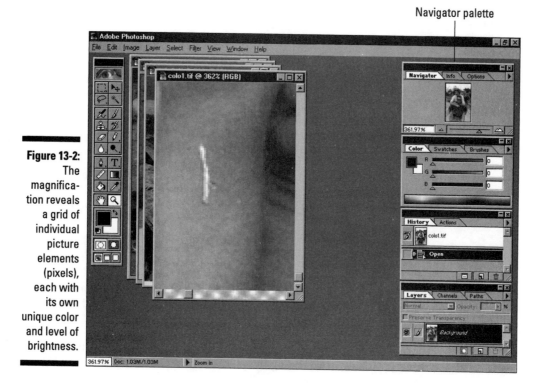

Figure 13-2:
The magnification reveals a grid of individual picture elements (pixels), each with its own unique color and level of brightness.

3. Click the brush in the top row, third from the left.

The brush you select directly affects the size of the cursor's action.

Before you begin your digital plastic surgery, observe the angle of the shadowing. The shadow is similar to the shape of the leg. You take some of the color from one place and copy (rubber stamp) it to another. So, as you work on this imperfection, the matching color and shading is at an angle.

1. **To use the Rubber Stamp tool, position the cursor approximately one inch to the left of the imperfection.**

2. **Press and hold down the Alt key and simultaneously click and release your mouse.**

   You just set the angle and distance relationship for the Rubber Stamp tool.

Figure 13-3:
Adobe
Photoshop
provides a
variety of
brush sizes
to meet your
painting
needs.

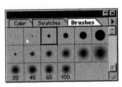

3. **Using this setting, position the cursor over the imperfection and click and drag to deposit color and shading.**

   Wow! What a tool!

   When you're done, you can zoom out.

To zoom out, click the zoom percentage box (refer to Figure 13-1) in the lower-left of the Photoshop screen, type **50** in the box, and press Enter. The photo returns to 50% of the full image. The scratch is gone. Nice job doctor.

Cropping images

Another advantage Photoshop gives you is the ability to isolate parts of photos. Frequently, you want only a portion of a picture. You use the Crop tool to do the job.

Select <u>W</u>indow⇨colo2.tif in the main menu. Colo2.tif comes to the front. If you want, you can grab and drag the photo to the middle of the screen by clicking, holding, and dragging in the photo's blue title bar. Notice that the file has some white at the bottom of the photo. Nasty little problem, huh. This is a job for the Crop tool.

1. **Click and hold your mouse over the Rectangular Marquee tool (first row, left column of the toolbox).**

   A selection of tools appears.

2. **Drag the cursor to the right to the Crop tool. Release your mouse to select it.**

   The toolbox now reveals the Crop tool, replacing the Rectangular Marquee tool, as shown in Figure 13-4. (As I mention in Chapter 12, right-pointing arrows in the lower corner of a tool's box indicate hidden selections.)

With the Crop tool selected, you can change the area of a graphics file.

1. **Starting in the upper-left corner (or any corner) of the photo, click and hold down your mouse. Drag the mouse to create a rectangle.**

   It doesn't matter where you draw it at this point.

2. **Release the mouse to reveal a dotted rectangle.**

3. **Click any of the nodes (little boxes) of the rectangle to increase the rectangle size until it covers the white area in the graphics file.**

4. **Press Enter.**

   The new area excludes the extraneous white.

Figure 13-4: Adobe Photoshop groups like kinds of tools together, such as the Marquee tools and the Cropping tool.

Adjusting images

Sometimes I think the features in Photoshop are endless. Even so, some of them are used more than others. Three bread-and-butter features offered by Photoshop are rotating canvas and color and brightness correction. Start with rotating canvas.

Reversing an image

You have one more thing to do with colo2.tif, and it's not a fix of an error, but an exercise of editor's license. You need to reverse the image because later in editing the image will be more useful flip-flopped. Of course, you wouldn't be able to reverse an image containing numbers or letters because the image would be bothersome to look at.

Select Image⇨Rotate Canvas⇨Flip Horizontal. You're finished with colo2.tif for the moment. Now it's time to go on to some other fix-its.

Adjusting hue

Sometimes a photo is fine by itself but is noticeably different in hue from other photos in a group. For example, select Window⇨colo3.tif in the main menu. Though this photograph is a great father and son shot, it has too much red in it for the picture to blend well with the others. You need to tone it down just a little.

1. **Select Image⇨Adjust⇨Selective Color.**

   The Selective Color dialog box appears (see Figure 13-5). You adjust the colors in this dialog box to shift the hue of a picture.

2. **Slide the Magenta setting to -20.**

   This alteration causes magenta shades to tone down just a bit (*desaturate*).

   If the Preview box is checked, you'll be able to watch your work improve as you make adjustment.

3. **Click OK.**

   You just color-corrected the image.

Adjusting brightness

Getting just the right degree of brightness and contrast are common challenges in video. Photoshop provides a way of making adjustments to brightness only, contrast only, or both. Select Window⇨colo4.tif in the main menu. The man in the photo is ever-so-slightly muddy. He needs a little light.

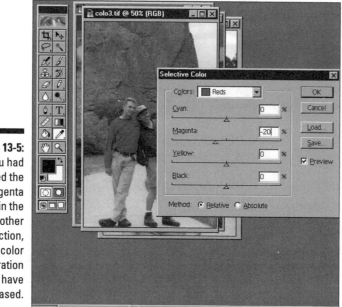

Figure 13-5:
If you had moved the magenta scale in the other direction, the color saturation would have increased.

1. **Select Image➪Adjust➪Brightness\Contrast.**

   The Brightness\Contrast palette appears.

2. **Slide the Brightness bar to the right to +25.**

   If the Preview box is checked, you can see the difference this change makes.

3. **When you're satisfied with how he looks, click OK.**

Creating New Images

As I explain in Chapter 12, Adobe Illustrator is a draw program. Photoshop is a paint program. A draw program sets properties for the space between points. A paint program sets properties for areas. In this section, you create an area equal in size and aspect ratio (the ratio of an image's width to its height) to a video frame. Once you make this area, you fill it with images and color. Sounds like fun!

Making a frame

Now it's time to make a new frame with the same aspect ratio as a video image, that is 4:3.

A conventional video image has an aspect ratio of 4:3 (4 picture elements in width for every 3 picture elements in height).

So, head this way:

1. **Select <u>W</u>indow⇨<u>N</u>ew in the main menu or press Ctrl+N.**

   The New dialog box appears (see Figure 13-6).

2. **Type** 320 **in the <u>W</u>idth text box.**

   The unit should be pixels.

3. **Type** 240 **in the <u>H</u>eight text box.**

   The unit should be pixels.

4. **Type** 150 **in the <u>R</u>esolution text box, making the resolution 150 pixels per inch.**

5. **Set the <u>M</u>ode to RGB Color.**

6. **Set the Contents to <u>T</u>ransparent.**

7. **Click OK to activate your choices.**

The frame you created is where you will put all the photos you've fixed. The frame will also contain text and some snazzy paint blends. Before you go further, notice the Layers palette on the right. Currently, it's one blank layer. That is about to change.

Figure 13-6: Making a new image requires some detailed work, but as you're about to see, the results are worth the effort.

New	☒
Name: Untitled-1	OK
	Cancel

Image Size: 225K

Width: 320   pixels
Height: 240   pixels
Resolution: 150   pixels/inch
Mode: RGB Color

Contents
○ White
○ Background Color
● Transparent

Adjusting source graphics

You're ready to place the four Colorado vacation trip photos in layers in the new frame. To do so, you have to change the photos' sizes. You adjust the height of the photos to equal the height of the new frame, while maintaining the photos' aspect ratios.

1. **Click the heading area of any one of the photos to activate it.**

2. **Select Image➪Image Size.**

   The Image Size dialog box appears (see Figure 13-7). If the Constrain Proportions box isn't checked, check it now.

3. **In the Pixel Dimensions section, type 240 in the Height text box.**

   This is the height of the new frame. Don't be confused that the width doesn't equal 320. You deal with the rest of the width space in a little bit.

   When changing an image size, smaller is always better, larger is usually a degradation of the image. When you make an image smaller, you are making the image's pixels smaller, causing the image to have more pixels per inch. Enlarging an image causes individual pixels to become visible, making the image look splotchy and jagged.

4. **Click OK.**

5. **Repeat these four steps for each of the other three photos.**

Figure 13-7:
The
Constrain
Proportions
option
maintains
the aspect
ratio of an
image.

Using color

Now you come to some more fun stuff. Manipulation of color is one of the most amazing features that Photoshop offers — and it has a lot of helpful features. In this little section, you do the following:

- ✔ Use color in the photos to determine the overall color of the screen.
- ✔ Fill areas with color.
- ✔ Create a gradient to tie the photo to the color background.

Picking colors

In the toolbox, you find a tool that looks like an eyedropper. Guess what it's called? Yup.

1. **Activate colo2.tif by clicking in its heading area.**

2. **Click the Eyedropper tool.**

   The cursor turns into an eyedropper when it passes over images.

3. **Position your cursor anywhere over the colo2.tif background (the landscape) and click.**

   When you click the background using the Eyedropper tool, that color becomes the foreground color in the toolbox Foreground Color box. You just picked a color.

Filling colors

Using the chosen color, you now make a background.

1. **Activate the new frame by clicking in its heading area.**

2. **Click the Paint Bucket tool in the toolbox.**

   You shouldn't have much trouble figuring out which tool that one is — *hint,* it's in the ninth row, left column.

3. **Place your cursor over the transparent area of the new frame and click.**

   Layer 1 of the new frame is filled with the same color as the one you chose from the landscape in colo2.tif.

Creating a gradient

Before assembling the image, you need to create a smooth transition from the multiple colors in the photo to the solid color background. You do this by creating gradient. You use the Linear Gradient tool to create a transition.

1. **Activate colo2.tif by clicking in its heading area.**

2. **Double-click the Linear Gradient tool in the toolbox.**

   The Linear Gradient tool is the eighth tool in the right column. By double-clicking the Linear Gradient tool, you open the Linear Gradient Options tab in the Navigator\Info\Options palette (see Figure 13-8).

3. **In the Gradient selection box, select Foreground to Transparent.**

4. **Check the Reverse box.**

5. **Place your cursor over the colo2.tif image at the girl's knees. Click and drag to the right edge of the frame and release.**

   The image is modified with a transparent to foreground color gradient. If it didn't work to your satisfaction, select Edit⇨Undo Gradient (or press Ctrl+Z) in the main menu and try again.

Linear Gradient tool   Linear Gradient tab

Figure 13-8:
Use the Linear Gradient tool to create a transition from one kind of image to another.

Assembling the image

The time has come to begin assembling the image. You drag the colo1.tif into the new frame. I think you're going to like this process.

1. **Click the Move tool in the toolbox.**

   The Move tool sits at the upper-right corner of the toolbox.

2. **Click colo2.tif and drag it into the new frame.**

   A copy of the image drops into the frame.

3. **Using your mouse or the arrow keys on the keyboard, adjust the image so that it fits trim against the left side of the frame, vertically filling the frame.**

4. **Click the X in the colo2.tif file to close it.**

   Now that the image is successfully copied to the new frame, you don't need it any more.

Working with layers

Notice that the Layers window has more than one layer in it now. To see it better, close the History\Actions palette and drag the Layers\Channels\Paths palette up to fill that space. Click the bottom edge of the window and drag it down, making the window taller.

1. **Click the right arrow at the upper-right corner of the Layers window.**

   A selection box appears.

2. **Click New Layer.**

   The New Layer dialog box appears.

3. **In the Name text box type** Colo 3 **background.**

4. **Click OK.**

   A new empty layer appears. Now, if you want, you can repeat the steps you just completed, starting with the section "Picking a color," for the other three photos:

   • Pick a color from the photo.

   • Fill the background.

     Change the gradient on the photo from transparent to foreground. (In the video, I stagger them left, then right, then left, and so on.)

   • Drag the image into the new frame.

   • Create a new layer for the next photo background.

And so on. Whether or not you choose to continue building the photo, take a look at the eyeballs in the Layers palette. If an eyeball is visible for a layer, the layer is visible. If the eyeball is not visible, the layer is not visible. You can toggle the eyeballs on and off by clicking in the Layers palette.

Creating Text in Photoshop

The final step in building the graphic for video is adding text. If you worked through Chapter 12, you created text in Illustrator. Some of the principles used there are used here, but there are also some major differences because Illustrator text is vector-based and Photoshop text is rastor-based.

A common question is which is better? The text in Illustrator or the text in Photoshop? You need to have experience with both so that you can make your own decision. So now you work with Photoshop text.

Text in Illustrator is much easier to use, more versatile, and capable of being changed — even in its final stages. Text in Photoshop is better looking; you can give it shadowing, it can have gradients, and other embellishments. But once you've created text in Photoshop and converted the file to a graphic for use in other programs, you can't change the text. In my work, I find it invaluable to pick and choose which of the two approaches is better (Illustrator or Photoshop) for each circumstance.

Adding text

To add text in Photoshop, you begin by naming the colo2 image in the new frame.

1. **Highlight Layer 2 in the Layers\Channels\Paths palette.**

2. **Click the Swatches tab in the Colors\Swatches\Brushes palette.**

3. **Click white to select it.**

   White becomes the new Foreground color.

4. **Click the Type tool in the toolbox.**

   The Type tool is the big T.

   Notice that the cursor becomes a strange figure with a box around it as you pass the cursor over the image.

5. **Click anywhere in the graphic area of the new frame.**

   The Type Tool dialog box appears (see Figure 13-9).

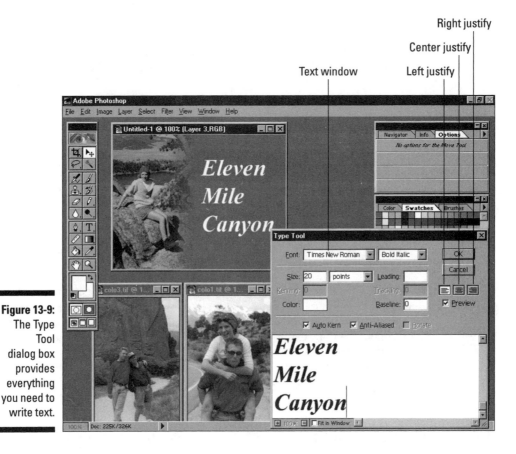

Figure 13-9:
The Type Tool dialog box provides everything you need to write text.

6. **Drag the Type Tool dialog box in such a way that you expose as much of the new frame window as possible.**

7. **Click the arrows to the right of the Font box and select Times New Roman and Bold Italic, respectively.**

8. **Make sure that the left-justify box is highlighted.**

   The left-, center-, and right-justify buttons enable you to make paragraphs much like a word processor.

9. **In the Size box, type** 20.

   This changes the type size to 20 points.

10. **Click in the text window to activate it.**

11. **Type** Eleven, **press Enter, type** Mile, **press Enter again, and type** Canyon.

The text simultaneously appears in the new frame as it appears in the text window. When you're satisfied with the size and font of the text, click OK. Notice that in the Layers window the text has its own layer.

Using Photoshop Images in Premiere

You're done using Photoshop. Good job! You can close it and open Premiere if you closed Premiere earlier. Now you import finished images that I created by using the process you just followed. All our work gets to have its moment of glory, after all.

1. **In Premiere, select File⇨Import or press Ctrl+I.**

   The Import window appears.

2. **Find the Chapter 13 folder that you copied from this book's CD to your hard drive.**

3. **Click mountain.wav, hold down your Shift key, click pic4.tif, and then click Open to import the files pic1-4.tif and mountain.wav.**

After you import these files, you're ready to build a graphics-based video.

Building a sequence of photos in Photoshop

Take a look at Figure 13-10. As you can see, the project is a sequence of photos with transitions between them. Below all the photos is an audio track. If you're reading this book chapter by chapter, your Premiere experience in Chapter 10 (plus Chapters 11 and 12) will make building this project simple. If you're skipping around and haven't yet read Chapter 10, you may want to refer to that chapter for information on using Premiere and the Timeline window.

1. **Lay mountain.wav on the Audio 1 track in the Timeline window.**

   The length of the audio clip extends out of the window to the right. You need to change units of time in the Timeline window.

2. **Click the Time Unit menu (see Figure 13-10) in the lower-left corner of the Timeline window.**

3. **Change the time unit to 1 Second.**

   You should now be able to see the entire audio track as shown in Figure 13-10.

Figure 13-10:
The entire
sequence is
made visible
by changing
the units at
the bottom
of the
Timeline.

Time Unit menu

4. **Lay pic1.tif on the Video 1A track in the Timeline window.**

5. **Change pic1.tif duration to 5 seconds.**

   See Chapter 12 for info on modifying duration.

6. **Lay pic2.tif on the Video 1B track in the Timeline window. Overlap pic1.tif by 1 second.**

7. **Change pic2.tif duration to 3 seconds.**

8. **Lay a Cross Dissolve transition between the clips.**

   See Chapter 10 for info on creating and previewing transitions.

9. **Follow the preceding steps to lay the other two Colorado images on the Timeline, each with the same duration of 3 seconds, the same overlap, and the same transition.**

10. **Drag the work area slider to cover all the image area.**

See Chapter 10 for info on creating and previewing transitions and for using the work area slider.

11. **Press Enter to watch your Preview.**

Congratulations! You've successfully created graphic images and built graphic images into a nice little video.

Chapter 14

Adding Animation to Your Video with Adobe After Effects

*O*nce upon a time, in a galaxy that today seems light years away, there was a breed of humanlike creatures who simply enjoyed basic video. This may be hard to imagine, but this primitive race of beings could sit in front of a television set for hours, watching a live broadcast of people just talking to each other. These programs had strange names, like "The Honeymooners" or "The Ed Sullivan Show."

Then something happened that changed these people. They became restless and wanted more and more stimulation. Simple talking images needed to have constant changing perspectives. Transitions from one scene to the next had to have special effects. The viewing environment of this alien people became so rarefied that they needed constant stimulation to maintain their attention.

What happened to these people? They were attacked by a mechanical monster called the *videotape recorder*. This voracious beast took over their world of visual communication. Because of it, a new world of special image processing was born. Within a few short timelines (these creatures call them "years"), people were unhappy with their viewing unless it was laced with things called *special effects* and *animation*.

And so we come to today — far removed from that naive, innocent culture. Today, video containing animation and special effects is not only normal, it is easy to produce. What a decade ago could be created only by using equipment costing many thousands of dollars can now be created on a personal computer equipped with software costing hundreds.

So, I have a simple question. Do you want your viewers to fidget in their seats fighting boredom, or do you want them on the edges of their seats wanting more? If your answer is the latter, you need some help with special effects. Help has arrived. In this chapter, I introduce you and your computer to Adobe After Effects.

You must have Premiere installed on your computer to do many of the things described in this chapter. For information on installing the Premiere 5.0 Tryout version that is on the CD that comes with this book, turn to Appendix B. You may also want to turn back to Chapter 10 if you need a brush-up on using Premiere.

Installing Adobe After Effects and the Sample Files

It's time to make magic in Adobe After Effects. This is pretty heady stuff, so if you're wearing a hat, you may want to make sure it's stretchable.

You need to install the tryout version of Adobe After Effects that's on the CD at the back of this book. You also need to download the Chapter 14 sample files from the CD-ROM. These sample files are stored on the CD-ROM in a subfolder named CHAP14, which is located in a folder named CLIPS. For steps on doing both, turn to Appendix B.

When you complete this chapter, you can delete the sample files from your hard drive to save space.

Getting Ready for Animation

As I mention in Chapter 10, Adobe Premiere is a powerful tool for assembling visual and audio media. Its strength lies in the ability it gives you to digitally connect and edit that media over a time continuum. You put audio and video clips on a timeline and create associations among the clips, such as transitions.

You can easily move the clips around the timeline, edit their beginning and end, and modify them, such as adjusting volume (see Chapter 11 for more on fading volume).

Premiere is called a nonlinear editing program — meaning that you can move things around and tinker with them to your heart's content, similar to the way you play with words and paragraphs in a word processor.

In contrast, Adobe After Effects is a compositing and animation software program. *Compositing* is just what the word implies — composing separate parts into a whole. After Effect's strength lies in the ability it gives you to compose layers of visual images into a single image while controlling animation effects for each layer. Simply stated, After Effects is an awesome generator of digital video special effects.

Quite often, a strength is also a weakness. For example, very powerful software programs tend to be hard to understand and use. Not so with Adobe After Effects. As you are about to see, a novice to After Effects can create powerful visual effects. But enough of this. You didn't come to this chapter to hear praises of Adobe After Effects; you came here to use it.

But before you jump in, let me show you what you are going to create in this chapter.

1. **Open Premiere and select File⇨Open in the main menu or press Ctrl+O.**

   The Open dialog box appears.

2. **Open the Chapter 14 folder you copied from the CD-ROM.**

3. **Click Open or double-click the clip aeend.mov.to open it.**

   The clip opens in the Source monitor.

4. **To play the clip, click the Source monitor and press the spacebar on your keyboard.**

   In the Premiere window, the monitor on the left is the Source monitor. See Chapter 10 for more information about the Source monitor.

   You can exit Premiere for now. You'll come back to it later in this chapter.

As you watch the clip, a word moves across a background. The word is actually *transparent,* which means that you are seeing through it to something else, in this case the flowers. Each letter is filled with video. Pretty neat, huh? You're going to make this special effect in just a few easy steps. But one thing before you move on: This one example, though quite powerful, is the tip of the iceberg of what you can easily learn to create using Adobe After Effects.

Setting Up an Animation Project

As I mention in Chapter 10, the Adobe Digital Media suite is a tag team affair. You can create a file in one program, such as Illustrator 8.0, and export the file to other programs, such as Adobe Photoshop 5.0 or Adobe Premiere 5.1. Conversely, Photoshop files work just as well in Illustrator and Premiere. And Adobe Premiere, Illustrator, and Photoshop files work in Adobe After Effects. Phew! I get worn out just thinking of the combinations.

Open the Adobe After Effects 4.0 Tryout version by clicking the Windows Start button. Then select Programs⇨Adobe⇨After Effects 4.0⇨Adobe After Effects 4.0 Tryout. The program opens.

Upon opening Adobe After Effects, your first inclination may be that you've made a mistake — not because it looks complex, but because it appears as though almost nothing is there. Be patient and use this little quiet moment to fasten your seat belt and check your rear view mirror, because you are about leave ordinary video in the dust. You are about to set up an animation project.

Importing files

You begin using After Effects by importing files. Just select File⇨Import⇨ Footage File (or press Ctrl+I). You'll probably go directly to the Chapter 14 folder, but if you don't, find and open the Chapter 14 folder in the Clips folder on your hard drive. Select flower.avi and flowers.tif and click Open. The two files appear in the Project window (see Figure 14-1). Still pretty unimpressive, but we're getting there.

Before going on, notice that each one of the two file types has a color assigned to it, one yellow and the other pink. Remember this. You'll see in just a little bit how these colors serve as road signs.

Also, click on flower.avi. A thumbnail appears at the top of the Project window, as shown in Figure 14-1. The thumbnail displays the first frame of the video and gives valuable information about the file's properties.

Making a composition

After you assemble some or all of your media, you're ready to define your composition. You may find that the steps you follow here are similar to some of the steps you follow when using Premiere to define a project. To create a new composition, follow these steps:

Thumbnail and file information

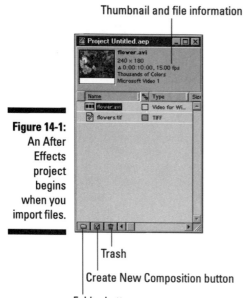

Figure 14-1:
An After
Effects
project
begins
when you
import files.

Trash

Create New Composition button

Folder button

1. **Click the Create a New Composition button at the lower-left side of the Project window (refer to Figure 14-1).**

2. **In the Composition Name text box type** Flower Show Logo.

3. **In the Frame Size section, check the Lock Aspect Ratio (4:3) button.**

4. **In the Width text box type** 240.

   The height automatically changes to 180.

5. **In the Frame Rate text box type** 15.

   Leave everything else as is. The Composition Settings window should look like the one Figure 14-2.

6. **Click OK.**

   The screen changes dramatically.

Working in the Time Layout Window

Adobe After Effects is a wonderful tool for adding the dimension of time to still objects. By adding time, you get to manipulate the still object in a number of ways, and you get to relate the still object to other still objects during that time period. You accomplish all of this in the Time Layout window.

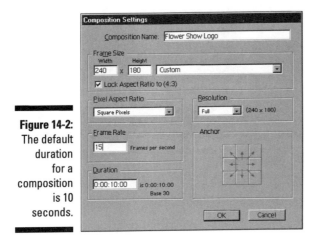

Figure 14-2:
The default
duration
for a
composition
is 10
seconds.

Making a composition

Adobe After Effects is full of little surprises. You're experiencing the first one. Everything you do in After Effects happens within a composition, which makes sense because this is a compositing software program.

When you created the composition, two additional windows appeared on the screen (jump ahead to Figure 14-3 to see the windows). The one at the top is the Program monitor. The Program monitor is where you watch previews of your animations. The long window at the bottom is the Time Layout window. The Time Layout window looks somewhat similar to Premiere's Timeline window. But looks can be deceiving. As I said at the beginning of this chapter, Premiere is an editing program. After Effects is a compositing program. You use an editing program timeline to order and relate clips over time (see Chapter 10 for more on the Premiere Timeline window). You use a compositing time layout to speed through the twists and turns of special effects. This will all make much more sense in just a moment.

Creating a layer

The power of Adobe After Effects lies in its capability to make multiple things happen simultaneously on the screen. For example, at the beginning of this chapter, you watched a finished movie of what you are now making. In this finished movie (aeend.mov), a word moves from right to left across the screen. The letters of the word are cut out, revealing moving video underneath. At the back of everything is a color background with nonmoving text on it. Each of these pieces has something happening to it that is different than what is happening to the other pieces.

Adobe After Effects enables you to work simultaneously with as many pieces of media as you like. You do this with _layers._ Layers allow you to create as many special effects for a composition as you want. These effects are isolated each to its own individual layer. As a result, you can have an infinite number of effects happening in numerous layers all at the same time. And After Effects keeps them all straight for you.

The time has come for you to place your media in the Time Layout window.

1. **Using your mouse, click and drag the file flower.avi into the Time Layout window.**

   The clip creates a row (layer) of information in the Time Layout window. Notice that the yellow indicator to the right stretches to "10s," which stands for ten seconds (see Figure 14-3). Also, notice that the opening frame appears in the Program monitor at the top of the After Effects screen.

2. **Click and drag flowers.tif into the Time Layout window.**

   A pink stretch of time appears to the right. The pink is a symbol to remind you that this is a graphic — as shown in the Project window. The first frame of flowers.tif fills the Program monitor (see Figure 14-3).

Notice that the flowers.tif image doesn't fit in the Program monitor. I made the file this way on purpose. I created a text image with room on either side of it. The image dimensions are equal to the frame height of 180 pixels. But the image width is much greater than the monitor width. Using the Time Layout window, you will set the flowers.tif layer properties so that the layer _crawls_ (that is moves) from right to left across the screen. And you will make the letters transparent, revealing the flowers video underneath. You adjust these settings with _keyframes,_ which are two points in time.

Defining an effect with keyframes

The chapter about Adobe Illustrator, Chapter 12, may help you understand animation keyframes. Adobe Illustrator is a draw program. You create two points (an in point, the beginning; and an end point — you're right — the ending), and the draw program connects the points with a line or a curve possessing properties as chosen by you. These properties might be color or stroke width or fill information for a box. (See Chapter 12 for more information on stroke width and fill information.)

Program monitor

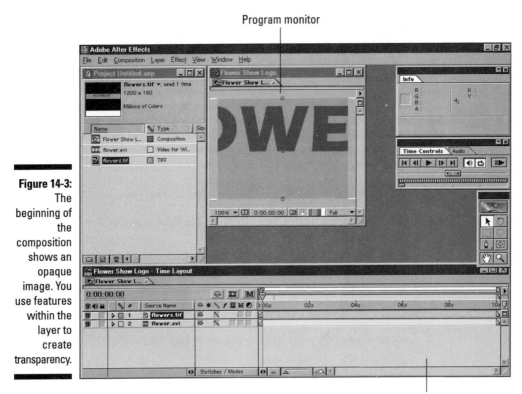

Time Layout window

Figure 14-3:
The beginning of the composition shows an opaque image. You use features within the layer to create transparency.

After Effects also works with points called keyframes. But, as I mentioned earlier, instead of being points on a piece of paper as in a draw program, *keyframes* are two points in time. You set the keyframes and then tell After Effects all the things you want to happen between these two points.

Now's the time (the in point) for you to work with keyframes.

1. **On the Time Layout window, click the right-pointing arrow to the left of the flowers.tif file.**

   A drop-down list appears showing three categories: Masks, Effects, and Transform (shown in Figure 14-4).

2. **Click the right-pointing arrow next to Transform.**

   If necessary, use the scroll bar at the right of the Time Layout window to see all five Transform effects. Notice in the upper-left corner of the window the number 0:00:00:00. This number indicates that you are at the first frame of this composition.

3. **Click the stopwatch to the left of the Position effect.**

   Notice that a black diamond appears on the Time Layout screen next to the Position effect. This is your first keyframe (see Figure 14-4). Notice the numbers to the right of the Position effect. They are 120 and 90. What do you think these two numbers represent? You got it. They are each one-half of 240 and 180. The flowers.tif image is currently parked in the middle of the image area. You are now going to change that.

4. **Click the number 120.**

   The Position window appears. In this window, you change the location of the graphic in relation to the image area. Now, you're going to leave the vertical location (Y-axis) alone and only mess with the horizontal location (X-axis). You are about to tell After Effects that you want the flowers.tif image moved to the right as far as possible without revealing any of the movie that is now beneath it.

5. **Type** 600 **in the X-axis text box.**

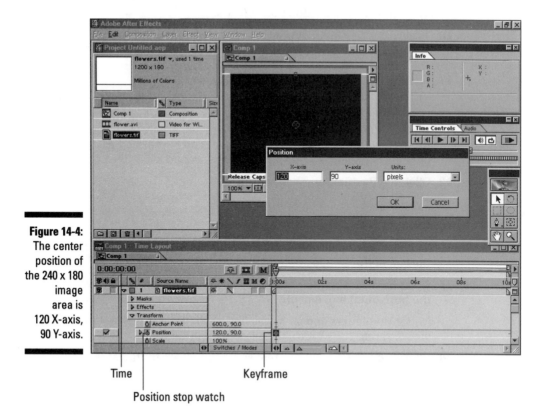

Figure 14-4:
The center position of the 240 x 180 image area is 120 X-axis, 90 Y-axis.

Time

Position stop watch

Keyframe

6. **Click OK.**

You can't really see what's going on. But you can change that.

7. **Click and hold the mouse over the 100% button in the Program monitor.**

A drop-down menu with choices for magnification appears.

8. **Drag up and release the mouse on 12.5%.**

The viewing area zooms out revealing a large area of nonviewing area. The nonviewing area is a kind of artboard that will hold your graphic outside the viewing area (the small box in the middle). As you can see, the flowers.tif image is where you want it — on the far-right of the viewing area and without revealing the image underneath it (skip ahead to Figure 14-5).

9. **Click the current time (0:00:00:00) in the upper-left corner of the Time Layout window (refer back to Figure 14-4).**

The Go To Time selection box appears.

10. **Type 928.**

After Effects knows where to insert the colons.

11. **Click OK.**

After Effects delivers you to the end of the composition. Notice that a grooved diamond appears in the Time Layout window in the Position effect row (see Figure 14-5). This is After Effects' way of telling you that it's in the groove (in the first keyframe) and is waiting for your next position command so that it can set the second keyframe.

12. **Click the Position numbers again.**

13. **Type -350 in the X-axis text box.**

14. **Click OK.**

A second keyframe appears on the Position effect row — this time at the end of the composition, as shown in Figure 14-5.

15. **Press the spacebar on your keyboard to watch a rough preview of the horizontal movement.**

Notice that letters appear as the flowers.tif graphic moves through the viewing area.

16. **Click and hold down your mouse on the 12.5% button at the lower-left corner of the Program monitor and drag down to change the zoom back to 100%.**

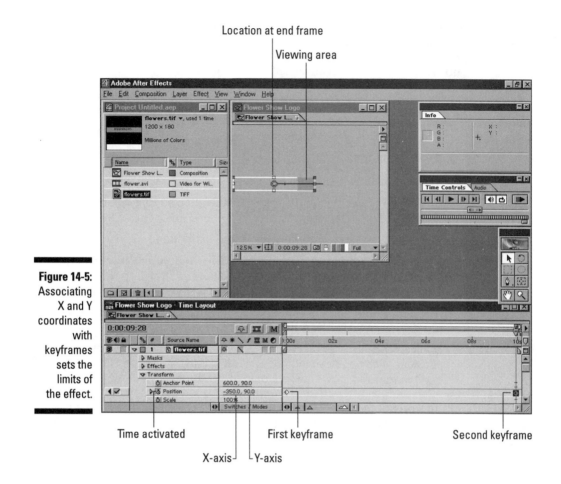

Figure 14-5:
Associating
X and Y
coordinates
with
keyframes
sets the
limits of
the effect.

This time, when you press the spacebar on your keyboard, you can see how the graphic moves through the viewing area. Don't worry about the speed of the movement. The speed has nothing to do with the speed of the movement of your animation.

Making a Transparency Effect

You're half way. You've set conditions on a layer — in this case movement of a graphic through the viewing area. Now you're going to add a third dimension to your project. You're going to define the relationship of the graphic to the other layer in the Time Layout window (see the earlier section "Creating a layer"). In this example, you cause the letters of the word to be transparent, creating the illusion that the letters are filled with moving flowers. The area outside the letters remains masked for the time being.

1. **Click the numbers in the upper-left corner of the Time Layout window.**

   The Go To Time selection box appears.

2. **Type** 500 **in the Go To Time text box.**

3. **Click OK.**

   You've moved to the middle of the composition so that you can see what is about to happen.

4. **Select Effect⇨Keying⇨Color Key in the main menu.**

   The Effects Controls window appears. The window may be partially hidden, so, if necessary, click in its heading and drag it to where it's clearly visible but not hiding the Program monitor.

   The letters were dark blue, but now that color has disappeared, revealing the image beneath (see Figure 14-6).

   What happened? When I created the flowers.tif graphic in Photoshop, the default *keying* (transparency) of After Effects was 100% blue, which is often referred to as "chroma blue." By entering into the Color Key effect, Adobe After Effects went looking for anything default blue and interpreted that filled area as transparent. Before leaving the Effects Control window, do a little fine tuning.

5. **Click 0 in the Edge Thin area.**

   The Slider Control window appears.

6. **Type a Value of** 1 **in the text box.**

7. **Click OK.**

8. **Click the 0 in the Edge Feather section.**

   The Slider Control window appears again.

9. **Type a Value of** 1.5 **in the text box.**

10. **Click OK.**

    Your effect looks beautiful.

11. **Close the Effect Controls window by clicking the X in its upper-right corner.**

12. **Press the spacebar on your computer to build and play the animation.**

    Way to go! Good looking, isn't it?

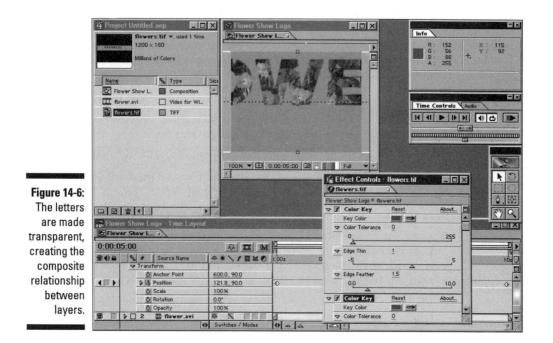

Figure 14-6:
The letters
are made
transparent,
creating the
composite
relationship
between
layers.

Because you are using the tryout version of Adobe After Effects 4.0, you are not able to save your work. But don't be bothered; remember that I showed you the finished product at the beginning of this chapter.

Using an Animation in Premiere

As a final step, I'd like to show you how you can schmooze an animation once you import it into Premiere.

1. **Exit Adobe After Effects and open Adobe Premiere.**

2. **Select File➪Import in the main menu.**

3. **Go to the Chapter 14 folder in the Clips folder on your hard drive and import the files announce.tif, flower logo.avi, and graduat.wav.**

4. **Drag announce.tif from the Program monitor to the Video 1A track in the Timeline window.**

5. **Right-click announce.tif in the Timeline window and select Duration. Change the duration to 10 seconds by typing 1000 in the text box.**

6. **Drag graduat.wav from the Program monitor to the Audio 1 track in the Timeline window.**

7. **Drag flower logo.avi from the Program monitor to the Video 2 track in the Timeline window.**

   You just created a transparency in Adobe After Effects. You're now going to create another one.

8. **Click the flower logo.avi clip to highlight it.**

9. **Select Clip⇨Video⇨Transparency (or press Ctrl+G) in the main menu.**

   The Transparency Settings dialog box appears. In this box, you will make logo.avi's blue background go bye-bye.

10. **In the Key type drop-down box, select Chroma.**

11. **Click within the blue in the Color box at the top of the dialog box; then click in various places in the blue Color box until the Sample window turns the graphic file into a blue tic tac toe image over the exposed background (see Figure 14-7).**

12. **Click and drag the preview slider at the bottom of the Sample window to see how your keyed image will look over the graphic.**

13. **Click OK.**

14. **Drag and stretch the blue work area slider to include the entire 10-second project.**

Figure 14-7:
The
Transparency
Settings box
enables you
to lay an
image on
top of
another
image and
to select a
transparent
color for
keying.

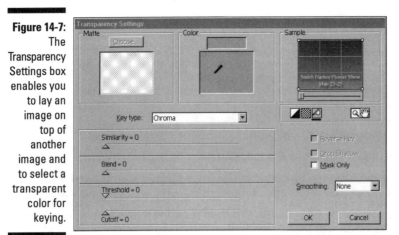

15. **Press Enter to preview the keying (transparency) effect you just created.**

   Your second key (transparency) exposes the still graphic in Premiere.

You just created an animated effect. Congratulations! If you're like me, you'll go bananas until you can get a full-fledged working version of Adobe After Effects 4.0.

Part V

Preparing Your Video for Sharing

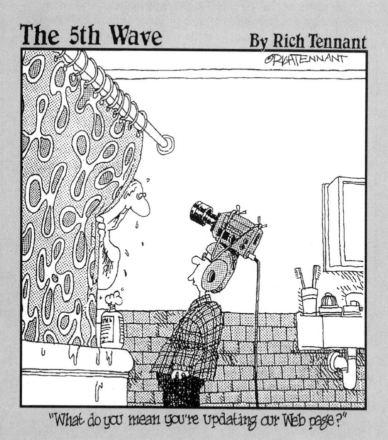

The 5th Wave   By Rich Tennant

ORICHTENNANT

"What do you mean you're updating our Web page?"

In this part . . .

I've got this friend who owns a complete digital video production system — digital video camcorder, computer, the works — and all he does is make digital video movies for his boss's PowerPoint presentations. My friend records videos, makes movies with his nonlinear editor, copies the movies to a CD, and puts the movies in PowerPoint presentations. His boss plays the presentations at seminars all over the country, using a laptop computer and an LCD projector — both of which he carries in a briefcase. So why am I telling you this? Because my friend is very successful doing unusual things with digital video. What unusual things would you like to do?

This part tells you some of the possibilities available with digital video. You find out how you can make amazingly high-quality VHS video. But that's only the tip of the electronic iceberg. You also learn about creating and exporting digital video to the World Wide Web, to tape, and to CDs. The discussions are quite candid. Some technology is still very young — perhaps too young to be taken seriously. Other technology is tried and true. I don't pull any punches. You get the straight story.

Chapter 15

Making Digital Video for the Web

*O*ne of the greatest love/hate relationships you'll have as a video producer is your relationship with the World Wide Web. Your tumultuous affair will be filled with glowing promises and shocking disappointments.

I love the World Wide Web. A large percentage of my workweek is spent productively scurrying about the Web's enormous wealth of information and services. But, then again, I hate the World Wide Web for all the things it ought to be able to do, hints that it does, and outright misleads you into thinking it has already perfected. Video on the Web is the epicenter of my love/hate relationships.

In this chapter, I show you some really neat video stuff you can realistically accomplish with the World Wide Web, while at the same time, I try to be candid and save you the frustration of attempting to do things that aren't yet possible. The day is quickly coming when video on the Web will be an extraordinary delivery medium. In the meantime, you want to make the most of what is currently possible. You may even have fun doing it.

Getting Ready for Video on the Web

Even in the best circumstances, video is very demanding on a computer. One of the most common compromises faced by video producers is selecting which information to sacrifice in order to make video work on a computer. Here are some of the normal challenges:

✔ **File size:** The most obvious problem is the size of video files. For example, a 9-minute, 30-second digital video file is 2GB (gigabytes). Therefore, a half-hour video of digital video quality is over 6GB! Your computer's hard drive is obviously never going to be used as a video warehouse.

✔ **Throughput:** Without the right hardware, you can't even play a full-motion video on a computer. You may recall all the computer system requirements discussed in this book in order to make digital video editing possible (see Chapters 8 and 9 about preparing a computer for digital video). A normal computer can't play a full-screen video.

✔ **Portability:** Say that you've edited your movie. It's a 20-minute masterpiece. Unfortunately, it's also the proverbial ship in a bottle. How do you get it out of your computer to give it to someone else?

Conveniently, answers exist to all these questions. Once you complete your editing, you can make movies that are much smaller, much less demanding in terms of throughput, and much easier to give to others. In this chapter, I show you how to prepare your video for sharing on the Internet. In Chapter 16, you work with video for multimedia CD-ROM. And in Chapter 17, I help you send your digital video to videotape.

This chapter describes features that are part of the normal operation of Adobe Premiere but are not available on the Adobe Premiere Tryout program that is on the CD at the back of this book, namely video capturing and file saving. If you want, this is a good time to purchase Adobe Premiere 5.1. Or you can still follow the discussion by referring to the figures throughout this chapter. Also, I describe features of an encoding program called RealProducer G2. RealProducer G2 is available from RealNetworks at www.real.com.

Preparing video for the Web requires some major compromises of video quality. But at least it can be done. This very day, you can make a movie for all the world to see on the World Wide Web. You basically have two ways to create such a video. One way is to make a normal AVI or QuickTime file. (An AVI file is the standard-type Windows-based movie file, and a QuickTime file is made to play on Macs and PCs with a special free player software program.) The other way is to encode a video file for on-demand playback.

AVI and QuickTime files

One way to put video on the Web is simply to store it there. By this, I mean you can make a movie in Adobe Premiere, upload the file to your Web site, and create a Web page that makes it possible to download the file to a computer. Or, even more simply, you can attach a video file to an e-mail letter. However, I don't put much stock in either of these ideas, so I won't waste your time with them. You probably would only try doing this once because a video file is *very* big (even when compressed). Most people find little or no pleasure sitting around for an hour waiting for a 10-second video to download. Instead, my suggestion is to create a RealVideo file, which I describe in just a moment.

Encoding on-demand video

The most effective way to put video on the World Wide Web is through encoding. *Encoding* is a process that does two things: Encoding compresses your video or audio file to a size small enough to play over the Internet, and encoding makes it possible for you to begin playing the video or audio file as it downloads rather than after it downloads. This encoding technology has come a long way in a short time. As I suggested at the beginning of the chapter, I am impatient with its quality over standard telephone lines and with current consumer modems, but I'm excited about the advances that are taking place to rectify the difficulties.

Working with the least common denominator

One of the most important decisions you'll make about your video for the Web is, unfortunately, also the toughest. You need to decide who will and who will not be able to watch your video. This is a crazy kind of censorship based on the size of modems and the age of processors. Here are some basic considerations:

✔ Many Internet users will not be able to watch your video, no matter what you do. In order to view any video on the Internet, computer owners need to have up-to-date Internet browsers such as Microsoft Explorer 4.0 or Netscape Communicator 4.0 and multimedia capabilities in their operating systems, including at least a 28.8 Kbps modem.

✔ Assuming your potential viewer has an up-to-date browser and operating system, the onus now falls on you. If you want just about anyone to be able to watch your video, you need to size and encode your video for working on a 28 Kbps modem. If you think your intended viewers are all more up to date, you can configure your video or audio to work within the limits of a 56 Kbps modem.

✔ Also, do your viewers want mono or stereo sound? This isn't a critical issue on the surface. But your decision can directly affect the size of your encoded video file.

It's time to make some video for the Web. In doing so, you'll get a feel for the strengths and weaknesses of this medium at this stage of its development. First, you export a file from Premiere.

Choosing a codec and configuration

If you've been following along in this book from chapter to chapter, you've already worked within Premiere, creating all kinds of exciting effects and transitions. In this and the next two chapters, you explore the exporting functions of Premiere.

If you haven't already installed Premiere and the sample files in the CLIPS folder from the CD at the back of this book, you need to do so before continuing. Turn to Appendix B for steps on doing both tasks. Turn to Chapter 10 for information on opening and using Premiere.

With Premiere running and the sample files on your hard drive, just do the following:

1. **In Premiere, select File⇨Import⇨File or press Ctrl+I to open the Import dialog box.**

2. **Open the Chapter 15 folder you copied from the CD-ROM, click the file 1copy.avi, and holding down the Shift key, click skiman.avi.; then click Open to import the files into the Project window in Premiere.**

3. **Drag the file skiman.avi on to the Video 1A track in the Timeline window.**

   See Chapter 10 for a full discussion on the Project and Timeline windows.

Now the video file rests on the Timeline. Before you do anything with the file, you need to find out about its properties.

1. **Right-click anywhere on the skiman.avi file on the Timeline.**

   A drop-down box appears.

2. **Click Get Properties.**

   The Properties for skiman.avi window appears (see Figure 15-1).

The properties window displays a bunch of fun and exciting information about the clip. It's over 4MB (can anyone say "diet"?!), and it's 6 seconds in duration. The average data rate is about 700K (kilobytes) per second, its image size is 240 x 180 pixels, and so on. Though all of this information relates to playback on the Internet, the most important detail is the data rate. A normal modem is able to communicate 28.8K of information per second. 700K just won't cut it. You've got some work to do, so. . . .

1. **Close the Properties window by clicking the X in the upper-right corner of the window.**

2. **Drag the work area to equal the length of the skiman.avi clip.**

Figure 15-1:
The data rate of a video clip needs to be small enough to stay within a 28 Kbps or 56 Kbps modem limit.

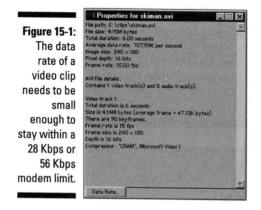

The work area slider is the blue bar at the top of the Timeline window. Click and drag the right end of the slider until it equals the length of skiman.avi.

Using the tryout version of Premiere (Premiere 5.0), you will not be able to perform the rest of the steps in this section. I suggest, however, that you follow these few steps to get an idea about how you can drastically reduce the size of the skiman.avi file. Don't worry too much that you can't export the skiman.avi file. I made a copy of it for you. It's over there in the Project window, and it's called 1copy.avi. You can open it after reading this section, or you can skip over there now if you like.

3. **From the main menu bar, select File⇨Export⇨Movie or press Ctrl+M.**

The Export Movie dialog box appears.

4. **Click the Settings button in the lower-right corner.**

The Export Movie Settings dialog box appears. This dialog box is almost identical to the Project Settings dialog box you find out about in Chapter 10. But the Export Movie Settings dialog box controls the configuration of your movie.

5. **Click the Next button.**

The Video Settings dialog box appears.

6. **To change the Frame Size, type** 80 **in the horizontal (h) text box and** 60 **in the vertical (v) text box.**

7. **To change the Frame Rate, type** 6 **in the Frame Rate text box.**

   The dialog box should look like the one in Figure 15-2.

8. **Click OK to accept your changes.**

   You're back at the Export Movie dialog box.

9. **Type the number** 1 **or some other more interesting name in the File Name text box.**

10. **Click Save.**

    Premiere compresses the movie clip.

11. **Play the new clip.**

    Or if you were unable to perform the export function because you're using the Adobe Premiere 5.0 Tryout version, double-click 1copy.avi in the Project window. The clip loads into the Source monitor (see Chapter 10 for info on using the Source monitor). You can now play the clip.

    As you can see, the file size and data rate are much smaller.

I know what you're thinking. This isn't a movie; it's a postage stamp with a twitch. Please don't shoot the piano player. Or, in this case, the postman. You can make a larger movie if you want. I'm using this as a safe example. At 6 frames per second, the video is 36 frames long. I'd rather you have a success with something very small as your first Web-based video instead of starting bigger and risk disappointment.

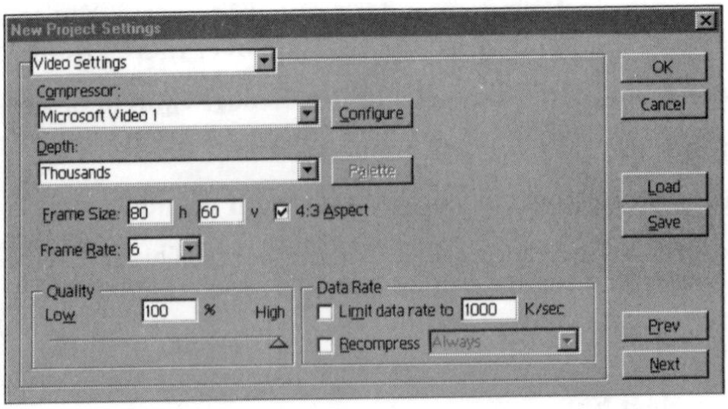

Figure 15-2: Changing size and frame rate drastically reduces size and throughput.

Right-click the movie clip to access the properties for this movie file. As you can see, this little critter has an average data rate of a little more than 32K (see Figure 15-3), which is definitely much smaller than it was before. And compression in the encoding process will also help.

You're finished with Premiere, so you can exit the program by selecting File⇨Exit or pressing Ctrl+Q.

You're probably getting the point by now. Video on the Web is in its infancy chronologically and developmentally.

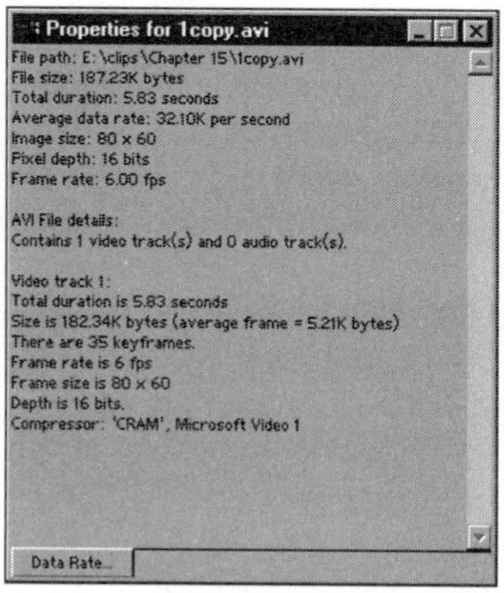

Figure 15-3:
The video is
sized down
considerably
to increase
its likeli-
hood of
successfully
playing on
the Internet.

Properties for 1copy.avi
File path: E:\clips\Chapter 15\1copy.avi
File size: 187.23K bytes
Total duration: 5.83 seconds
Average data rate: 32.10K per second
Image size: 80 x 60
Pixel depth: 16 bits
Frame rate: 6.00 fps

AVI File details:
Contains 1 video track(s) and 0 audio track(s).

Video track 1:
Total duration is 5.83 seconds
Size is 182.34K bytes (average frame = 5.21K bytes)
There are 35 keyframes.
Frame rate is 6 fps
Frame size is 80 x 60
Depth is 16 bits.
Compressor: 'CRAM', Microsoft Video 1

Data Rate...

Putting Your Movie on the Web

This book doesn't delve into all the important stuff you need to know to create a Web site. When it comes to creating Web pages, I recommend *FrontPage 2000 For Dummies* by Asha Dornfest.

But if you'd like to see right now how the 1copy.rm file works on the World Wide Web, open your browser and go to www.digitalproduct.com. When you get there, select Samples. When you get to the Samples page, select Video On Demand. On this page, you can find a sample of the 1copy.rm file and three more files, each slightly larger. Observe your computer's ability to properly play each of the files.

Encoding the movie for streaming

Now, I propose a little side trip. I want to show you how you can use RealProducer G2 (by RealNetworks) to encode the 1copy.avi file for playing on the Internet. You can purchase your own copy of RealProducer G2 online at www.real.com.

1. **If you have RealProducer G2, click the Windows Start button and select Programs⇨ Real⇨RealProducer G2 to open RealProducer G2.**

   The RealProducer G2 program opens (see the figure in this sidebar).

2. **Fill out the information boxes in the window.**

   Under Clip Information, type 1copy.rm (RealNetwork files use the file extension .rm)

and then fill out the rest of the boxes in this area. Under Target Audience, select 28K modem, under Audio Format select No Audio, and under Video Quality select Normal Motion Video.

3. **Click Start to encode the file.**

   The encoding takes only a moment.

That's all it takes to create a file that can be played on the World Wide Web. I've included the 1copy.rm file in your Chapter 15 folder. If you have installed RealPlayer on your computer, you can play the file from your hard drive. Simply open RealPlayer and select File⇨Open. Find and open the Chapter 15 folder in the Clips folder on your hard drive. Open 1copy.rm, and RealPlayer plays the file for you automatically.

Target audience

Filename   Audio info   Video quality

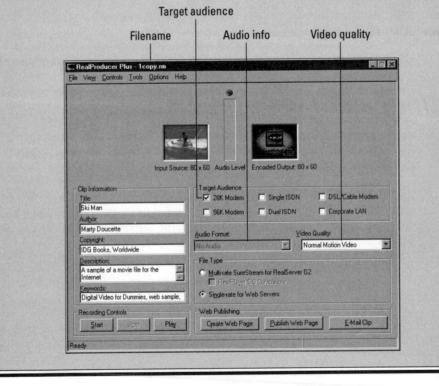

Chapter 16

Using Digital Video in Multimedia

*O*ne of the most challenging parts of making a video on a computer is creating a foolproof way to successfully play it on someone else's computer. In this chapter, I tell you about some of the limitations you face and some of the ways you can successfully work within those limitations.

Most often, when people make video for playing on computers, they are making the video to play within a multimedia authoring program such as Microsoft PowerPoint or Macromedia Director. Multimedia relates to video, audio, and graphics and so is about using sights and sounds for your message.

A multimedia authoring program controls the circumstances for using the sights and sounds. Here is a very simple example. Wearing your video producer's hat, you create a video in Adobe Premiere. Then wearing your multimedia author's hat, you use PowerPoint to make a button on the screen. If someone presses the button, PowerPoint begins playing your video within PowerPoint.

In this example, you created (exported) what Adobe Premiere calls a "movie" and made the movie so that it can be played by other computer programs, such as a multimedia authoring program. Because of their sheer size and memory requirements, multimedia files used within multimedia programs are often stored on CD-ROM.

Earlier in this book, I show you how you can create nonlinear editing projects by using Adobe Premiere. In this chapter, you find out how to make those projects into movies by exporting them from Premiere for use on CD-ROM. Exporting is one of the easiest steps in digital video production; unfortunately, that's a little like saying jumping out of an airplane is easy. Sure it is, but leaving the plane is only the beginning of the story. Likewise, once you export a movie, getting it to properly deploy can be tough — sometimes *very* tough.

Why? Anyone who has owned a computer even a little while knows that things can easily get crazy. Software programs don't always like each other. This probably isn't a revelation to you but something made in one computer program won't always automatically work as intended in another computer program. When you export a file from Premiere, you naturally hope that it will be able to play on another computer and in another computer program, such as PowerPoint. The good news is that it probably can. But the possibility of problems always exists. This chapter helps you successfully export movies that work on other people's computers. One of the difficulties you may face is related to that funny little coffee cup holder affectionately referred to as your CD-ROM drive.

Exporting Movies via CD-ROM

When you export a movie from Adobe Premiere for someone else's use, you're giving them one humongous file. As I mentioned earlier, for that reason, the usual mode of multimedia file transport is via CD-ROM. As a multimedia author, you use a CD recorder to record on (burn) disks. A recordable disk is called a CD-R (Compact Disk–Recordable). When you record (burn) the disk, you make the disk playable on CD-ROM (Compact Disk–Read Only Memory) drives. The disk at the back of this book is a CD disk made to play in your CD-ROM drive. These days, CD recorders are inexpensive and durable. As a result you can easily share files as large as 500MB and more.

Quite often, people use recordable drives such as Zip drives for transferring large files. This is a very good way to transfer files, but Zip drives aren't on every computer. CD-ROM drives are standard on almost every computer.

Living with the limitations

CD-ROM is great for trading large files, but it can have its limitations during playback. For one thing, many older CD-ROM drives are still in use. These drives are slow and unable to handle much information at one time. But even the newer drives don't play back at the same speed that hard drives do. So, although you can create a movie that plays well on a computer's hard drive, you may find that it plays poorly or not at all on a CD-ROM drive.

Finding the right balance

The speed of a CD-ROM drive is not the only challenge to good playback of a movie file. By its very nature, multimedia tends to max out a computer. The speed of a computer's processor(s), the amount of RAM, and the kinds of peripheral hardware and their connections can individually and collectively impact multimedia playback.

When exporting a video file, you need to understand a little bit about what other computers can bear, such as their storage and data rate capacities. You can easily be too liberal and create a big, beautiful video file that is simply too much for most computers to handle. Or you can be too conservative and create a limited version that is unnecessarily ugly. Your challenge is to compromise and to create a good-looking movie that plays well on numerous other computers.

Although multimedia isn't about storage and data rates — it's about adding sight and sound to a presentation — you must be aware of those issues when exporting movies from Premiere. During export, you have to do some file tweaking — such as changing resolution and compression — to increase the chances of successful playback on as many computers as possible. Your decisions during the exporting process can have a long-lasting impact on the playback limitations of your digital video files.

As does Chapter 15, this chapter describes features that are part of the normal operation of Adobe Premiere but that are not available on the Adobe Premiere Tryout version that is on the CD at the back of this book, namely video capturing and file saving. However, you can still follow the discussion by referring to the figures throughout this chapter.

Choosing your compression

Selecting your file compression isn't all that hard. You simply have to predict the operating system(s) your movie will be played on and whether the movie will be played back from a CD-ROM or a hard drive. Here's how you can compress a movie:

> For the sake of example (and vainly assuming that you have cheerfully read and worked through at least one chapter from among Chapters 10 through 14), you can now import any video file from one of the chapter folders you copied from the CD-ROM to your hard drive.

1. **Open Premiere.**

   If you haven't already downloaded Premiere 5.0 from the CD at the back of this book, please see Appendix B for steps on doing so. Turn to Chapter 10 for information on opening and using Premiere.

   If you need to, you can turn to Chapter 10 and Appendix B for information about copying the chapter folders to your hard drive.

2. **Import the file of your choice by pressing Ctrl-I and then selecting the file of your choice from its chapter folder.**

3. **Click OK.**

   The file loads into the Project window in Premiere.

   See Chapter 10 for information on the Project window, as well as the Timeline window mentioned in the next step.

4. **Drag the video or graphic file from the Project window to the Video 1A track in the Timeline window.**

5. **Click anywhere within the Timeline window to activate it.**

   You must activate the Timeline window in order to export (save) a file.

   As I mentioned earlier in this chapter, the Adobe Premiere 5.0 Tryout program that's on the CD at the back of this book doesn't allow you to save files. However, you can still follow this discussion by referring to the figures in this chapter.

6. **To begin exporting, select File➪Export➪Movie in the main menu bar.**

   The Export Movie dialog box appears.

7. **Select Settings.**

   The Export Movie Settings dialog box appears.

8. **Click the down arrow to the right of File Type.**

   A dialog box appears showing the kinds of export options available (see Figure 16-1). For now, focus on just two file types — Microsoft AVI and QuickTime.

9. **Leave the File Type set as the default Microsoft AVI.**

   Before leaving the dialog box, notice the other file types. Microsoft AVI and QuickTime are generic types of movie files. The others are for specialized uses. For example, Animated GIF is a file type specifically for use with the Internet.

Figure 16-1:
Microsoft
AVI is the
most
commonly
used file
type for
exporting
and playing
movies on
Windows-
based
computers.

Export Movie Settings

General Settings

File Type: Microsoft AVI   Advanced Settings

Range:
  Microsoft AVI
  TIFF Sequence
  Targa Sequence   ☑ Open When Finished
  QuickTime
  GIF Sequence
Current Se Animated GIF
  Filmstrip
Video Set Flc/Fli
Compress Windows Bitmap Sequence
Frame Size
Depth: Thousands, Quality: 100%

Audio Settings

OK
Cancel
Load
Save
Prev
Next

Making a multimedia presentation

Adobe Premiere is popular among multimedia authors as a movie-making tool for their multimedia applications. The most widely used multimedia authoring program is Microsoft PowerPoint. PowerPoint enables you to easily insert a video file right into a PowerPoint page. If you have PowerPoint installed on your computer and want to make a slide show containing a movie, open the program and select Insert⇨Movies and Sounds⇨Movie from File. If you want, you can select one of the movies that comes on the CD at the back of this book.

By selecting Insert⇨Movies and Sounds⇨Movie from File and then selecting the movie, you place the video file in the slide show. The inserted video starts when you click it during a PowerPoint slide show.

If you are a little adventuresome and would like to find out about a full-blown professional multimedia authoring program, check out www.macromedia.com. There you'll be able to read and try out a number of very good authoring programs.

Microsoft AVI and QuickTime

For most multimedia uses, you normally would choose one of two types of export — Microsoft AVI and QuickTime.

- ✔ **Microsoft AVI:** AVI is short for Audio-Video Interleaved. AVI is a file extension, such as in movie.avi. Microsoft Windows contains a multimedia program called the Media Player. You can see the Media Player by clicking the Windows Start button and selecting Programs⇨ Accessories⇨Multimedia⇨Media Player. Media Player recognizes and plays movies with AVI extensions.

- ✔ **QuickTime:** QuickTime is also a media player. Created by Apple, QuickTime files play on Mac, Windows, and UNIX platforms that are equipped with the QuickTime software. QuickTime movies are designated with the .mov extension, such as in movie.mov.

Selecting the right codec

A successfully exported video file is one that works as intended for someone else. To accomplish this feat, you have to save the file in a digital fashion that can be recognized on another computer and probably in a software program other than Premiere.

To ensure that you don't overwhelm the capacity of other computers, you must compress the file, and in doing so, you must use a method that other computers can recognize and decompress.

As I mention in Chapter 15, *codec* is the shorthand term for compression and decompression. So when you export a video file, you have to select a codec that will work on other people's computers, which you do as follows:

1. **From the main menu bar, select File⇨Export⇨Movie or press Ctrl+M.**

   The Export Movie dialog box appears.

2. **Click Settings.**

   The Export Movie Settings dialog box appears.

3. **With the File Type Microsoft AVI selected, click the Next button.**

   You're now in the Video Settings dialog box.

4. **Click the down arrow beside the Compressor selection box.**

   A selection of codecs for AVI files appears. The selection list differs somewhat from one computer to the next; Premiere loads in codecs to this list, but other software programs do, too. For example, the software that comes bundled with a capture card will usually load in a proprietary codec for capture and export of video with that card.

5. **Click Cinepak Codec by Radius.**

   Cinepak (available in Microsoft AVI and QuickTime versions) is a dependable codec for movies on CD-ROM. Cinepak works well for high compression and fast decompression. These two characteristics greatly enhance a CD-ROM's capability of keeping up with the file during playback. By "keeping up," I mean that you see and hear every frame of video correctly.

If you intend to distribute movie files on CD-ROM for copying and playback on a hard drive, Cinepak may be overkill. The default Microsoft Video 1 codec should work fine for playing a movie from a hard drive.

Setting the right levels

Part of your work of video production is experimentation. I don't know anyone who works with multimedia CD-ROM who hasn't spent many hours experimenting, trying to get the ratios of compression and quality properly balanced. The relationship of frame size and frame rate is one of those areas of experimentation.

Framing your multimedia file

Generally, most multimedia authors keep frame size within the 320 x 240 range. On a video screen with 640 x 480 resolution, 320 x 240 is a quarter of the screen size. A smaller resolution has a much smaller data rate.

And usually, frame rate works best at 15 frames per second or less. A computer works half as hard playing 15 frames in a second than it does playing 30 frames in a second (standard video frame rate).

If you know the computer power of everyone who will see your video, you may be able to select a larger frame size and a faster frame rate. If you don't, my generalizations are definitely your outer limits.

Dialing the right data rate

The Cinepak codec allows you to adjust data rate. *Data rate* is the amount of video information that is processed during each second of playback. In the world of CD-ROM, data rate is directly related to the age of the drive. Older drives are as slow as 2X (double-speed). Newer CD-ROM drives are many times faster.

As a general rule, if you don't know who will be playing your movie, be conservative. A double-speed CD-ROM drive can handle a data rate up to 200K (kilobytes) per second.

After you select your file type, such as Microsoft AVI, and when you choose your codec, frame size, frame rate, and data rate, you're ready to export the movie. Click OK to return to the Export Movie dialog box. Type your movie's name in the File Name text box and click Save. Premiere begins exporting your movie file.

When Premiere finishes the export process, a clip window appears in Premiere, allowing you to play your exported movie. Your movie is now ready to be incorporated into a multimedia application and burned onto a CD-R (recordable disk).

Chapter 17

Outputting Digital Video to Tape

- -

In This Chapter

▶ Preparing your movie for export to tape

▶ Controlling your tape recorder

▶ Recording the movie

▶ When you want to make dubs

- -

*I*f you've put a lot of effort into creating a video project, you'll find the procedure for exporting to tape simple and satisfying — simple in procedure, satisfying in quality of outcome. I have to admit that I'm occasionally tempted to laugh out loud at how easy, powerful, and beautiful nonlinear editing has become. Exporting to video is the capstone.

In Chapter 9, I describe capture cards and their software. In that chapter, I explain the important handshake that occurs between the capture card and the nonlinear editing software program. And I illustrate the communication link between the capture card and the MiniDV camcorder. If these terms are a little fuzzy to you, I highly recommend that you read Chapter 9 before you tackle this chapter.

This chapter has a bookend relationship with Chapter 9. Instead of bringing video in from the camcorder, the capture card and software are sending video out to the camcorder. And, just as in Chapter 9, your nonlinear editing software plays a major role.

As I mention in Chapter 9, capture and playback of digital video require a capture card. For that reason, I can't give you hands-on capture and playback experience in this book. In this chapter, I show you some of the important things you need to know in order to understand how to export video to MiniDV and VHS tape.

So, with my apologies, prepare to look over my shoulder for the next few pages. I'm hunching my shoulders to give you a better view. For sake of illustration, I'm using the Pinnacle DV300 capture card and software in this book.

Setting the Presets

I installed Adobe Premiere 5.1 before installing the capture card and the capture software. Because I followed the proper order of installation, the DV300 software setup included adding plug-ins into Adobe Premiere 5.1.

You start seeing the evidence of the Pinnacle plug-ins from the moment you open Premiere. As usual, Premiere opens with the New Project Settings dialog box with the General Settings option already selected (see Figure 17-1).

By clicking the down arrow to the right of Editing Mode, you see that the drop-down list includes miroINSTANT Video. By selecting this option and clicking OK, you activate the Pinnacle plug-ins within Premiere. The plug-ins cause the miroINSTANT Video software to activate a connection between your computer and video monitor via your capture card. From this time forward, anything in your Premiere program monitor will also be on your video monitor.

Figure 17-1:
Thanks to the Pinnacle DV300 software, you can access the miroINSTANT Video Editing Mode plug-in with just a click of the mouse in the New Project Settings dialog box.

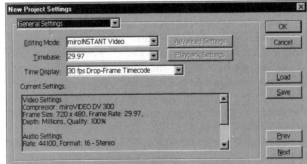

Pinnacle provides a commanding presence in Adobe Premiere — for a good reason. When you run Adobe Premiere with the DV300 plug-ins installed, your computer becomes an integrated nonlinear editing system. Not only are you within Premiere, you also activate the DV300 software and capture card, and you send a signal through the IEEE 1394 cable to your camcorder and the attached monitor. Whew! All this happened simply by opening Premiere and using the miroINSTANT Video editing mode. Figure 17-2 shows how a project might look with the miroINSTANT Video Editing Mode activated.

Figure 17-2: By selecting the miroINSTANT Video editing mode, you dedicate Adobe Premiere to operate as a MiniDV non-linear editor.

Why is the miroINSTANT Video editing mode so significant? Actually, for two reasons — playback and transitions. The miroINSTANT Video editing mode plays back your video using the DV300 capture card. You can use the monitor connected to your camcorder to watch full-screen playback. Also, when previewing a rendered project on the Timeline, the playback of transitions and effects is smooth, without interruption. Basically, you're a full-fledged editor capable of watching and recording transitions in real time. Awesome!

Exporting to MiniDV Tape

When you complete your project and are ready to export it to videotape, the miroINSTANT Video editing mode provides another important function — handling of the camcorder controls during recording. To make a videotape version of your project, select File⇨Export⇨Export to Tape. An Export to Tape dialog box appears (see Figure 17-3).

In the Export Options area, check Activate Recording Deck. That's all you have to do. The miroINSTANT Video plug-in flawlessly exports your project to your MiniDV tape.

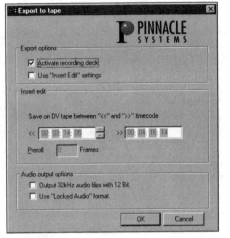

Figure 17-3:
The Export
to Tape
dialog box
permits
miroINSTANT
Video to
control your
camcorder
during
recording.

Using the same Export to Tape procedure, you can simultaneously make a VHS or S-VHS version of your video. Just connect the VHS or S-VHS outputs of the DV300 capture card to the inputs of a VHS or S-VHS recorder. You can then connect your monitor to the recorder. That way the video plays through your recorder to your monitor. To record, press the Record button on your VCR.

Part VI
Making Cool Stuff with Digital Video

The 5th Wave   By Rich Tennant

"...and here's yet another photo of Marsha and I ruining a perfectly good shot of the back of Uncle Leo's head."

In this part . . .

Υou wanna make a home movie. But you're kinda
embarrassed because that's all you want to do? No
problem. This part has lots of stuff just for you.

In fact, this part has lots of stuff for lots of people —
how-to stuff about shooting and editing digital video
home movies, weddings, and special 3-D photo galleries.

You get a double reward in this part: You have fun working
your way through it, *and* when you put your new knowledge to use, folks will be asking for more of whatever it is
you produce.

Chapter 18

Putting 2-D Photos into 3-D Space

• •

In This Chapter

▶ Making something marvelous of the mundane

▶ Building layers for a special effect

▶ Creating an illusion of 3-D

▶ Putting together the pieces in Premiere

• •

*I*n this chapter, you find out about converting simple photographs into an exciting 3-D gallery. Plain old photo albums are great. But once in awhile, you may want to create a special presentation of your vacation or construct a presentation for your high school reunion. A digital video 3-D gallery adds a special flair and a touch of professionalism to your photos.

I don't give you detailed step-by-step procedures in this chapter because here the focus is on using creative thinking in nonlinear editing. But if you want to get into the how to's, please check out some of the earlier chapters in this book. In the various sections in this chapter, I discuss working with Adobe Premiere and Adobe Photoshop. For information on downloading tryout versions of these two programs from the CD at the back of this book, see Appendix B. For information on opening and using the two programs, please see Chapter 10 (Premiere) and Chapter 13 (Photoshop). For information about adding background music, please refer to Chapter 11.

Looking at a Sample 3-D Gallery

The 3-D gallery illustrated in this chapter is only an example of what you can do. It incorporates a number of easy procedures that you can use to create altogether different ideas, which is the whole idea behind this chapter.

You also need to download the Chapter 18 sample files from the CD-ROM. These sample files are stored on the CD-ROM at the back of this book in a sub-folder named CHAP18, which is located in a folder named CLIPS. See Appendix B for information on copying the files to your hard drive. See Chapter 10 for steps on locating and opening the files once they are on your hard drive.

Selecting images for your video gallery

When you make a video gallery, you need to carefully choose what you want to show. Video isn't like a photo album where you can jump from one picture to the next. Video is linear; you have to watch one image to get to the next.

When making your choices, try to determine what will be important to your viewer. Then prioritize your selections based on their relative importance to the overall theme. Consider whether information is more important than aesthetics. The important thing is to determine a basis for your choices; then stick with your logic. But remember, you are selecting images for your viewer, not for yourself.

When you complete this chapter, you can delete these sample files from your hard drive to save space.

In the Chapter 18 folder, you will find the clip that you work with in the following steps. So, to look at a finished 3-D gallery, just march this way.

1. **Open Premiere.**

2. **Click File⇨Open or press Ctrl+O.**

   The Open dialog box appears.

3. **Find your Chapter 18 folder on your hard drive and open the clip vacation.avi.**

   The clip loads into the Source monitor.

   See Chapters 10 and 11 for information on using the Source monitor.

4. **Press your spacebar to play the clip.**

As you play and replay the clip, notice that the following things happen in this order:

1. **The video opens with music and a picture of a beach and pier.**

2. **A girl appears.**

3. **A photograph zooms to the middle of the screen.**

4. **The photograph moves to the left.**

   Amazingly, the photo passes between the pier pilings and the girl. This effect is a multilayered 3-D one that I show you how to perform in this chapter.

5. **As soon as the photo disappears to the left, a new photo begins to appear and enlarge in the middle of the pier.**

6. **The procedure repeats two more times.**

7. The girl and music fade away, leaving the picture of the beach and pier.

This simple but visually compelling little project took about two hours to make. At that point, I could have quickly added a large number of additional photos. Let me show you how you can make a similar gallery with your own photos.

By the way, I created the movie clip you just watched in Adobe Photoshop 5.0 and Adobe Premiere 5.1. I could have created the sequences using Adobe After Effects 4.0. But, for the sake of simplicity, I used only Photoshop and Premiere. Because you are most likely using the tryout versions of Photoshop and Premiere, in places where you can't save or export files, I've provided you with sample files.

Developing an Idea

When working creatively, you can begin a number of ways. Most often, for me, creative work starts with a responsibility. I am supposed to make something that people will like. Fortunately, I enjoy the responsibility. In the example in this section, I was asked to create an interesting presentation of a family's vacation photos.

First, I developed an idea. I looked through the photos for a thread that connected the photos to establish a theme. The vacation photos had the "connections" of family time, sun, and proximity to water.

After some mulling, I noticed a connection between two photos — one taken underneath a pier, the other of young woman, back to camera, staring out at the surf (see Figure 18-1). BOING! I had an idea. I would make a gallery of photos emerging from the center of the pier structure. The girl would appear to be looking at the photos. I would layer her image onto the pier image in such a way that the photos could pass between her and the pier structure. The effect would be three-dimensional. It sounded like fun, so I decided to do it.

Figure 18-1: An idea begins with a unifying thread.

Capturing Photos to Video

After you develop the idea, you begin selecting the images to capture into your computer. The thing to remember about capturing is that high-quality images take up lots of space in a computer. And, just as important, capturing images can take lots of time, which is why you need to distill your selection based on your idea. Then, once you have a workable number of images, you can begin capturing.

In Chapter 9, I show you how to capture video into your computer. Here are some ways you can capture photos:

- **Digital photo:** The first and most obvious way is by using a digital still camera or a digital video camcorder with a photo mode. A digital still photo is easily converted to a computer graphic file with the software that comes with the camera.

- **Scanned snap shots:** You can make a digital still with a scanner. Simply scan a photo, and your scanner converts the image to a computer graphic file.

- **Photo board:** The oldest and least expensive method of capturing photos is by videotaping them. To do so, place a photo flatly on any surface (preferably not a white surface because white messes up the camcorder's aperture setting). Record the photo(s) and then use your computer's video capture board to create a computer graphic file.

Resizing the Images

In this section, you use Photoshop to prepare images for the 3-D gallery. You can follow along using Photoshop if you like. Or you can skip using Photoshop and simply read my suggestions. It's up to you. If you want to use Photoshop, open the files vacate01.tif through vacate06.tif in your Chapter 18 folder.

After you capture the images, you can take them into Adobe Photoshop to resize and crop as needed. (Figure 18-2 shows the group of photos you will work with.) See Chapter 13 for more on resizing images.

You need to resize the images to conform them to the screen size of video. In my example, I want to resize images to fit within a 320 pixel by 240 pixel image area because 320 x 240 is the 4:3 aspect ratio that's consistent with a television screen. See Chapter 10 for more on aspect ratio.

Many of the images in Figure 18-2 don't have a 4:3 aspect ratio. So I place all the images over a single background of the correct aspect ratio (the pier image).

Figure 18-2:
Photos are often taken both vertically and horizontally. Horizontal pictures more closely match video aspect ratio.

Here is the basic rule for resizing images with aspect ratios other than 4:3: Make their longest dimension fit within the acceptable limit. A tall image's longest dimension is its height. The height needs to be changed to 240 pixels. When you use Photoshop's image size function, make sure the Constrain Proportions box is checked before you modify pixel size.

With all the images resized, it's time to do some magic. It's time to put the girl's image into the pier image.

Creating Special Effects

The term *special effects* can mean a lot of things. Basically though, a special effect is a manipulation of a graphic, a video clip, or a portion of sound in some unusual, noticeable fashion. In this section, I show you how to begin making a special effect with Adobe Photoshop.

The Adobe Photoshop toolbox has some hidden tools. (See Chapter 13 for information about the toolbox and its inhabitants.) One of them is the Magnetic Lasso tool. This tool resides behind the Lasso tool (second row, left column) Using the Magnetic Lasso tool, you can highlight the girl's shape (see Figure 18-3). Once you highlight the figure, you are ready to copy it (see Chapter 13 for more on copying).

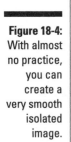

Figure 18-3:
The
Magnetic
Lasso tool is
attracted to
the edges of
a shape.

After you copy an image, select File⇨New or press Ctrl+N to create a new window. The new window equals the size of the object in the Clipboard. You'll need to create the window with a transparent background. Then paste the image into the new window. The image is now isolated (see the result in Figure 18-4). You are ready to layer the image.

Figure 18-4:
With almost
no practice,
you can
create a
very smooth
isolated
image.

Working with Layers

Layering is Photoshop's way of placing numerous images on top of each other in a graphic while maintaining individual control of each image. I discuss layering in Chapter 13. In creating the 3-D photo gallery, you lay each image on its own layer (see Figure 18-5).

If you were to lay photos on top of each other on a table, the top-most layer is the one that's visible. You have to remove a photo to see the next one in the pile. Adobe Photoshop layers work in somewhat the same manner. Except, rather than removing images, you simply make them invisible. In Chapter 13, I tell you how you can make layers visible or invisible. Take a look at the eyeball(s) in the Layers palette (refer to Figure 18-2). If an eyeball is visible for a layer, the layer is visible. If the eyeball is not visible, the layer is not visible. You can toggle the eyeballs on and off by clicking in the Layers palette.

Also, you can see through part of a layer to a layer or layers below. You accomplish this effect with transparency. You lay an image on a layer and leave everything other than the image transparent. In Chapter 13, I show you how you can make portions of an image transparent.

Figure 18-5:
Each image
is on its own
layer. For
convenience,
you can give
layers
unique
names.

The Power of Superimposition

Believe it or not, you now have everything you need to create the 3-D photo gallery file. If you were using the full version of Photoshop 5.0 (as opposed to the tryout version that's on the CD at the back of this book), you could save the image as a Photoshop file (Photoshop files use the .psd extension). But, just to be helpful, I created a copy of the gallery for you and named the file gallery.psd.

You can now close Photoshop and open Premiere. Once in Premiere, import gallery.psd from the Chapter 18 folder to the Premiere Project window (see Chapter 10 for steps on importing files into Premiere). The Layer Selection dialog box automatically appears (see Figure 18-6) because you are importing a Photoshop (.psd) file. The Layer Selection dialog box asks you to select how you want to import the file (as merged or individual layers). Select Background layer to begin the import process. You are selecting the bottom layer and building the image, layer by layer in Premiere.

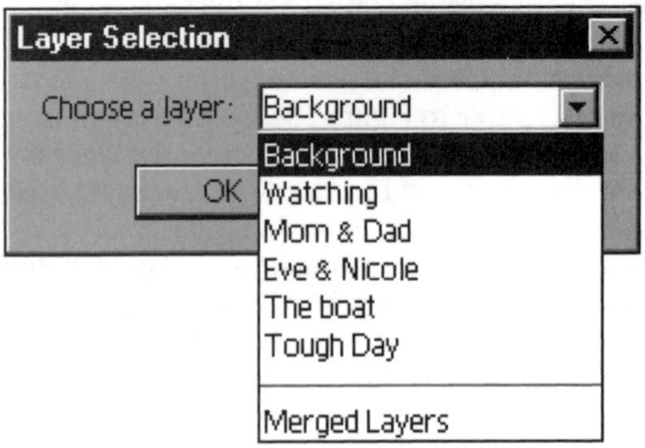

Figure 18-6:
The layers of a Photoshop file are individually or corporately available for use in Premiere.

Layer Selection

Choose a layer: Background

Background
Watching
OK Mom & Dad
Eve & Nicole
The boat
Tough Day

Merged Layers

In this section, you can follow along using the Premiere 5.0 Tryout version if you like. Or you can skip using Premiere and simply read my suggestions. If you want to use Premiere, set your project frame size to 320 x 240. I show you how to set frame size in Chapter 10.

Because you use more than one layer from the file, rename the images as you import them into the Project window. For example, you can click the name of the first image and change it from gallery.psd to Background. As you import the other layers, continue naming each image. For example, I named the Watching Photoshop layer the same name when I imported it into Premiere. This way you won't confuse one layer from the other. Layer by layer, import and name each clip.

After you import the clips, begin constructing the Timeline (again, see Chapter 10 for information on constructing a timeline). The Background layer goes on Video 1A or 1B in the Timeline. Give the Background layer a duration of 40 seconds — equaling the length of the entire project. All the other layers will be handled in a special way on special tracks.

Video 2 is a special track. On Video 2, you can superimpose images containing transparency, such as the layers from the Photoshop file. But you need five such layers. So create tracks 3 through 6. In Chapter 13, I discuss adding tracks to the Timeline.

Once you create the tracks, place an image layer on each track. Give each of the images a duration of 8 seconds. Last, place the Watching image on track 6. Premiere interprets the order of tracks in such a manner that the highest number is on top. The lowest number is in the background. By putting the Watching layer on the highest track, all motion will happen between the young woman and the background. This is how you can create a 3-D effect.

In Chapter 12, I discuss the procedure for creating motion for illustrations and graphics. Using those procedures, you can create a motion for each of the photo images.

Fading an Image In and Out

The last thing you do (other than add music) is to make the Watching layer fade in at the beginning and out at the end. In Figure 18-7, notice that the Watching track is now expanded. (Check out Chapter 11 for more on expanding tracks.) You do this by clicking the expanding arrow at the left of the Timeline. The track expands, showing the Alpha Key layer (again, see Figure 18-7). *Alpha Key* is special color information that interprets transparency. Add a handle at each end and turn the rubber band down at each end. This is how you control fading in and fading out. In Chapter 11, I tell you how to work with handles and rubber bands.

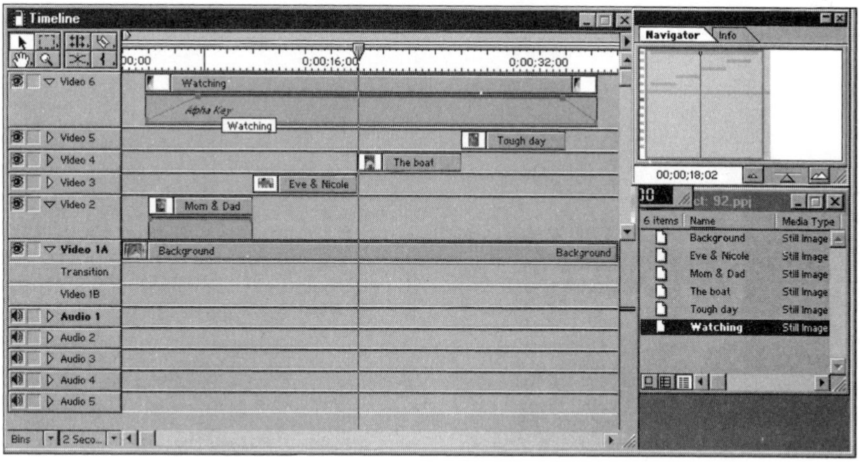

Figure 18-7:
The Alpha Key was imported with the layer from Photoshop. This is how Premiere knows what is supposed to be transparent.

Chapter 19

Making an Enjoyable Home Movie

*H*ere's a plea from all the huddled masses who have ever sat in a darkened living room, unable to escape, desperately trying to act politely interested while being tortured beyond the limits of human video-watching endurance. For all these wretched people everywhere I cry out: Stop punishing your friends and relatives with bad video! Whatever the pounds of sugar and dozens of eggs they owe you, no matter how many lawn mower blades of yours they've dulled, nothing they've done deserves this kind of retribution. In the name of all that is decent and kind, have pity on these poor people.

Decide! Do you want an appreciative audience? Wouldn't it be nice for people to ask for more? Really. I mean it. People asking if you have anything else you can show them! This can actually happen.

I have a little home movie that I want you to watch. I made it with neighborhood kids and their parents. The whole process of shooting and editing took about half a day. The actual home movie was shot and edited for video, but I made a smaller version for you to play in Adobe Premiere. Open Premiere and play brian.avi from the Chapter 19 folder on your hard drive.

For steps on downloading the tryout version of Premiere that comes on the CD-ROM at the back of this book, turn to Appendix B. You also need to download the Chapter 19 sample files from the CD-ROM. These sample files are stored on the CD-ROM in a subfolder named CHAP19, which is located in a folder named CLIPS. When you complete this chapter, you can delete these sample files from your hard drive to save space. For information on opening and using Premiere and the sample files, go to Chapter 10.

This video (for which I have won numerous brownie points from neighborhood parents and kids) is an example of what you can do creatively to present a bunch of otherwise boring stuff. All you really see in my video is a bunch of kids running and playing, except that material (which might otherwise be mind numbing) is fascinating — because I show it from a new perspective and as part of a story.

In this chapter, I walk you through steps that can assure positive neighborhood notoriety. As you'll see, I use a storyboard approach (see Chapter 6 for the lowdown on storyboarding). I use a keyframe from each section of the video to explain the development of the whole idea.

Creating a Story

A few years ago, home moviemakers had an excuse. They recorded video, and then they played the video for whomever they could trick or persuade into watching it. Little could be done to modify the order and magnitude of the recorded video. As a viewer, all you could do was hope that your host would press the fast forward button on his remote control and that the button would somehow get stuck. Fortunately, nonlinear editing for the home moviemaker has changed all that, or at least it offers the opportunity for change. Now, with digital video and nonlinear editing, you can record to your heart's content, capture what you want, and build the video any way you desire.

Usually, the most effective way of creating fun and fascinating video is by placing the captured video into a story. People often miss or simply don't know the importance of story, so allow me to explain.

First, you've got your video clips. You've got pictures of the kids and the dog(s), pictures of relatives and friends, pictures of interesting places, and pictures of meaningful events. In and of themselves, these clips are only half of what you need. You can't make an interesting video with just these video clips — no matter how well they were shot and no matter how interesting they appear. You have to add a second element — you have to put the video clips into a story. You must give viewers a logical basis and a compelling need to watch your video. Otherwise, you're punishing them with unrelated, poorly presented bits and pieces of information. That's why home movies are often so awful. They may be filled with incredible video clips, but they're lacking in the all-important second element — a story.

In my example, I created a story centering on one of the kids in my neighborhood — his name is Brian (see Figure 19-1). This doesn't mean that I'll necessarily exclude any of the other kids or their parents from the video. By creating a story about Brian, though, I give the viewer a way to connect with all the other people in the video. The opening segment offers the viewer the opportunity to emotionally connect with the main character of the story.

Figure 19-1:
The freehand drawing of Brian's name implies that the video is being presented by him.

Setting the Borders

The next moment in this story is important to the viewer. This is where a sort of promise is made by the video producer (you) to the viewer. In my example, Brian says that this video is about his day (see Figure 19-2). In this way, Brian tells the viewer a number things:

✔ The entire story is seen through Brian's eyes.

✔ Brian is the narrator.

✔ The video is sort of a chronological depiction of events from a six-year-old's perspective.

✔ The events happen within a day.

Your challenge is to live up to each of these four points. As I mentioned a moment ago, the video I present on the CD-ROM is a somewhat abbreviated version of a video that pretends to portray Brian's entire day. Even with this shortened version, though, you can pick up an implication of the movement of time throughout a portion of the day.

Figure 19-2:
Opening
statements
define the
perspective
and limita-
tions of a
story.

Establishing and Maintaining the Fable

Brian's narration is obviously critical to the story. His phrases tell you how to interpret a sequence through his eyes. In the opening scene following the titles, Brian is running from two girls (his sisters). In actuality, when I shot the video, Brian was racing with (and losing to) his sisters. I edited the clip only to show Brian while he was still ahead. In the narration, Brian says "Sometimes my day starts out rough." By adding this narration, the producer stays within the "fable" to imply the beginning of the day (time border) and Brian's need for shelter (story border).

One of the most important responsibilities you have in storytelling is not to break the rule of the fable. In my example story, "Brian's Day," the producer promises that the story is being seen through Brian's eyes. Once establishing that point, the producer can't violate the rule, which is why Mrs. Fisk bends down to speak directly into the camera (see Figure 19-3). By having Mrs. Fisk bend down, the producer assures the viewer that this is Brian's story about his day.

You may be wondering how and when I recorded Brian's voice (that really is Brian's voice in the video) and where the script came from. I created the narration in a little multistep process, which I've used many times over the years.

Figure 19-3:
You can manipulate the angle of your camera in relationship to the characters being filmed to create various and strong subjective reactions in your viewers.

First, after capturing all the clips, I created a roughly edited version of the video, which took all of 15 to 20 minutes. Once I had the pieces laid together on the Timeline, I decided the only audio worth keeping was Mrs. Fisk saying "Hi Brian." So I deleted all the other audio. See Chapter 10 for information on using the Premiere Timeline. See Chapter 11 for working with audio in Premiere.

Next, I wrote a rough draft of the narration script and kept shortening it and simplifying it until it was just a series of 18 short phrases. Brian isn't old enough to read yet, so I needed phrases that would be easy to remember and say.

Once I was sure about what I wanted, I asked Brian to sit in front of the camera, pressed the record button, read a phrase, and asked him to repeat it. He got some of the phrases right on his very first try. Others took a little directing. But, all in all, Brian performed the narration in about ten minutes.

Then I captured the narration as a series of audio clips (just as though I was capturing video), imported them into Premiere, and added them to the Timeline. See Chapter 9 for more on capturing.

Peopling the Landscape

I'm not telling you something you don't already know when I say it can be tough to get people to be themselves on camera. Frankly, children are easier to set at ease than adults are. Children usually forget about the camera within seconds. They have more important things to focus their attention on (as you can see in Figure 19-4). Adults can be tough. Just watch the Sunday morning news talk shows where politicians pretend to act naturally. And they are pros.

So what do you do with that wonderful, deep, personable person who turns to cardboard as soon as the camera begins to record? How do you help him or her? If you figure that out, please let me know. My experience ranges from total failure to limited success in this area.

Here's a suggestion from years of recording people on camera. The biggest problem you usually face when confronted with a person who freezes on camera is that you don't have the luxury of patience. When you're recording, you're recording. No one else is willing to wait while you help a frozen adult melt a little. My advice, if you want to call it that, is to laugh it off. Some people simply can't function in front of a camera. When you encounter these people (and you will, I promise), keep your composure, try to show compassion toward their embarrassment, and just keep going with your recording.

Figure 19-4:
Action on video appears most natural when the subjects don't pay attention to the camera.

Making Funny Funny

People get very serious about what makes something funny. I guess that's logical when you consider all the kazillions of dollars that are spent by advertisers who are betting that you will think an advertisement is so funny that you'll resurrect from your TV-watching stupor to remember a brand name the next time you go shopping. How else can you explain lizards electrocuting frogs so that you'll remember to buy a particular kind of beer?

Fortunately, you don't have to spend lots of money to be funny. You just have to be funny. So how do you do that? Well, I don't know, just be funny. When producing a video, funny can be slapstick, and it can be subtle. Usually, it emerges from the cleverness (both intended and unintended) of a moment.

Surprise is a good tool for creating a funny moment. In "Brian's Day," I use a number of still images of Brian in a Bartles and James sort of stance with people appearing around him. Then, as a surprise, I throw in moving video of Jackson the dog trying to lick Matthew the brother (see Figure 19-5).

Maybe even more important than making funny be funny is ensuring that serious is serious. I'm serious. My worst memories as a producer come from people laughing at the wrong time.

Figure 19-5:
You can cue
humorous
responses
by using
visual and
audible
surprises.

Here is a word of advice from a graduate of the school of hard knocks. People are callous when they watch video. People will laugh at things in video that they would never consider laughing at in real life.

Video separates us from reality to the degree that we are separated from people's feelings. For example, if something odd is in a picture showing a funeral, people will laugh. I guarantee it. It doesn't matter how tragic the circumstance. If you're the producer, you'll know what it means to feel mortified. Take much care in your handling of serious moments.

Maintaining Point of View

After you establish a point of view in a video (such as seeing a day through a child's eyes), you have to maintain that point of view. Maintaining a point of view requires occasionally reestablishing the viewer's relationship with the character. You accomplish this with creative camera location.

As I said earlier, in this example video, the viewer sees a day through Brian's eyes. But maintaining relationship is a subjective endeavor. For example, if I were to use a stationary camera setting to record Brian riding his bike, the viewer might feel unconnected to Brian. However, I used a moving camera to record Brian on his bicycle, giving the viewer the feeling that he or she is moving with Brian — thereby reconnecting the viewer with Brian (refer to Figure 19-6 and watch the movie to see how I accomplish this effect).

The procedure for reconnecting can be quite simple. In this case, reconnecting is a matter of first showing Brian from the front as he rides his bicycle while he says "But most of all, I like to ride my bike" and then showing him from the back. By reestablishing this relationship, you have new energy and interest to feel and see what Brian is experiencing.

To maintain any kind of energy in a video, you need to determine what's interesting, and then cut it in half. The best and easiest way to create interesting and exciting video is to have less of it. You maintain people's interest by giving them just enough in order to understand your message and no more.

Figure 19-6:
As a producer, you occasionally need to help the viewer reestablish the point of view by creatively implying a subjective connection.

Making the End a Beginning

Most good stories end with a beginning. A storyteller closes a loop in time. In "Brian's Day," the story begins with Brian identifying himself and saying that you are about to see his day. Brian ends the story by saying that he has performed his task. But this task ends with someone saying hello to him, just as in the beginning of the story (see Figure 19-7). And Brian's last words are his invitation for you to come over to his house — a beginning.

The task of closing a story is easy or difficult based on how well you lived up to the promises you made at the beginning of the story. In "Brian's Day," you committed to depicting a day through a child's eyes, and you committed to presenting what he might consider a day. If you live up to these commitments, you can simply have the character say good-bye at the end.

Now it's your turn. What kind of story do you want to tell?

Figure 19-7:
You can close a story by implying completion.

If it's worth the effort, go for it!

One enjoyable part of making a video is the chance to use your imagination. A story helps you be creative — to see the finished product in your mind's eye and to look for ways to make the idea happen. The story in this chapter, "Brian's Day," needed video of Brian on his bicycle, from Brian's perspective. The simplest way to achieve this was by riding in front of and behind Brian to establish the shots as he toured the neighborhood.

Chapter 20

Producing a Digital Video Wedding

. . . .

. . . .

*I*f there is a made-in-heaven use for digital video, it has to be weddings. The combination of a MiniDV camcorder (which is based on a miniaturized digital video format) and computer-based nonlinear editing system (for example, a computer using Adobe Premiere) make affordable and possible what could not be imagined a couple of years ago in wedding videography. Beautiful and vibrant are terms often attributed to newlyweds. Those adjectives are now being used for wedding videos, too.

Until recently, most weddings were recorded and edited in VHS or S-VHS formats (see Chapter 2 for more on formats). The editing and special effects capabilities of these two formats are limited. As I explain in this chapter, weddings require lots of editing and special effects, not only because weddings are important, but also because they pose special kinds of problems.

This chapter helps you plan and produce a knockout wedding video. In some ways, I feel a little guilty. After you make a beautiful wedding video, you're going to become more popular than you may want to be. By the way, I know a place where you can order boxes of rice by the case.

Wedding Videos Have Parts

Producing a wedding video can be lots of fun, but it can also be tough. Some of the simplest ceremonies can provide you with incredible recording opportunities. And some of the most elaborate ceremonies can leave you virtually no opportunities for any kind of worthwhile recording. Here's an example of what I mean.

Most weddings are performed in churches. In many instances, pastors of small congregations are more apt to allow you to record close to the front of the church. Smaller congregations often have fewer weddings and, therefore, are less likely to have strict procedures for what can and cannot be done by videographers at such ceremonies. In contrast, pastors of larger churches are sometimes overworked and overbooked. Frequently, larger churches have strict guidelines for what can be done by the videographer (which you may discover only when you arrive for the wedding, so be sure to ask in advance). Sometimes, the videographer is not allowed anywhere except the back of the church, which is not the best location for recording a wedding video.

So what can you do if you're limited in what you can shoot at the ceremony? Fortunately, the wedding ceremony itself is only a part of what the newlyweds will enjoy seeing in their finished video. In fact, a wedding video may have multiple parts — for example, photographs showing their early friendship in progress, their engagement period, their wedding preparations, and their wedding ceremony (such as the smiling couple in Figure 20-1) and reception. If you keep these parts in mind, you can create a very meaningful video — even when you're limited in how you can record the actual ceremony. And as you will see later in this chapter, digital video makes a world of difference in turning a tough problem into an easy solution.

In terms of a creating a wedding video's parts, I use what I call a *weighting factor* — which isn't something official or carved in stone, but is a good rule of thumb. If I get lots of good recording at the ceremony, I devote 60 percent of the video to this part, 30 percent to the reception, and the remaining 10 percent to the friendship and engagement stages and to the wedding preparations. On the other hand, if opportunities to record at the wedding ceremony are limited, I may devote only 20 percent of the video to the ceremony, and perhaps 40 percent to the reception, and the remaining 40 to all else.

Most often, I don't have a clue about the weighting factor until after I record the wedding and reception. Following the reception, if I find I have problems, I start seeking help from the newlyweds' friends and relatives. I ask them to provide me with photos and video from earlier times in the couple's relationship. Usually, I get more help than I need.

Figure 20-1:
The
wedding
ceremony is
only one
part of a
wedding
video.

Preparing for the Ceremony

I know this may sound dumb, but you need to know the wedding couple enough to understand what they will want in the video. Too often videographers impose their own preferences and standards on the wedding video to the chagrin of the newlyweds. For example, if the couple is deeply religious, find out whether they would like to include special images or religious symbols in their video. Also, you might ask them whether anyone other than the immediate family should receive special attention in the video. And, if circumstances dictate, should anyone *not* appear in the video?

Develop a shot list with the couple. A *shot list* is a list of the people and the sequence of events that the couple want recorded. When making this list, be sure to caution the couple that this list is only a wish list. You may not be able to record everything they want. But at least you can create a mutual road map.

Finding audio solutions

On the day of the wedding, your first concern is to resolve your audio needs. No matter how beautiful the visual part of video is, ultimately the sound is at least equally important. First, you must somehow record the marriage vows.

Second, you need to record the minister's (rabbi, justice of the peace, ship captain) voice. Third, you need to record the music.

As I mention in Chapter 5, you can record the vows with a wired or a wireless microphone. However, you may run into a situation where neither of these options is possible. When all else fails, I suggest you place a battery-operated recorder as close as possible to where the vows are taken. Turn the recorder on before the wedding begins — and remember to collect it at the end! You can later record the audio from the recorder directly into your computer using the line input on your computer's sound card (see Chapter 8 for more on sound cards).

You can access a sound recorder application by clicking the Windows Start button and then selecting Programs⇔Accessories⇔Multimedia⇔Sound Recorder. The Sound Recorder can record the playback from your tape recorder as a .wav file (see Chapter 11 for more about .wav files). After you record the .wav file, you can import it into Premiere. Your only challenge is to match the audio with the speakers' lip movements in the video. But, believe me, it can be done. Just about anyone who has edited video has synchronized audio with lip movements a number of times.

For steps on downloading the tryout version of Premiere that comes on the CD-ROM at the back of this book, turn to Appendix B. For information on opening and using Premiere, go to Chapter 10.

If you use the microphone on your camcorder, be careful not to locate your camcorder near the music source or near the speakers for the music system. In addition to headaches during the ceremony, you'll also have worse head-aches during the editing stage as you try to overcome the imbalance of the sound on your videotape.

Determining your limits

Whether you like it or not, you can't avoid calling attention to yourself when you use a camcorder at a wedding. But you can help avoid detracting the guests' attention from the wedding ceremony itself.

One of the most useful tools I have in my arsenal as a videographer is *tactful boldness.* By this I simply mean taking advantage of whatever shot is immediately available, though I always try to set up for a shot when attention is diverted somewhere else. A good example of tactful boldness is the wedding processional, like the one shown in Figure 20-2. (Along with noticing the lovely young ladies, notice that the camcorder height is appropriate for the two being recorded.)

Without undue attention, you can position yourself (holding your camera, rather than using a tripod) at the front of the church when people are looking the other way. By taking this position, though, you need to communicate to the minister that you know what you're doing and that you know when and how to retreat without being noticed. Obviously, that moment is when the bride begins to come down the aisle. If you handle this moment correctly, you will most likely be trusted throughout the rest of the ceremony. By the way, no matter how polite you may be, you'll score zero with the minister if you're not dressed appropriately.

Figure 20-2:
The front-of-the-sanctuary position is probably acceptable when attention is toward the back.

Here's my basic ethic of recording: Never do something for which you haven't received permission or been asked to perform. Before the ceremony, ask the bride, the bride's parents, and the minister if you have their permission to discreetly move about the sanctuary during the ceremony. Though not always, usually you'll receive permission. Either way, though, you have demonstrated courtesy and professionalism.

Seeing a Wedding through a Videographer's Eyes

After you tell someone that you are recording their wedding, you are no longer a pedestrian. You are part of the wedding party. You are the historian. Accept your role with pride — but also with humility. From the time you arrive, your role is only to be the videographer. You're not a mother or a husband, a friend or a relative. You're the person who's making the wedding video.

Getting all the principals on tape (balance)

As the videographer, you must forget who your friends are. Everyone at the wedding is your friend. Your clients, whether you're being paid with dollars or a spaghetti dinner, are the wedding couple and the wedding party. No one is more important than the bride and groom and their parents; among the rest of the wedding party, no one is less important than anyone else.

Whatever you do, you must show impartiality in your recording. I emphasize this because it is so hard to maintain. No matter what scoundrel you know one member to be, no matter how much more attractive one of the families appears on camera than the other, balance is your job. But, no matter how hard you try, balance is built-in impossible unless you're using two cameras. By virtue of where you set your tripod (assuming you're situated somewhere at the front), one side of the wedding party will automatically look into the camera and one will look away. So what can you do?

Recording what's necessary (somehow)

A videographer's number one virtue is an elephant's memory. I take great pains to remember the people, for one reason or another, I couldn't get on camera during the ceremony. Then I seek out those people during the reception and get lots and lots of flattering video. If anything, I tend to overcompensate by giving them too much attention.

Virtue number two is being an advocate for the unattractive family member. At every event, I make a concerted effort to see with my heart rather than my eyes. My heart has yet to fail me. I look for the person who may be easily overlooked or who seems to be intentionally avoiding my lens. I figure that if I give special attention to that person, everything else will take care of itself. And it almost always does. Inevitably, when the wedding couple reviews my finished work, they react with glee that I recorded Aunt Norma or Cousin Dick. They wonder how I knew that I should include her or convince him to agree to being recorded.

Looking for the interesting

A wedding videographer is a storyteller. Your main story line, of course, is the wedding. And you have no trouble identifying the hero and heroine. But much of the quality of the story is in its depth and its surprising twists and turns of plot provided by the supporting cast — the wedding guests. Spend a lot of your time pointing your camcorder at them (as I'm doing in Figures 20-3 and 20-4).

Figure 20-3: Always keep an eye trained on the bride and groom to record the unexpected guest.

Figure 20-4:
Sometimes, a layered shot of guests admiring the newlyweds is very effective.

Looking for a Postproduction Theme

At the beginning of this chapter, I said that digital video makes affordably possible what couldn't even be imagined a couple of years ago. This is partly because of the broadcast quality of MiniDV and partly because of what's possible during the editing stage (postproduction stage) as a result of nonlinear editing programs. You can now perform magic. You can make a little look like a lot, you can mask imperfections, you can imbue beauty and energy into the unattractive and lifeless. Digital video not only allows you to be a storyteller, it also *makes* you one almost by default. You find yourself imagining and playing with "what-ifs" rather than fiddling and struggling to make machines perform correctly.

One useful postproduction what-if is establishing a symbol of the wedding. Each wedding is different and each provides you with its own symbol. For the wedding illustrated in this chapter, I chose the figures on top of the wedding cake (see Figure 20-5) as the symbol. The decoration on a cake is hardly an original idea for a symbol, but as you'll see in the next section, such decorations can add magic to the video.

Figure 20-5:
A figurine
atop a
wedding
cake, such
as the one
shown in
this figure,
can serve
as a symbol
of the
wedding in
the wedding
video.

Putting It All Together

Now, humor me please by looking at a portion of the wedding video. The clip that I want you to see is named wedding.avi, and it's stored on the CD-ROM at the back of this book. To make the clip play properly, you'll probably need to copy it temporarily on your computer's hard drive.

To copy the file to your hard drive, you need to download the Chapter 20 sample file from the CD-ROM. The sample file is stored on the CD-ROM in a subfolder named CHAP20, which is located in a folder named CLIPS. See Appendix B for steps on downloading chapter folders to your hard drive.

When you complete this chapter, you can delete this sample file from your hard drive to save space.

After you have the file on your hard drive, open Premiere. (See Appendix B for steps on downloading the tryout version of Premiere from the CD-ROM; see Chapter 10 for steps on opening and using the program.)

To open the movie file that you'll be using in this section, follow these steps:

1. **Select File⇨Open or press Ctrl+O.**

   The Open dialog box appears.

2. **Open the Chapter 20 folder on your hard drive and highlight wedding.avi.**

3. **Click Open.**

   The movie opens in the Premiere Source monitor. See Chapter 10 for information on using the Source monitor.

4. **Click anywhere in the Source monitor and press the spacebar to play the wedding.avi movie.**

As you play the video, notice that the figurine serves as a background theme to the video. Also notice that I inserted transitions for five wedding video parts. (See Chapter 10 for information on using transitions.) The Vows part of the video has actual moments from the wedding. I included the transitions just so you can get a feel for the order of a wedding video.

In the vows portion, you see the following:

✔ The procession of the bride

✔ The bride's father "giving her away"

✔ The couple turning toward each other

What you just watched (if you humored me) in less than a minute actually took place over a ten-minute period during the wedding. Your job as the magic-making chronicler of the wedding is to find ways to compress the wedding without hurting it. If you edit the video with tender loving care, you can make the video teem with life.

Notice that the transitions are cutouts of the couple (see also Figure 20-6). I did this using Adobe Photoshop. (See Chapter 18 for information on how to do these cutouts by using special effects. In that chapter, I take you through a procedure for isolating and cutting out a part of one graphic and laying it onto another graphic.) The special effect is an easy way to provide a special touch to the wedding video.

Who owns wedding photographs? If you want to use photographs from other weddings in a video you're creating, you must receive permission from the photographer in order to use them. If the wedding photos were made by a studio, be prepared not to receive permission to use them in the video.

Figure 20-6:
Cutouts of
actual video
can be
effective
wedding
symbols.

Part VII
The Part of Tens

The 5th Wave   By Rich Tennant

"...and here's me with Cindy Crawford. And this is me with Madonna and Celine Dion..."

In this part . . .

So you want to know what all this digital video stuff costs? You want some ideas about what products are available? This part answers those questions and more. The two chapters in this part give a number of specific examples of almost every kind of equipment and software you might need for your digital video production system. And if you don't find what you're looking for, you are given a number of World Wide Web links (addresses) for searching and researching to your heart's content.

Chapter 21

Ten Great Digital Video Web Sites

1 hate clutter. You wouldn't know it if you looked in my garage (or in my office, or in my sock drawer). But I do, I really do.

More than anything else, I hate brain clutter. If you're like me, you spend way too much energy just trying to keep information out of your brain so that you can have some space and time to deal with all the stuff you already know and have to do something about.

So, with some guilt, I offer you a bunch of information about ten Web sites that, in one way or another, are dedicated to digital video. However, I assure you, olive branch in hand, that they are not infested with wastrel brain invaders.

In fact, the Web sites are positively informative and somewhat inspiring in a technological sort of way. Who knows, you may even have some fun visiting them — kind of like finding matching socks.

www.hypertech.co.uk/vidsite/mainframe.html

I think it's only right that my first recommendation, the Hypertech Multimedia Guide Web site, is an educational site.

This Web site, from the eastern shores of the Atlantic, provides practical overviews of digital and desktop video. Quoting the authors on the opening page of the educational portion of the site:

> We're not a developer or reseller of hardware and/or compression tools so our opinion should be completely unbiased. In such a rapidly changing technological area, we know this is unlikely to be comprehensive which is why we've provided links to other useful pages, particularly those containing the technical stuff.

The Hypertech Multimedia Guide is broken into six segments: Formats, Capture, Editing, Compression, FAQs, and Links. You'll find it fascinating and fulfilling, and you'll still make it home in time for tea.

www.vidy.com

Because digital video begins with the camcorder, my first recommended commercial site deals with video production. Welcome to the *Videography* magazine Web site. Contributing authors are people who actually shoot video for a living.

This online magazine covers subjects that range far beyond digital video. But, frankly, in the last year or so, the magazine has devoted a large portion of its space to digital video — because digital video is the future of videography. If you're like me, you'll catch yourself ogling at the showcased equipment. And you may find yourself a little overwhelmed by some parts of the articles. But, mostly, you'll probably find yourself admiring talented people talking in an engaging way about video production. And you'll learn a lot.

www.digitalproducer.com

As much as *Videography* magazine is about the big picture of video production, *Digital Producer Magazine* focuses on the big picture of digital video production. This Web-based magazine provides the latest releases on hardware and software as well as updates on changes in the landscape of manufacturers and digital video-related services. If you want, the publishers will even deliver the magazine to your e-mail box in time for your morning coffee and Solitaire break.

www.dv.com

DV Live magazine is a great resource for insight into the strengths and weaknesses of specific hardware and software. The publishers even offer you back issues! In each issue, *DV Live* provides fascinating comparison charts for everything from camcorders to hard drives.

And then there are the ads. Lots and lots of ads. Sure the reading is kind of loud with hucksters. Sure you need to hold onto your wallet. But should you expect anything different? You're in the City Market of Digital Video. Like the publishers claim: This is DV Live!

www.adobe.com

If you want to know about the most widely used software programs in desktop publishing, go to the Adobe Systems, Inc. Web site. Adobe employs some of the most creative and gifted software developers to be found anywhere. Most of their applications are considered benchmarks in the industry. The Adobe Web site is a virtual gold mine of information.

www.canondv.com

You want to know what your options are in camcorders? Want to know what kind of options and accessories are available? Go to the Canon Corporation Web site. This site is dedicated to digital video products. You'll see that Canon even offers you membership in a camera owners' club.

www.real.com

Those of you who like living and working on the cutting edge of technology should give some thought to producing digital video for intranets and the Internet. If such possibilities interest you, you have a friend in RealNetworks. As I discuss in Chapter 15, Web-based video is a promising, almost-there technology. RealNetworks is one of the most prominent pioneers and ongoing developers in this field. The site provides up-to-date news and information about the world of streaming audio and video as well as numerous free programs and upgrades.

www.macromedia.com

Ten years ago, the future of interactive multimedia seemed squarely fixed in a circular disk called CD-ROM. Macromedia, a manufacturer of interactive authoring software programs, was there and was one of the leaders in the burgeoning industry. That was a decade ago. Today, the future of interactive multimedia seems focused on the World Wide Web. Macromedia is still there, and, amazingly, continues being the leader in multimedia development. Have you been "shocked" on the Web? If so, you already know about Macromedia. If not, hold on. (*Shocked* is a Macromedia term for powerful, on-demand animation on the World Wide Web.)

As you will see on the Web site, Macromedia multimedia is a world of its own. Rumor has it that some people go to the site and never return. You will be offered an amazing amount of information about authoring as well as product information, samples, and educational (and employment) opportunities.

www.xingtech.com/store

There's got to be a better way. Someone has got to come up with a way to present high-quality video on a computer screen without special hardware! Er, excuse me. Someone has. It's called MPEG 1. A company called Xing has it. They would like you to try their software free for 30 days.

Xing would like you to go to their Web site to download and then test a trial version of their encoder and player. If you really like the encoder and player and have a use for the technology, Xing will charge you a lot of money to purchase the software. Many people think the money is worth it — including me. You get to make your own decision without spending any money. What a country!

www.sgi.com

Silicon Graphic is one of the industry's best known developers of high-end UNIX-based visualization systems. Yeah? And so what does this have to do with recommended Web sites about digital video? Nothing actually. Except that big-deal-name Silicon Graphics has recently also become a major player in the development of low-cost Windows NT digital workstations.

Affectionately called the SGI 320 and 540 workstations (marketing people no doubt burned double-time midnight oil to come up with such imaginative names), these little machines are actually amazing. They do things — good things — to graphics and video that I never even imagined possible. I'll let you check out the Web site to see what I mean. I'm not saying you'll necessarily run out and buy one of these machines, but a significant number of people are doing just that — running, not walking, to buy these machines.

My only reservation, and I confess being gun shy, is that they are so new and so revolutionary that I'd like to wait a version or two to give the technology some time to mature. Maybe you're braver than I am. And maybe I'm paranoid.

Chapter 22

Selecting Your Toys

· ·

· ·

*O*nce upon a time, someone with a keen sense of reality tagged film and video production gear as "toys." The name stuck, probably for good reason. The term says more about the users than it does about the equipment. People who seriously use video production gear still aren't sure what they'll do when they grow up — even though many of them have children (and grandchildren) of their own. After all, video production itself is only a child of the entertainment industry. So how serious can you get?

In this chapter, you get a tour of equipment and software that together equal a full-fledged digital video production and nonlinear editing suite. Depending on what your individual needs are and what you can afford at one time, you can start just about anywhere in building your own suite.

Making Your Choices

So what do you want to play with? Do you want to be very grown up, controlled, and fiscally sound and only frowningly dabble in a few inexpensive necessities? Or do you want to jump fully clothed into a vat of electronic slush and make a complete idiot of yourself? Most of us restrain ourselves enough to fall somewhere in between. We don't want anyone laughing at our toys because they're dime store stuff, but we also want to somehow justify our decisions. And that's good, because that means we'll enjoy our toys now *and* when the rent is due.

I'm not going to tell you what digital video gear you ought to own. But I will tell you about some of the products out there that are worth the asking price. And I'll tell you my preferences. Most of the preferences are based on some degree of logic and experience, but, in the end, they are still just preferences. They may or may not fit you and your needs. That is fine. Life would be boring and nonprogressive otherwise.

This chapter is a kind of digital video outfitting store. It outfits you for the video production environment using high-quality, consumer-priced equipment. If you want to start in digital video for the least amount possible (assuming you already own a Pentium-class computer), you can start for under $2,000 by purchasing a single CCD digital video camcorder and a digital video capture card. If you want to fully equip yourself for the successful world of the digital producer, you can have it all for $13,000 to $20,000.

Production Gear

Based on your budget, you'll have to determine how far you can go in equipping yourself for production. If necessary, you can select the basics now and supplement with the niceties later. Just remember one thing: Your image and your sound will never be better than they are on the original tape.

Selecting a camcorder

When choosing a high-quality digital camcorder, keep these things in mind:

- **Lens quality:** Size counts when it comes to a lens. The larger the lens, the greater the degree of light and image collection quality. Good cameras have interchangeable lenses. And, customarily, a professional lens exceeds the image quality of the recording medium. Believe me, manufacturers will let you know when their lens achieves these criteria.

- **Pixels:** The term *pixels* is an abbreviation for pixel elements, or the number of dots that together comprise a picture. Basically, the more pixels in an image of a fixed size, the greater the resolution quality of that image. Some good cameras offer as much as 410,000 or more pixels per CCD (or equivalent).

- **CCDs:** The size and number of charged couple devices (CCDs) affects the quality of the recorded image. A high-quality digital video camera has three CCD chips. One-third inch CCDs are considered a good minimum.

- **Audio options:** A high-quality camcorder should be able to record audio using XLR (as described in Chapter 5) balanced-type microphones. This allows professional quality recording.

- **Time code:** A high-quality camcorder should be able to record time code. Time code is necessary for frame-accurate editing. Frame accuracy is essential for videotape control in identifying clips and for editing.

✔ **IEEE 1394 interface:** The camcorder needs a digital video in and out connection. The in and out connection is how you send out and receive back video in a digital format. IEEE 1394 is a standard that ensures compatibility among digital video equipment. I explain IEEE 1394 in Chapters 1 and 2.

✔ **Special features:** Features will vary from one camcorder to the next, but some features are vital. The camcorder should be able to record in fully automatic, semiautomatic, and fully manual modes. Also, the camcorder should offer 16:9 aspect ratio for future video use. (See Chapter 10 for details on aspect ration.) And the camcorder should offer the zebra function and the optical image stabilizer, both of which are discussed a bit later in this chapter.

Sony DCR-TRV9

This Sony DV camcorder uses a ¼-inch color CCD chip with 680,000 pixels specially designed for use with MiniDV tapes. The camera includes an advanced color viewfinder.

Details

15x optical zoom lens. Allows extreme close-up shots with digital zoom.

Manual focus. Allows greater control over the recorded images.

3 ½-inch Swivelscreen color LCD (Liquid Crystal Display) and color viewfinder. Provides a clear, accurate color image, even in bright sunlight.

Super SteadyShot picture stabilization. Includes image stabilization system using motion sensors that compensate for camcorder or operator movement without deterioration of image quality.

6-Mode auto exposure. Includes the Portrait, Beach & Ski, Sports Lesson, Landscape, Spotlight, and Sunset & Moon modes, which enable you to choose preset aperture openings and shutter speeds. (See Chapter 3 for more on aperture.)

Photo mode. For high-quality still images; can record up to 750 individual still images.

Selectable white balance. Includes Auto, indoor, outdoor, hold only.

PCM stereo digital audio. Provides CD-like sound in a 12-bit, 32 kHz recording mode.

IEEE 1394 interface. Enables you to connect your camcorder to a computer. IEEE 1394 provides digital-to-digital transfer of audio and video information.

Time code. Provides drop-frame time code for accurate frame editing.

Built-in speaker with volume control. Enables you to immediately review recorded material.

You can see a list of Sony products online at www.sel.sony.com/SEL/consumer/ss5/office/camcorder/digitalvideoproducts/dcr-trv9_specs.shtml.

Canon XL1

Canon advertises this camcorder as follows: "The full potential of digital video in one extraordinary camcorder. Unparalleled optics plus interchange-able-lens versatility." For once, someone isn't exaggerating. The Canon XL1 epitomizes one of those rare moments when technology transcends itself. This high-quality camcorder is capable of performing more than probably you'll ever need.

Details

Optical image stabilized 16X zoom lens. An optical 16X (32X digital) standard lens is included with the XL1. At present, this is the longest lens for a digital video camcorder. The resolution quality of the XL1 camera lens is 600 TV lines. The actual recording quality of the MiniDV standard is 500 TV lines. Therefore, the XL1 takes full advantage of MiniDV. The camcorder is fitted with a variable angle prism for image stabilization, has a neutral density filter, manual focus and zoom rings, and an automatic focus function.

The XL1 is made to accommodate interchangeable lenses. This capability permits a potential range of focus between 24 and 2160 mm. An optional 3X wide-angle lens is available.

3 CCDs. The XL1 provides a separate CCD for each primary color (red, green, blue). This 3-chip process achieves broadcast-quality color reproduction.

Pixel shift. Canon uses a complex technology to combine low light capabili-ties with normal light signal clarity. The XL1 uses a rather large pixel (72 square microns) for collecting light in extreme low light conditions. For normal light clarity, Canon uses a process of pixel shifting for a perceptible pixel density. *Pixel shifting* is based on the fact that the green of RGB contains 60 percent picture detail with red and blue combining for 40 percent. The XL1 electronically shifts green the equivalent of ½ pixel horizontally and vertically from red and blue pixels. This gives a perceivable pixel depth approximate to 410,000 pixels per CCD.

SuperRange optical image stabilization. The XL1's image stabilization com-bines a conventional stabilizing sensor with an additional low-frequency vibration-sensing function.

Shooting options. The XL1 provides a wide range of shooting features, including normal movie mode, digital photo mode, and frame movie mode. The digital photo mode allows more than 500 still pictures per video tape.

In addition, the XL1 allows automatic, semiautomatic, and manual control. This video camcorder can be set for shutter priority (image speed control) and aperture priority (light control). You can also dial a wide range of settings to override automatic exposure readings.

The XL1 also provides a convenient zebra pattern which is typical of professional camcorders. The zebra pattern informs you through the viewfinder when your light setting exceeds 80 IRE, the maximum facial lighting. The zebra function can be turned on and off using the XL1's menu options.

4:3 and 16:9 aspect ratios. The XL1's menu options include a switch for shooting in either the 4 to 3 aspect ratio (current television and VCR standards) or in 16 to 9 aspect ratio (future digital television standard).

Four-Channel Digital Audio System. Canon hit a home run with the XL1's audio capabilities. In addition to DAT- (digital audio tape) quality 16-bit stereo, the XL1 offers up to four channels of simultaneously recorded sound. Each of the four signals can be output independently, providing you with extraordinary editing capabilities.

Balanced sound. An important option that comes with the XL1 is the option to use balanced-type microphones. This capability enables you to use studio-quality microphones, eliminating all traces of electronic hum.

Digital video input and output. The XL1 provides an IEEE 1394 serial bus connection for digital to digital transfer to and from a computer.

Time code. The XL1 offers drop-frame time code for accurate frame editing.

I discuss camcorders in detail in Chapter 3. You can also find Canon on the Web at www.canondv.com.

Choosing your tripod

What has four wheels and flies? Correct. A garbage truck. What has three legs and a zipper? Correct again. A tripod bag. Is there a connection between these two tidbits of wisdom? Actually, yes. The surest way to distinguish your work from what is carried in one of those flying trucks is to use those three legs in the zippered bag. If you're serious about your work, and I know you are, you may need a tripod.

The Bogen/Manfrotto Series 501 Head and 2-Stage Tripod

When talking about a tripod, you actually are referring to two separate pieces of equipment — a head and a tripod. A head is the equipment that holds the camcorder, making it possible for you to turn the camera from left to right (panning) and up and down (tilting). You can think of the tripod as the legs that hold up the camcorder and head.

The Bogen/Manfrotto 501 Head is made for lightweight MiniDV camcorders. It features a quick release sliding plate for balancing the camcorder. The head can be adjusted for an acceptable amount of drag for performing smooth tilts and pans. The head provides a full-size platform for the camcorder and a leveling bubble for setting your shot.

The tripod and head are conveniently collapsible to 28 inches for knee shots and expandable to 66 inches for tall Adam's apple shots. The tripod base has a spreader for floor settings and spiked feet for outdoor shooting.

I discuss tripods in detail in Chapter 6.

Making sound decisions

Here's a common video production problem. You've got this not-so-great spot to set up your camcorder. Say that you're 75 feet from your subject. You can zoom in and pick up most of what you'll visually need. The only real problem is the sound. Between you and your star is an audience of coughing, sneezing, yawning, whispering people. Okay, you know where I'm talking about. You're shooting your child's school play.

Your camcorder's microphone is worse than worthless. It's picking up everything except your child's kazoo masterpiece. But, no problem! Unbeknownst to your first-grader's friends and teachers, she's wearing a wireless microphone hidden in her platypus costume. Because of your camcorder's advanced audio features, you can dial out the camcorder microphone and input symphony-quality balanced digital sound. It wouldn't be much better in a studio. You accomplish this with a wireless microphone.

Samson UHF Series One UM1 Micro Diversity System

A wireless microphone is actually three pieces of equipment: a microphone, a transmitter, and a receiver. The microphone collects the sound. The transmitter turns the sound into a radio signal. The receiver picks up the radio signal and turns it back into sound. The receiver is connected to the camcorder.

Samson's UM1 Micro Diversity System offers three choices of microphones: a hand-held mic, a lavalier mic (for wearing on your lapel), and a headset mic. The transmitter is small and can be worn on a belt. The receiver is housed in a compact package and provides crystal-clear reception for digital-quality sound. Because of the receiver's small size (2.63 inches wide, 4.21 inches high, and 0.91 inches in diameter), the UM1 fits easily on a MiniDV camcorder. The supplied XLR to mini-XLR cable provides balanced sound.

I discuss sound in detail in Chapter 5.

Letting there be light(s)

Camcorders love lots of light. Your camera's CCDs hunger for luminance. For that reason, you sometimes have to provide you own light. Most of the time, you'll be able to handle lighting needs if you come properly equipped with some basic fixtures. Here's what I use.

Lowel Tota/Omni GO kit

The Tota/Omni kit has three professional lights — two Omni and one Tota.

The Omni light is a spotlight with an adjustable focus that allows you to adjust the intensity of the center of the light source. The Omni light has barn doors for cropping the light's throw. (*Barn doors* are folding plates that are on the top, bottom, and sides of the light. The barn doors can be adjusted to make the lighted area either wide, narrow, tall, or slim.) This feature is particularly useful when you need to light one area while leaving an adjacent area unaffected by the light source. The Omni light is typically your primary (key) light on your foreground. You crop the light with the barn doors, which prevents casting shadows on the background.

The Tota light is a general area wash, sometimes referred to as a soft light. Typically, you use the Tota light to serve as a general area light that washes the background while providing a secondary light source for the foreground.

I discuss a lot of lighting techniques in Chapter 4.

Editing Equipment

As wide open and outdoorsy as production can tend to be, post-production (the editing phase) elicits contrasting thoughts of long hours in a sedentary position, doing the same thing over and over, trying to get it just right. The editing environment is where you'll be spending most of your otherwise free hours as a budding digital producer, so why not at least make it efficient and semicozy? The following sections recommend ways for doing so.

Furniture

Am I serious? Yup. Furniture is a good place to start. In my years of helping people integrate their editing systems, the one thing that they have always thanked me for is my insistence on purchasing the right furniture for the job.

I've personally done it both ways. I've pieced together the equipment and then gone to the local office supply store to buy folding tables and bookshelves. And I've purchased professional editing furniture. I can't begin to tell you the difference in efficiency and personal satisfaction in doing it right. A good editing desk isn't cheap. So I suppose that if you need to cut back somewhere, this could be the place. But at least give it a lot of thought first.

Winsted Edit Desk

In my opinion, the Winsted Corporation offers the most complete and innovative line of consoles and workstations for the video and broadcast industries. Their modular components are as attractive as they are ergonomically engineered.

I have a 60-inch-wide digital desk with a curved table top. The 30-inch-deep work surface and 20-inch-deep adjustable riser are finished in mar-resistant black granite laminate and black contour edge molding. The Edit Desk features metal and plastic tracks to channel video and monitor cords out of sight. Numerous options are available, such as a paper tray that attaches to the underside of the desk and a mini-tower support well that holds your computer tower off the floor.

Versatility is key to matching your needs with desktop editing consoles. Shelves can be ordered complete or custom designed from in-stock components. Many different basic styles are available. Optional decorative colored accent trim can be ordered to add a touch of flair to your work environment.

Editing equipment and software

I've chosen what I believe is a relatively economical, very good computer for nonlinear editing. You can find bargain basement alternatives. I just can't recommend them to you. Experience has shown me that you must have a lowest common denominator of performance. Once you've set that standard, feel free to purchase the most economical equipment that conforms to your minimum needs. The reverse approach is to buy the cheapest equipment, hoping that it will work in the demanding nonlinear environment. Been there, done that. Won't ever do it again. Fortunately, dollar for dollar, fast and rugged computers don't cost a whole lot more than slower delicate ones. See Chapter 8 for more on selecting a computer and making it ready for digital video.

Intergraph TDZ 2000 GL2

My system of choice is the Intergraph TDZ 2000 GL2 workstation. I've personally made this commitment because Intergraph is one of the best in graphics-oriented computer systems and Intergraph offers many of its high-end features in its lower-end computers, such as the GL2.

Intergraph is a pioneer in graphics workstations. Having made its name in interactive graphics on the RISC/UNIX platform, Intergraph brought its graphics technology and system design experience to the open platform in 1992. They've been leading the pack ever since.

Every computer is different, one from the other. So you need a measuring rod for choosing a computer powerful enough to meet your nonlinear editing demands. The following specifications about the TDZ 200 GL2 are sufficient for a "powerful enough" computer.

These specifications may or may not make a lot of sense to you. I'm not going to bore you with explanations of what everything means. Fortunately, you can buy a computer without understanding all that goes into it. Again, you can use these specifications as a basis of comparison.

Chassis style. Ultra-tower.

Processor. Pentium II, single 450 MHz (upgradeable to dual); 32K Level 1 cache; 512B Level 2 cache.

Memory. 128MB 100 MHz SDRAM DIMM.

RealiZm II 3D Graphics subsystem. A powerful, cost-effective dynamic 3-D graphics rendering system that supports real-time, interactive performance in true color at all supported standard resolutions up to 2.5 million pixels including both 4:3 and 16:9 ratio aspects.

Display monitors: Intergraph offers a comprehensive lineup of high-resolution monitors certified and approved for Intergraph systems. I've selected the 21-inch model. This may seem extravagant, but hey! My wife and I sit here looking at this thing for hours some days. Plus, 21 inches is enough screen real estate to accommodate all the windows you'll use in your nonlinear editing program.

Disk storage subsystem. Wide Ultra-SCSI channel, a single 4.2GB system drive, and dual 18.2GB A/V drives. You will use the system drive for all your applications. The two striped A/V drives are dedicated for storage of your nonlinear editing files.

Card expansion slots. Six full-length slots: four PCI, one ISA, and one AGP.

CD-ROM. 32X EIDE preinstalled.

Floppy disk drive. A 3.5-inch diskette, 1.44MB preinstalled.

Audio. Multimedia keyboard. This multimedia keyboard is basically acceptable for nonlinear editing. You may choose to add some speakers to your system.

I discuss nonlinear editing computer details in Chapter 8. You can also find out much more about Intergrah computers at www.intergraph.com.

Pinnacle miroVIDEO DV300

As important as your computer is to your editing work, you're no where without your capture card. The capture card (sometimes referred to as a video recorder) enables your computer to digitize and export video. See Chapters 9 and 17 for more information on capture cards and digitizing.

Details

The Pinnacle miroVIDEO DV300 card provides an easy-to-use high-speed IEEE-1394 digital scanning, capturing, editing, and printing solution for your camcorder and computer. The DV300 comes with DVTools software for frame-accurate camcorder control from your computer! All video is captured through the IEEE-1394 port, keeping the video completely digital.

Following are the system requirements recommended by DV300. Read this list carefully. If you can make neither heads nor tails of the information, you may want to talk to a computer salesperson.

- ✔ 300 MHz or faster Pentium PC
- ✔ Windows 95, Windows 98, or Windows NT 4.0
- ✔ 1 free bus mastering 1x32 PCI 2.1 slot
- ✔ 64MB RAM
- ✔ 2GB free system hard disk space
- ✔ 9GB A/V rated Ultra Wide SCSI hard disk (Ultra Wide SCSI controller built-in on DV300)
- ✔ 24 bit Graphics card with overlay support
- ✔ CD-ROM drive

You can find details on computer digital video capture in Chapter 9. You can find out a lot about Pinnacle capture cards by checking out the Web site at www.pinnaclesys.com.

Sony DRV-1000

Okay. Frill you say. I don't think so. If you're going to be a serious digital editor, you're going to need a MiniDV recorder. You can use your camcorder for this, but that's not ideal. You're not going to find a more economical or convenient video tape recorder than the DRV-1000. It's designed to be installed in your PC. Using your mouse, you can operate the DRV-1000 as a fully functional player. It reads time code, can search, and can be used for batch digitizing. The DRV-1000 has digital video input and output plus S-VHS and composite outputs.

Flip back to Chapters 9 and 17 for info on computer control of the digital video camcorder.

OmniMusic Library

I cannot think of a more useful editing tool than production music. Unless you've completed a 30-minute training program, watched it in its completed form, and realized that your program is booooooring, you won't be able to appreciate the importance of adding music.

With a music library like OmniMusic, you can create logo music for a customer or sports team, add suspense to a detailed training segment, or add sweetly emotional undercurrents to an anniversary party. You name the subject, the OmniMusic library has appropriate musical background.

I show you how to use music in your video production in Chapter 11.

One More Than Ten

Okay. I know. This chapter is about my ten recommendations for digital video toys. I'm sorry, but I have to squeeze in one more favorite. I hope you don't mind. This isn't exactly a digital video toy. It's a "how-to" for playing with the toys.

Anyone who purchases a nonlinear editing system quickly becomes very interested in in-depth training. It happens every time. You buy this awesome system, quickly fall in love with all you can do, and then you get very, very hungry. You want to know how to become an expert. You have everything you need except expertise.

One of the best remedies I know is provided by a company called Total Training, Inc. Total Training provides a number of videotape-based training programs. For example, you receive in-depth training in Adobe Premiere 5.1 and Adobe After Effects 4.0. The prices of the training series are reasonable and the training is great. To make your investment a safe one, Total Training, Inc. provides a free trial offer.

Where to Go to Buy the Toys

In general, you're not going to find digital production and editing equipment at your corner computer store. Computer-based video production is a specialized industry. If you live in a large city, I'd suggest checking your Yellow Pages for video production equipment dealers. Regarding your computer, I suggest that you purchase it already configured and tested rather than saving a buck by assembling it yourself. I base my reasons on my experience with hours and hours of frustration, attempting to make peripherals work and finding no one willing to assume responsibility for incompatibility. As a general rule, if you're not already a computer engineer, you don't need to try to become one now. I suggest you buy your system already assembled and tested by the vendor.

If you can't find what you're looking for locally, check out www.digital product.com — where you'll find everything discussed in this chapter and in a lot more detail.

Part VIII
Appendixes

The 5th Wave   By Rich Tennant

"...and now, a digital image of my dad trying to cheat at a game of golf."

In this part . . .

In the chapters throughout this book, I've tried to cover all that you need to know to be a top-notch digital videographer. But I have more helpful info to share in this part.

Appendix A provides sample forms and checklists to use in video production. Appendix B is essential: It tells you how to copy or install all the neato stuff from this book's CD-ROM onto your computer.

Appendix A
Producer's Forms

· ·

*V*ideo production is tough enough when everything is going right. You
don't need to build in the "Oops! Factor." This appendix provides some
simple aids that may make a big difference in your work — even if you're just
planning to videotape your dog's graduation from obedience school. Believe
me, you don't need to have problems sneak up and bite you in the end. Ouch.

This appendix provides forms that you may use in conjunction with Chapters 6
and 7.

Creating a Take Board

One of the simplest ways to ensure a pleasant editing process is by using a
"take board" at the beginning of each recording segment. Of course, use of a
take board may not always be necessary or possible. But if you are recording
something that may later require a lot of cutting and pasting, it's a good idea
to use a take board.

Figure A-1 is a sample take board. If you plan to use one a lot, I suggest you
purchase a small dry erase board. Use a permanent marker to create the
lines and categories. Then use a dry erase marker to fill in the information.

Date: Time:	Production:
Tape #:	Scene #:
Shot #:	Take #:
Special info:	

Figure A-1:
A typical
take board
contains all
the
information
you need to
identify a
specific
shot.

Preparing a Log Sheet

If you do any extended videotaping that will later require editing, you may want to use a log sheet during production. A log sheet is a simple form that lists pertinent information regarding the order of recording and details about individual shots.

See Figure A-2 for an example log sheet.

DATE:

LOCATION:

TAPE	SCENE	SHOT	TAKE	COMMENT

Figure A-2:
A log sheet
helps you
keep up
with the
specifics of
each shot in
a recording.

Getting Permission with a Talent Release Form

Something that I have never experienced (and never want to experience) is having a person complain that I recorded him or her without permission. Such an ugly possibility is easily avoided by means of simple courtesy. *Always* request permission to videotape someone. And, when appropriate, get written authorization. The only exception to this might be crowd scenes or wide shots of people in public places.

Figure A-3 illustrates a little form that I wrote myself. I am not a lawyer, but a lawyer has told me the form is basically okay. You're welcome to use this form as a guide, but *be sure* and ask an attorney if it fits your particular circumstances.

Figure A-3:
A signed permission form is a good way to ensure that you are free to use a person's image and voice.

PERMISSION FORM

I, _____, grant unconditional permission to

_____ to videotape my likeness and my voice for the purpose of

_____ video program(s). I further grant unconditional permission

the use of my likeness and my voice for any reason associated with the video program(s).

I unconditionally permit editing of my likeness and voice in any manner. I unconditionally

permit the use of my likeness and voice in a for-profit video production.

This permission is granted without expectation of any financial reimbursement to me.

Name (print) _____

Date _____

Signature _____

Guardian (print) _____

Guardian signature _____

Appendix B

About the CD

*H*ere is a sample of the programs that you find on the *Digital Video For Dummies* CD-ROM:

- ✔ MindSpring, a popular Internet service
- ✔ Netscape Communicator and Microsoft Internet Explorer, the two most popular Web browsers
- ✔ Demo versions of Sound Forge 4.5 and Sound Forge XP 4.5 for your sound editing needs
- ✔ Adobe Premiere 5.0, Adobe Illustrator 8.0, Adobe Photoshop 5.0, and Adobe After Effects 4.0 Tryout programs (fully functional except for the Save and capture functions)
- ✔ Sample audio, video, and graphics files used throughout this book

System Requirements

Make sure that your computer meets the minimum system requirements listed in this section. If your computer doesn't match up to most of these requirements, you may have problems using the contents of the CD-ROM. (*Note:* These requirements are for using this CD. For requirements for a full-fledged nonlinear editing system, see Chapter 8.)

- ✔ A PC with a 486 or faster processor
- ✔ Microsoft Windows 95 or 98 or Windows NT 4.0 or later
- ✔ For best performance, Windows 95, 98 or NT 4.0 with at least 16MB of RAM installed
- ✔ At least 120MB of hard drive space available to install all the software from this CD-ROM (less space if you don't install every program and sample file)
- ✔ A CD-ROM drive — double-speed (*2x*) or faster
- ✔ A sound card for PCs
- ✔ A monitor capable of displaying at least 256 colors or grayscale
- ✔ Recommended: A modem with a speed of at least 28.8K

If you need more information on the basics, check out *PCs For Dummies,* 7th Edition, by Dan Gookin (published by IDG Books Worldwide, Inc.). Or read *Windows 95 For Dummies,* 2nd Edition; or *Windows 98 For Dummies,* both by Andy Rathbone (both published by IDG Books Worldwide, Inc.).

Using the CD through the HTML Pages

1. **Insert the CD into your computer's CD-ROM drive.**

   Give your computer a moment to take a look at the CD.

2. **Open your browser.**

   If you don't have a browser, follow the easy steps as described in the following section, "Using the CD from the Directory Structure," to install one. For your convenience, we have included Microsoft Internet Explorer, which is an installation-savvy browser.

3. **Select File⇨Open (Internet Explorer).**

   The browser opens a dialog box.

4. **In the dialog box that appears, type** D:\START.HTM **and click OK.**

   If the letter for your CD-ROM drive is not D, replace D with the correct letter. You now see the file that walks you through the contents on the CD.

5. **To navigate the CD interface and go to a topic of interest, simply click that topic.**

   You go to an explanation of that topic and the files on the CD and how to use them or install them on your computer's hard drive.

6. **To install a particular file or program, click its name to launch the install program.**

   The program or file is automatically installed. Because you are using a browser to install this software, you will be asked to select either "Save this file" or "Run this file from its current location." Select "Run this file from its current location" when this dialog box pops up. The program you selected will now be installed on your hard drive.

   If you are installing the multimedia files, the procedure is the same. When you click the name of the chapter, the CD automatically copies all sample files for that chapter to your hard drive in a folder called Clips.

7. **After you finish with the interface, close your browser as usual.**

You may not have sufficient space on your hard drive to temporarily store the multimedia files used as examples within the chapters. If that's the case, just keep the CD-ROM in your CD-ROM drive and use the files from this drive as you need them. Though the response time from the CD-ROM drive will be slower than from your hard drive, the multimedia files should still work properly.

Using the CD from the Directory Structure

If you are using a browser that does not support software installation, you will need to follow these steps to install the software. You can always install Internet Explorer 5.0 (included on the CD-ROM), which is an installation-savvy browser.

1. **Double-click the file named License.txt.**

   This file contains the end-user license that you agree to by using the CD. When you finish reading the license, close the program, most likely NotePad, that displayed the file.

2. **Double-click the file named Readme.txt.**

   This file contains instructions about installing the software from this CD. You may find it helpful to keep this text file open while you use the CD.

3. **Double-click the folder for the software or files you are interested in.**

   Be sure to read the descriptions of the programs and files in the next section of this appendix (much of this information also shows up in the ReadMe files). These descriptions give you more precise information about the programs' folder names and about finding and running the installer program.

4. **Find the file named Setup.exe, or Install.exe, or something similar, and double-click that file.**

   The installer for the program you selected now walks you through the process of setting up your new software.

What You'll Find

Here's a summary of the software on this CD-ROM and steps for downloading them from the CD-ROM to your computer's hard drive. The installation process for each program includes an uninstall feature so that you can uninstall the programs when you like.

Sound Forge 4.5 and XP 4.5 demos by Sonic Foundry

Sound Forge 4.5 enables you to put powerful audio-processing tools and effects to work on your desktop. Sound Forge XP is the version that you will probably want to use if you are new to the world of audio processing, while Sound Forge 4.5 is designed for professional use. For your convenience, we include both demo versions on the CD-ROM.

For more information, visit Sonic Foundry's Web site at www.sonicfoundry.com.

To run these programs, you need to have DirectX Media Runtime 6.0 installed on your system. If you don't have this program, check out www.microsoft.com/directx/default.asp for the latest version available for download.

Folder on CD-ROM: PROGRAMS\SOUNDFRG

MindSpring Internet Service Provider

In case you don't have an Internet connection, the CD-ROM includes sign-on software for MindSpring, an Internet Service Provider.

For more information and for updates of MindSpring, visit the MindSpring Web site at www.mindspring.com.

You need a credit card to sign up with MindSpring Internet Access.

If you already have an Internet Service Provider, please note that MindSpring Internet Access software makes changes to your computer's current Internet configuration and may replace your current settings. These changes may stop you from being able to access the Internet through your current provider.

Folder on CD-ROM: PROGRAMS\MDSPRING

Microsoft Internet Explorer 5.0

Microsoft Internet Explorer is one of two major players in the Web browser market. However, just in case you don't have the latest version (at the time of publication), we include a copy of Microsoft Internet Explorer 5.0 on this CD-ROM. You can always find the latest information about Internet Explorer at the Microsoft support site: www.microsoft.com/ie.

Folder on CD-ROM: PROGRAMS\MS_IE

Netscape Communicator Suite 4.5

Netscape Navigator is the other major Web browser and comes as part of the Netscape Communicator Suite (Version 4.5) that we include on this CD-ROM. Whether you use the Netscape or Microsoft Web browser is largely a matter of personal preference. Check out both. You can find the latest versions and important updates on the Netscape support site at www.netscape.com/ browsers/index.html.

Folder on CD-ROM: PROGRAMS\NETSCAPE

Adobe image processing programs

Adobe is a leader in graphics-related desktop publication applications. Among Adobe's many offerings is a group of programs that together comprise a nonlinear editing software suite. This CD-ROM includes a tryout version of each of the programs in the suite.

For additional information about the following programs, go to www.adobe.com.

Adobe After Effects 4.0 Tryout Version

Adobe After Effects is a great program for layering and manipulating numerous images on the screen at one time. After Effects is often called a 2-D animation program. But that's just the beginning.

Folder on CD-ROM: PROGRAMS\AFTEREFF

Adobe Illustrator 8.0 Tryout Version

Adobe Illustrator is a draw program. With Illustrator, you can create the simplest to the most elaborate drawings of images and text — while maintaining the ability to easily modify individual parts of the drawings. Illustrator is great for many nonlinear editing needs, such as screens requiring text or drawings on top of video images.

Folder on CD-ROM: PROGRAMS\ILLUST8

Adobe Photoshop 5.0 Tryout Version

Adobe Photoshop is a paint program. With Photoshop, you can change and correct images. A robust paint program such as Photoshop is critical to nonlinear editing.

Folder on CD-ROM: PROGRAMS\PHOTOSHP

Adobe Premiere 5.0 Tryout Version

Adobe Premiere is a nonlinear editing program. Premiere is an easy-to-use, powerful, and cost-effective solution for your computer-based editing needs.

Folder on CD-ROM: PROGRAMS\PREMIERE

Clips folder and contents

The CD-ROM includes a folder named CLIPS that contains the following graphics, video, and audio files:

Chapter 10 (Folder: CHAP10)

- ✔ Girl1.mov
- ✔ Jars1.mov

Chapter 11 (Folder: CHAP11)

- ✔ Jetski3.mov
- ✔ Natural1.wav
- ✔ Shore.mov
- ✔ Shorestill.bmp
- ✔ Versatile.wav

Chapter 12 (Folder: CHAP12)

- ✔ Illusend.mov
- ✔ Sailing.wav
- ✔ Shorestill.bmp
- ✔ Sun.ai
- ✔ Wind Tours.ai

Chapter 13 (Folder: CHAP13)

- ✔ Colo1.tif
- ✔ Colo2.tif
- ✔ Colo3.tif
- ✔ Colo4.tif
- ✔ Colorado.avi
- ✔ Mountain.wav
- ✔ Pic1.tif
- ✔ Pic2.tif
- ✔ Pic3.tif
- ✔ Pic4.tif

Chapter 14 (Folder: CHAP14)

- Aeend.mov
- Announce.tif
- Flower logo.avi
- Flower.avi
- Flowers.tif
- Graduat.wav

Chapter 15 (Folder: CHAP15)

- 1copy.avi
- 1copy.rm
- Skiman.avi

Chapter 18 (Folder: CHAP18)

- Gallery.psd
- Vacate01.tif
- Vacate02.tif
- Vacate03.tif
- Vacate04.tif
- Vacate05.tif
- Vacate06.tif
- Vacation.avi

Chapter 19 (Folder: CHAP19)

- Brian.avi

Chapter 20 (Folder: CHAP20)

- Wedding.avi

In several chapters in this book, you work with the multimedia files stored in the preceding chapter folders. As you need each chapter folder from the CD-ROM, I ask you to download the folder to your hard drive.

To download the multimedia files from the CLIPS folder on the CD-ROM, follow these steps (or you can, of course, install these files through the CD's interface):

1. **Go to your desktop and open Windows Explorer.**

2. **In Windows Explorer, find your CD-ROM drive (generally D).**

3. **On your CD-ROM drive, open the CLIPS folder.**

   Within the Clips folder, you find individual multiple .EXE files, each named after a chapter (for example, CHAP10.exe).

4. **To automatically copy all files from a chapter folder to a folder called Clips on your hard drive, double-click the chapter file.**

   This step automatically creates a Clips folder on your hard drive and copies the chapter folder to the Clips folder on your hard drive.

When you complete a chapter, you can delete the chapter folder from your hard drive to save space.

If You've Got Problems (Of the CD Kind)

We tried our best to compile programs that work on most computers with the minimum system requirements. Alas, your computer may differ, and some programs may not work properly for some reason.

The two likeliest problems are that you don't have enough memory (RAM) for the programs you want to use, or you have other programs running that are affecting installation or running of a program. If you get error messages like `Not enough memory` or `Setup cannot continue`, try one or more of these methods and then try using the software again:

✔ Turn off any antivirus software that you have on your computer. Installers sometimes mimic virus activity and may make your computer incorrectly believe that it is being infected by a virus.

✔ Close all running programs. The more programs you're running, the less memory is available to other programs. Installers also typically update files and programs. So if you keep other programs running, installation may not work properly.

✔ Have your local computer store add more RAM to your computer. This is, admittedly, a drastic and somewhat expensive step. However, if you have a Windows 95 PC, adding more memory can really help the speed of your computer and allow more programs to run at the same time. This may include closing the CD interface and running a product's installation program from Windows Explorer.

If you still have trouble with installing the items from the CD, please call the IDG Books Worldwide Customer Service phone number: 800-762-2974 (outside the U.S.: 317-572-3993).

Index

• *D* •

Notes

WHAT DOES DRAMATICA WRITER'S DREAMKIT DO?

"DreamKit blows away the competition in price and power . . . and it takes much less time to use than getting a master's degree in creative writing."
- Mac World

What no other program can!

Dramatica Writer's DreamKit guides you through the story creation process and ensures that your story structure works.

Unique query system!

The Writer's DreamKit query system leads you through a series of thought-provoking questions to nail down the perfect story structure.

The Writer's DreamKit predicts how other parts of your story should play out.

Start with just an idea, a scene, a joke, or a conversation! Watch how your story takes shape.

Be as sketchy or detailed as you want and expand as you go along.

10% off! When you fax or mail this coupon

Dramatica Writer's DreamKit

Go to www.digitalproduct.com for details and pricing

Canon XL1

**Digital
From
Start . . .**

The only MiniDV with Interchangeable Lenses.

All You Need

*A complete line
of video production
and nonlinear editing
equipment and supplies*

* Canon
* Intergraph
* Adobe
* Lowel
* Samson

* Sony
* JVC
* Avid
* SGI
* Many More

Intergraph TDZ 2000 GL2

. . .To Finish!

All the computing power you need (and more)

For Less

**Go to
www.digitalproduct.com
for details and pricing**

IDG Books Worldwide, Inc., End-User License Agreement

READ THIS. You should carefully read these terms and conditions before opening the software packet(s) included with this book ("Book"). This is a license agreement ("Agreement") between you and IDG Books Worldwide, Inc. ("IDGB"). By opening the accompanying software packet(s), you acknowledge that you have read and accept the following terms and conditions. If you do not agree and do not want to be bound by such terms and conditions, promptly return the Book and the unopened software packet(s) to the place you obtained them for a full refund.

1. **License Grant.** IDGB grants to you (either an individual or entity) a nonexclusive license to use one copy of the enclosed software program(s) (collectively, the "Software") solely for your own personal or business purposes on a single computer (whether a standard computer or a workstation component of a multiuser network). The Software is in use on a computer when it is loaded into temporary memory (RAM) or installed into permanent memory (hard disk, CD-ROM, or other storage device). IDGB reserves all rights not expressly granted herein.

2. **Ownership.** IDGB is the owner of all right, title, and interest, including copyright, in and to the compilation of the Software recorded on the disk(s) or CD-ROM ("Software Media"). Copyright to the individual programs recorded on the Software Media is owned by the author or other authorized copyright owner of each program. Ownership of the Software and all proprietary rights relating thereto remain with IDGB and its licensers.

3. **Restrictions on Use and Transfer.**

   (a) You may only (i) make one copy of the Software for backup or archival purposes, or (ii) transfer the Software to a single hard disk, provided that you keep the original for backup or archival purposes. You may not (i) rent or lease the Software, (ii) copy or reproduce the Software through a LAN or other network system or through any computer subscriber system or bulletin-board system, or (iii) modify, adapt, or create derivative works based on the Software.

   (b) You may not reverse engineer, decompile, or disassemble the Software. You may transfer the Software and user documentation on a permanent basis, provided that the transferee agrees to accept the terms and conditions of this Agreement and you retain no copies. If the Software is an update or has been updated, any transfer must include the most recent update and all prior versions.

4. **Restrictions on Use of Individual Programs.** You must follow the individual requirements and restrictions detailed for each individual program in the "About the CD" appendix of this Book. These limitations are also contained in the individual license agreements recorded on the Software Media. These limitations may include a requirement that after using the program for a specified period of time, the user must pay a registration fee or discontinue use. By opening the Software packet(s), you will be agreeing to abide by the licenses and restrictions for these individual programs that are detailed in the "About the CD" appendix and on the Software Media. None of the material on this Software Media or listed in this Book may ever be redistributed, in original or modified form, for commercial purposes.

5. **Limited Warranty.**

   (a) IDGB warrants that the Software and Software Media are free from defects in materials and workmanship under normal use for a period of sixty (60) days from the date of purchase of this Book. If IDGB receives notification within the warranty period of defects in materials or workmanship, IDGB will replace the defective Software Media.

   (b) IDGB AND THE AUTHOR OF THE BOOK DISCLAIM ALL OTHER WARRANTIES, EXPRESS OR IMPLIED, INCLUDING WITHOUT LIMITATION IMPLIED WARRANTIES OF MERCHANTABILITY AND FITNESS FOR A PARTICULAR PURPOSE, WITH RESPECT TO THE SOFTWARE, THE PROGRAMS, THE SOURCE CODE CONTAINED THEREIN, AND/OR THE TECHNIQUES DESCRIBED IN THIS BOOK. IDGB DOES NOT WARRANT THAT THE FUNCTIONS CONTAINED IN THE SOFTWARE WILL MEET YOUR REQUIREMENTS OR THAT THE OPERATION OF THE SOFTWARE WILL BE ERROR FREE.

   (c) This limited warranty gives you specific legal rights, and you may have other rights that vary from jurisdiction to jurisdiction.

6. **Remedies.**

   (a) IDGB's entire liability and your exclusive remedy for defects in materials and workmanship shall be limited to replacement of the Software Media, which may be returned to IDGB with a copy of your receipt at the following address: Software Media Fulfillment Department, Attn.: *Digital Video For Dummies,* IDG Books Worldwide, Inc., 10475 Crosspoint Blvd. Indianapolis, IN 46256, or call 800-762-2974. Please allow three to four weeks for delivery. This Limited Warranty is void if failure of the Software Media has resulted from accident, abuse, or misapplication. Any replacement Software Media will be warranted for the remainder of the original warranty period or thirty (30) days, whichever is longer.

   (b) In no event shall IDGB or the author be liable for any damages whatsoever (including without limitation damages for loss of business profits, business interruption, loss of business information, or any other pecuniary loss) arising from the use of or inability to use the Book or the Software, even if IDGB has been advised of the possibility of such damages.

   (c) Because some jurisdictions do not allow the exclusion or limitation of liability for consequential or incidental damages, the above limitation or exclusion may not apply to you.

7. **U.S. Government Restricted Rights.** Use, duplication, or disclosure of the Software by the U.S. Government is subject to restrictions stated in paragraph (c)(1)(ii) of the Rights in Technical Data and Computer Software clause of DFARS 252.227-7013, and in subparagraphs (a) through (d) of the Commercial Computer–Restricted Rights clause at FAR 52.227-19, and in similar clauses in the NASA FAR supplement, when applicable.

8. **General.** This Agreement constitutes the entire understanding of the parties and revokes and supersedes all prior agreements, oral or written, between them and may not be modified or amended except in a writing signed by both parties hereto that specifically refers to this Agreement. This Agreement shall take precedence over any other documents that may be in conflict herewith. If any one or more provisions contained in this Agreement are held by any court or tribunal to be invalid, illegal, or otherwise unenforceable, each and every other provision shall remain in full force and effect.

CD Installation Instructions

Using the CD through the HTML Pages

1. **Insert the CD into your computer's CD-ROM drive.**

   Give your computer a moment to take a look at the CD.

2. **Open your browser.**

   If you don't have a browser, follow the easy steps as described in the following section, "Using the CD from the Directory Structure," to install one. For your convenience, we have included Microsoft Internet Explorer, which is an installation-savvy browser.

3. **Select File⇨Open (Internet Explorer).**

   The browser opens.

4. **In the dialog box that appears, type** D:\START.HTM **and click OK.**

   If the letter for your CD-ROM drive is not D, replace D with the correct letter.

   You now see the file that walks you through the contents on the CD.

5. **To navigate the CD interface and go to a topic of interest, simply click that topic.**

   You go to an explanation of that topic and the files on the CD and how to use them or install them on your computer's hard drive.

6. **To install a particular file or program, click its name to launch the install program.**

   The program or file is automatically installed. Because you are using a browser to install this software, you will be asked to select either "Save this file" or "Run this file from its current location." Select "Run this file from its current location" when this dialog box pops up. The program you selected will now be installed on your hard drive.

   If you are installing the multimedia files, the procedure is the same. When you click the name of the chapter, the CD automatically copies all sample files for that chapter to your hard drive in a folder called Clips.

7. **After you finish with the interface, close your browser as usual.**

You may not have sufficient space on your hard drive to temporarily store the multimedia files used as examples within the chapters. If that's the case, just keep the CD-ROM in your CD-ROM drive and use the files from this drive as you need them. Though the response time from the CD-ROM drive will be slower than from your hard drive, the multimedia files should still work properly.

Using the CD from the Directory Structure

If you are using a browser that does not support software installation, you will need to follow these steps to install the software. You can always install Internet Explorer 5.0 (included on the CD-ROM), which is an installation-savvy browser.

1. **Double-click the file named License.txt.**

   This file contains the end-user license that you agree to by using the CD. When you finish reading the license, close the program, most likely NotePad, that displayed the file.

2. **Double-click the file named Readme.txt.**

   This file contains instructions about installing the software from this CD. You may find it helpful to keep this text file open while you use the CD.

3. **Double-click the folder for the software you are interested in.**

4. **Find the file named Setup.exe, or Install.exe, or something similar, and double-click that file.**

   The installer for the program you selected now walks you through the process of setting up your new software.

For descriptions of the software and folders on the CD and details about using them, see Appendix B.

IDG BOOKS WORLDWIDE
BOOK REGISTRATION

Register This Book and Win!

We want to hear from you!

Visit **http://my2cents.dummies.com** to register this book and tell us how you liked it!

- Get entered in our monthly prize giveaway.

- Give us feedback about this book — tell us what you like best, what you like least, or maybe what you'd like to ask the author and us to change!

- Let us know any other *For Dummies*® topics that interest you.

Your feedback helps us determine what books to publish, tells us what coverage to add as we revise our books, and lets us know whether we're meeting your needs as a *For Dummies* reader. You're our most valuable resource, and what you have to say is important to us!

Not on the Web yet? It's easy to get started with *Dummies 101*®*: The Internet For Windows*® *98* or *The Internet For Dummies*® at local retailers everywhere.

Or let us know what you think by sending us a letter at the following address:

For Dummies Book Registration
Dummies Press
10475 Crosspoint Blvd.
Indianapolis, IN 46256

™

...FOR
DUMMIES

BESTSELLING
BOOK SERIES